We'Moon 2014
Gaia Rhythms for Womyn

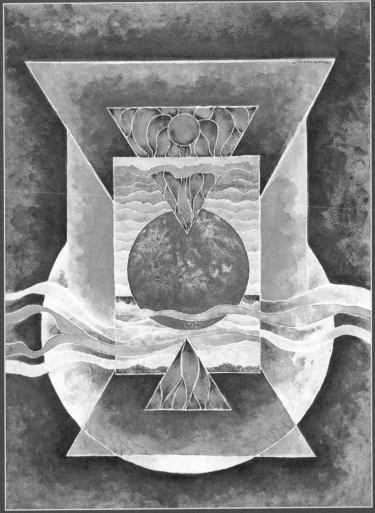

Dance of the Five Elements   © *Diane Lee Moomey 2010*

Radical Balance

33rd Edition of We'Moon

published by
Mother Tongue Ink

WE'MOON 2014: GAIA RHYTHMS FOR WOMYN
SPIRAL, STURDY PAPERBACK BINDING AND UNBOUND EDITIONS
© MOTHER TONGUE INK 2013

We'Moon Founder/Crone Editor: Musawa
We'Moonagers: Sue Burns, Barb Dickinson
Special Editor: Bethroot Gwynn
Graphic Design: Sequoia Watterson
We'Moon Creatrix/Editorial Team: Bethroot Gwynn,
Barb Dickinson, Sequoia Watterson, Sue Burns
Production Coordinator: Barb Dickinson
Production Assistant: Ecole Venskytis
Proofing: Sher Vadinska, EagleHawk, Sandra Pastorius
Promotion: Sue Burns, Myshkin, Susie Schmidt
Retail Sales: Ecole Venskytis
Order Fullfillment: Susie Schmidt, Jillian Hocking
Accounts Manager/Promotions: Sue Burns

Mother Tongue Ink
P.O. Box 1586, Estacada, OR 97023
All correspondence:
P.O. Box 187
Wolf Creek, OR 97497

www.wemoon.ws

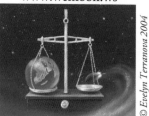

Balance

© *Evelyn Terranova 2004*

Astrological data provided by Astro Computing Service/Starcrafts Publishing, 334-A Calef Hwy., Epping, NH 03042 www.astrocom.com

This eco-audit applies to all We'Moon 2014 *products:*

Order directly from Mother Tongue Ink
To Order see p. 231. Email: weorder@wemoon.ws
US toll-free: 877-693-6666 Local/International: 541-956-6052
Wholesale Accounts: 503-288-3588

In the Spirit of We'Moon
Celebrating 30 Years ~ An Anthology of We'Moon Art and Writing
ISBN: 978-1-890931-75-9 • $25.95

We'Moon 2014 Datebooks: • $18.95
Spiral ISBN: 987-1-890931-88-9
Sturdy Paperback ISBN: 987-1-890931-89-6
Unbound ISBN: 987-1-890931-90-2
The Last Wild Witch
ISBN: 978-1-890931-59-4 • $18.95

Other *We'Moon 2014* Products:
We'Moon on the Wall • $14.95
ISBN: 987-1-890931-91-9
We'Moon Cover Poster • $10
ISBN: 987-1-890931-93-3
2014 Greeting Cards (6) • $9.95
ISBN: 987-1-890931-92-6

2014

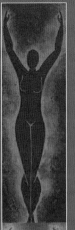

JANUARY

S	M	T	W	T	F	S
		(1)	2	3	4	
5	6	7	8	9	10	11
12	13	14	(15)	16	17	18
19	20	21	22	23	24	25
26	27	28	29	(30)	31	

FEBRUARY

S	M	T	W	T	F	S
						1
2	3	4	5	6	(7)	8
9	10	11	12	13	(14)	15
16	17	18	19	20	21	22
23	24	25	26	27	28	

MARCH

S	M	T	W	T	F	S
						(1)
2	3	4	5	6	7	8
9	10	11	12	13	14	15
(16)	17	18	19	20	21	22
(23)	24	25	26	27	28	29
(30)	31					

APRIL

S	M	T	W	T	F	S
		1	2	3	4	5
6	7	8	9	10	11	12
13	14	(15)	16	17	18	19
20	21	22	23	24	25	26
27	(28)	29	30			

MAY

S	M	T	W	T	F	S
				1	2	3
4	5	6	7	8	9	10
11	12	13	(14)	15	16	17
18	19	20	(21)	22	23	24
25	26	27	(28)	29	30	31

JUNE

S	M	T	W	T	F	S
1	2	3	4	5	6	7
8	9	10	11	(12)	13	14
15	16	17	18	19	(20)	21
22	23	24	25	26	(27)	28
29	30					

JULY

S	M	T	W	T	F	S
		1	2	3	4	5
6	7	8	9	10	11	(12)
13	14	15	16	17	18	(19)
20	21	22	23	24	25	(26)
27	28	29	30	31		

AUGUST

S	M	T	W	T	F	S
					1	2
3	4	5	6	7	8	9
(10)	11	12	13	14	15	16
17	18	19	20	21	22	23
24	(25)	26	27	28	29	30
31						

SEPTEMBER

S	M	T	W	T	F	S
	1	2	3	4	5	6
7	(8)	9	10	11	12	13
14	15	16	17	18	19	20
21	22	(23)	24	25	26	27
28	29	30				

OCTOBER

S	M	T	W	T	F	S
			1	2	3	4
5	6	7	(8)	9	10	11
12	13	14	15	16	17	18
19	20	21	22	(23)	24	25
26	27	28	29	30	31	

NOVEMBER

S	M	T	W	T	F	S
						1
2	3	4	5	(6)	7	8
9	10	11	12	13	14	15
16	17	18	19	20	21	(22)
23	24	25	26	27	28	29
30						

DECEMBER

S	M	T	W	T	F	S
	1	2	3	4	5	(6)
7	8	9	10	11	12	13
14	15	16	17	18	19	20
(21)	22	23	24	25	26	27
28	29	30	31			

◯ = NEW MOON, PST/PDT   ◯ = FULL MOON, PST/PDT

Warm Women
© *Khara Scott-Bey 2005*

Cover Notes

Planetary Alignment © *Julie Dillon 2010*

In my illustration, "Planetary Alignment," I wanted to depict a woman who has an important part in maintaining balance in a complex system, but who does so with confidence and ease. She is in control of herself and her surroundings in an environment that is airy, open and free.

Columbia Gorge ¤ *Dana Logan 1995*

My first visit to the Columbia Gorge was during a storm so violent the wind whipped water from the river with rain and splashed it in every direction making me doubt gravity. The next day the Columbia was so still the blue sky reflected off the water making the looming dark cliffs appear suspended in air. It was this primal magic I attempted to capture in my drawing.

Dedication

Each year, we donate a portion of our proceeds to an organization doing good work that resonates with our theme—bringing positive change to the world and to the lives of women. We are drawn to two organizations, in particular, that are both doing the work of Radical Balance: MissRepresentation of the US and Maman Shujaa of the Democratic Republic of Congo.

MissRepresentation is a non-profit social action campaign established to shift people's consciousness around gender stereotypes, and ultimately transform culture so that all people may fulfill their potential. Written and directed by Jennifer Siebel Newsom, the film "Miss Representation," exposes how mainstream media contribute to the distorted and degrading representation of women in positions of power and influence in America.

MissRepresentation.org offers age-appropriate curricula for classrooms, from Kindergarten to University level, designed to help students think more critically about media and the damaging effects of gender stereotypes. The curriculum challenges media's disparaging portrayals of women and girls, which contribute to the underrepresentation of women in leadership. Students are encouraged to speak out, celebrate empowering media, challenge negative imagery, and work for change in their world.

Maman Shujaa, founded by activist Neema Namadamu, is a leadership core of grassroots women's rights activists based in Congo, described as one of the worst places in the world to be a woman, rife with rape and conflict. Maman Shujaa, translated "Hero Women," works to mobilize, enlighten, and engage women as advocates for women's rights and Persons With Disabilities (PWD). Maman Shujaa runs a Media Training Center, providing computer and internet literacy skills for women. The program is creating a core of strength and connection among women, sharing their stories of survival and developing healing solutions for peace and transformation in their country. Says Neema Namadamu: "I'm not interested in making a little noise—I'm looking to CHANGE THE PARADIGM!"

Join us in supporting these two amazing, change-making organizations. Learn more about Neema Namadamu and Maman Shujaa at www.namadamu.com and MissRepresentaion at www.missrepresentation.org.

Barbara Dickinson © Mother Tongue Ink 2013

Table of Contents

Introduction

Moon Calendar: Radical Balance

Appendix

We'Moon 2014 Features:

Astrologers: Gretchen Lawlor, Heather Roan Robbins, Sandra Pastorius, Susan Levitt, Mooncat!, Beate Metz; **Introduction to the Theme**: Bethroot Gwynn; **Holy Days**: Rose Flint; **2014 Lunar Phase Card:** Susan Baylies; **Herbs:** Sue Burns; **We'Moon Cycles:** Musawa.

Me Facing Me
¤ *SunRae 2006*

What Is *We'Moon*? A Handbook in Natural Cycles

We'Moon: Gaia Rhythms for Womyn is more than an appointment book, it's a way of life! We'Moon is a lunar calendar, a handbook in natural rhythm, and a collaboration of international womyn's culture. Art and writing by wemoon from many lands give a glimpse of the great diversity and uniqueness of a world we create in our own image. We'Moon is about *womyn's spirituality* (spirit'reality). We share how we live our truth, what inspires us, how we envision our reality in connection with the whole earth and all our relations.

Wemoon means "women." Instead of defining ourselves in relation to men (as in *wo*man or *fe*male), we use the word *wemoon* to define ourselves by our primary relation to the natural sources of cosmic flow. Other terms wemoon use are *womyn* and *wimmin*. We'Moon is a moon calendar for wemoon. As wemoon, we seek to be whole in ourselves, rather than dividing ourselves in half and hoping that some "other half" will complete the picture. We see the whole range of life's potential embodied and expressed by wemoon and do not divide the universe into gender-role stereotypes. We'Moon is sacred space in which to explore and celebrate the diversity of she-ness on Earth. We'Moon is created by, for and about womyn: in Her image.

Wemoon means "we of the moon." The Moon, whose cycles run in our blood, is the original womyn's calendar. Like the Moon, wemoon circle the Earth. We are drawn to one another. We come in different shapes, colors and sizes. We are continually transforming. With all our different hues and points of view, we are one.

We'Moon culture exists in the diversity and the oneness of our experience as wemoon. *We honor both.* We come from many different ways of life. At the same time, as wemoon, we share a common mother root. As makers of We'Moon, we are glad when wemoon from varied backgrounds contribute art and writing. When material is borrowed from cultures other than your own, we ask that it be acknowledged and something given in return. Being conscious of our sources keeps us from engaging in the divisiveness of either *cultural appropriation* (taking what belongs to others) or *cultural fascism* (controlling creative expression). We invite you to share how the "Mother Tongue" speaks to you, with respect for both cultural integrity and individual freedom.

Lunar Rhythms: Everything that flows moves in rhythm with the Moon. She rules the water element on Earth. She pulls on the ocean's tides, the weather, female reproductive cycles and the life fluids in plants, animals and people. She influences the underground currents in earth energy, the mood swings of mind, body, behavior and emotion. The Moon's phases reflect her dance with Sun and Earth, her closest relatives in the sky. Together, these three heavenly bodies weave the web of light and dark into our lives.

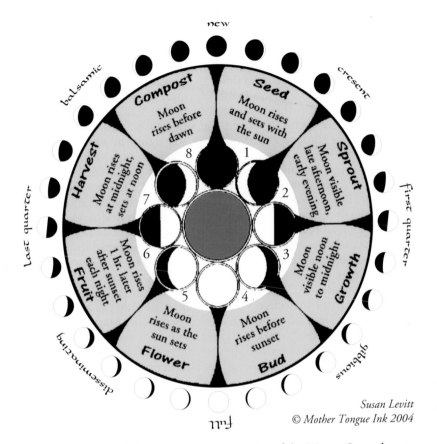

balsamic

crescent

Compost
Moon rises before dawn

Seed
Moon rises and sets with the sun

Sprout
Moon visible late afternoon, early evening

Harvest
Moon rises at midnight, sets at noon

last quarter

first quarter

Growth
Moon visible noon to midnight

Fruit
Moon rises 1 hr. later after sunset each night

Flower
Moon rises as the sun sets

Bud
Moon rises before sunset

8

1

7

2

6

3

5

4

disseminating

gibbous

full

Susan Levitt
© Mother Tongue Ink 2004

Gaia Rhythms: We show the natural cycles of the Moon, Sun, planets and stars as they relate to Earth. By recording our own activities side by side with those of other heavenly bodies, we may notice what connection, if any, there is for us. The Earth revolves around her axis in one day; the Moon orbits around the Earth in one month ($29\frac{1}{2}$ days); the Earth orbits around the Sun in one year. We experience each of these cycles in the alternating rhythms of day and night, waxing and waning, summer and winter. The Earth/Moon/Sun are our inner circle of kin in the universe. We know where we are in relation to them at all times by the dance of light and shadow as they circle around one another.

The Eyes of Heaven: As seen from Earth, the Moon and the Sun are equal in size: "the left and right eye of heaven," according to Hindu (Eastern) astrology. Unlike the solar-dominated calendars of Christian (Western) patriarchy, We'Moon looks at our experience through both eyes at once. The **lunar eye** of heaven is seen each day in the phases of the Moon as she is both reflector and shadow, traveling her $29\frac{1}{2}$-day path around the Earth in a "Moon" Month (from each new moon to the next, 13 times in a lunar year). Because Earth is orbiting the Sun at the same time, it takes the Moon 27⅓ days to go through all the signs of the Zodiac—a sidereal month. The **solar eye** of heaven is apparent at the turning points in the Sun's cycle. The year begins with Winter Solstice (in the Northern Hemisphere), the dark renewal time, and journeys through the full cycle of seasons and balance points (solstices, equinoxes and the cross-quarter days in between). The **third eye** of heaven may be seen in the stars. Astrology measures the cycles by relating the Sun, Moon and all other planets in our universe through the backdrop of star signs (the zodiac), helping us to tell time in the larger cycles of the universe.

Measuring Time and Space: Imagine a clock with many hands. The Earth is the center from which we view our universe. The Sun, Moon and planets are like the hands of the clock. Each one has its own rate of movement through the cycle. The ecliptic, a 17° band of sky around the earth within which all planets have their orbits, is the outer band of the clock where the numbers are. Stars along the ecliptic are grouped into constellations forming the signs of the zodiac—the twelve star signs are like the twelve numbers of the clock. They mark the movements of the planets through the 360° circle of the sky, the clock of time and space.

Whole Earth Perspective: It is important to note that all natural cycles have a mirror image from a whole earth perspective—seasons occur at opposite times in the Northern and Southern Hemispheres, and day and night are at opposite times on opposite sides of the Earth as well. Even the Moon plays this game—a waxing crescent moon in Australia faces right (☽), while in North America it faces left (☾). We'Moon uses a Northern Hemisphere perspective regarding times, holy days, seasons and lunar phases. We'moon who live in the Southern Hemisphere may want to transpose descriptions of the holy days to match seasons in their area. We honor a whole earth cultural perspective by including four rotating languages for the days of the week, from different parts of the globe.

Whole Sky Perspective: It is also important to note that all over the Earth, in varied cultures and times, the dome of the sky has been interacted with in countless ways. The zodiac we speak of is just one of many ways that hu-moons have pictured and related to the stars. In this calendar we use the Tropical zodiac, which keeps constant the Vernal Equinox point at 0° Aries. Western astrology primarily uses this system. Vedic or Eastern astrology uses the Sidereal zodiac, which bases the positions of Signs relative to fixed stars, and over time the Vernal Equinox point has moved about 24° behind 0° Aries.

Musawa © Mother Tongue Ink 2008

Moon Goddess
© Lisa Noble 2003

How to Use This Book
Useful Information about We'Moon

Time Zones: All aspects are in Pacific Standard/Daylight Time, with the adjustment for GMT and EDT given at the bottom of each page. To calculate for other areas, see "World Time Zones" (p. 226).

Signs and Symbols at a Glance is an easily accessible handy guide that gives brief definitions of commonly used astrological symbols (p. 227).

Pages are numbered throughout the calendar to facilitate cross referencing. See Table of Contents (p. 5) and Contributor Bylines and Index (pp. 191–201). The names of the days of the week and months are in English with four additional language translations: Laadan (See page 32, Introduction to the Theme), Farsi, Spanish and Mandarin.

Lunar Calendar Moon Theme Pages mark the beginning of each moon cycle with a two-page spread near the new moon. Each *Moon Page* is numbered with Roman numerals followed by the theme for that month (e.g., **II: Synergy**) and contains the dates of that *Moon's* new and full moon, and solar ingress.

Year at a Glance Calendars are on pp. 3 and 228. **Month at a Glance Calendars** can be found on pp. 212–223 and include daily lunar phases. Susan Baylies' **Lunar Phase Card** features the moon phases for the entire year on pp. 224–225.

Annual Astro Portraits: To find your astrological portrait for the year by Gretchen Lawlor, turn to "Star Map" (p. 20) for the page featuring your portrait.

Holy Days: There is a two-page Holy Day spread for all equinoxes, solstices and cross-quarter days. These include feature writings by Rose Flint, accompanied by additional art and writing.

Planetary Ephemeris: Exact planetary positions for every day are given on pp. 206–211. These ephemerides show where each planet is in a zodiac sign at noon GMT, measured by degree in longitude in Universal Time.

Asteroid Ephemeris: Exact positions of asteroids for every ten days are given for sixteen asteroids in the zodiac at midnight GMT on p. 205.

Astrology Basics (Refer to sample calendar page, p. 10)

Planets: Planets are like chakras in our solar system, allowing for different frequencies or types of energies to be expressed. See Mooncat's article (pp. 203-204) for planetary attributes.

Signs: The twelve signs of the zodiac are a mandala in the sky, marking off 30° segments in the 360° circle around the earth. Signs show major shifts in planetary energy through the cycles.

January
Januar

DDD   lundo

♊   Monday
      17

Moon Phase

$D \triangle \Psi$ 1:38 am
$\check{Y}R$ 2:28 am
$D \square \sigma$ 12:51 pm
$D \triangle \mathring{H}$ 9:02 pm

Month

Day of the Week

Moon Phase

Planet Glyphs

Retrograde

Aspect between Planets

σσσ   mardo

♊   Tuesday
♋   18

$\check{Y} \rightarrow \approx$ 2:20 pm
$D \divideontimes \, 4$ 2:21 pm
$D \mathcal{S} \, \female$ 3:02 pm   v/c
$D \rightarrow \female$ 8:01 pm

Sun Sign

Moon Sign Glyph

Moon Void of Course

Ingress

Sun in Aquarius 10:23 am PST

☿☿☿   merkredo

♋   Wednesday
♌   19

DApG   9:20 am
$\odot \rightarrow \approx$ 10:23 am
$D \square \, 4$ 2:36 pm   v/c
$D \rightarrow \female$ 7:58 pm
$\odot \mathcal{S} \, D$ 8:40 pm

Apogee (or PrG for Perigee)

Lunar Quarter Phase

Eclipse Information

Full Moon in ♌ Leo 8:40 pm PST
Total Lunar Eclipse 8:45 pm PST (1.325 mag.)
Eclipse visible from the Americas

Sample calendar page for reference only

Glyphs: Glyphs are the symbols used to represent planets and signs.

Sun Sign: The Sun enters a new sign once a month (around the 20th or so), completing the whole cycle of the zodiac in one year. The sun sign reflects qualities of your outward shining self. For a description of sign qualities, see "Sun Signs" (pp. 12–14).

Moon Sign: The Moon changes signs approximately every $2^{1}/_{2}$ days, going through all twelve signs of the zodiac every $29^{1}/_{2}$ days (the sidereal month). The Moon sign reflects qualities of your core inner self. For descriptions see "Moon Signs and Transits" (pp. 15–17).

Moon Phase: Each calendar day is marked with a graphic representing the phase of the Moon. Although the Moon is not usually visible in the sky during the new or dark moon, we represent her using miniscule crescent moon graphics for the days immediately before and after the actual new moon or conjunction.

Lunar Quarter Phase: At the four quarter-points of the lunar cycle (new, waxing half, full and waning half moons), we indicate the phase, sign and exact time for each. These points mark off the "lunar week."

Day of the Week: Each day is associated with a planet whose symbol appears in the line above it (e.g., ☽☽☽ is for Moon: Moonday, Monday, Luna Day, lundi, lunes). The names of the days of the week are displayed prominently in English with translations appearing in the line above them. The languages—Laadan (See page 32, Introduction to the Theme), Farsi, Spanish and Mandarin—rotate weekly, in this order, throughout the calendar.

Eclipse: The time of greatest eclipse is given, which is near to, but not at the exact time of the conjunction (☉☌☽) or opposition (☉☍☽). Locations from where eclipses are visible are also given. For more information, see "Eclipses" (p. 18).

Aspects (□△☍☌✶⊼): These show the angle of relation between different planets. Daily aspects provide something like an astrological weather forecast for the day, indicating which energies are working together easily and which combinations are more challenging. See "Signs and Symbols at a Glance" (p. 227) for a brief explanation of each kind.

Ingresses (→): Indicates when the Sun, Moon and other planets move into new signs.

Moon "Void of Course" (☽ v/c): The Moon is said to be "void of course" from the last significant lunar aspect in each sign until the Moon enters a new sign. This is a good time to ground and center yourself.

Apogee (ApG): This is the point in the orbit of a planet or the Moon that is farthest from Earth. At this time, the effects of transits (when planets pass across the path of another planet) may be less noticeable immediately, but may appear later on.

Perigee (PrG): This is the point in the orbit of a planet or the Moon that is nearest to Earth. Transits with the Moon or other planets, when they are at perigee, will be more intense.

Direct or Retrograde (D or R): These are times when a planet moves forward (D) or backward (R) through the signs of the zodiac (an optical illusion, as when a moving train passes a slower train that appears to be going backward). When a planet is in direct motion, planetary energies are more straightforward; in retrograde, planetary energies turn back in on themselves and are more involuted. See "Mercury Retrograde" (p.18).

Musawa © Mother Tongue Ink 2000

SUN SIGNS AND SUN TRANSITS

The Sun is the source of light, life, and will. Each month the Sun brings us a fresh lens and fresh medicine as it brings our attention to the unique gifts and challenges of its sign. The Sun sign we're born under does not define us, but it does describe our core spark and psyche's structure.

Sharing the Light © *Julie O. 2008*

All the rest of the planets reflect the Sun's light.
How we use it is up to us.

♒ **Aquarius** (Jan 19–Feb 18): During Fixed Air Aquarius, we assess our communities and explore our philosophies of love and collaboration. Are we really living by our philosophies; and if not, do we need to change our life, or our ideas? True collaboration is a balance of empowered, emotionally-connected equals.

Aquarians know how to work the room. They're far-sighted, and can sometimes see what everyone else needs better than they can see themselves and their intimate beloveds. Ideas are their food, but those must arise from authentic experience. To know what their community thinks and feels is their gift and challenge.

♓ **Pisces** (Feb 18–March 20): During Mutable Water Pisces month, we turn inwards to our tender places and intimate dreams. Our energy may be low, but this can help us do less and process more, review the story of our year, compost its lessons, and dream the future before we begin a new cycle. Our challenge is to stay grounded in the moment.

Pisces-born people carry an ephemeral, chameleon-like ability to reflect and connect with others, sensitively responding to all circumstances. They can flow around obstacles and absorb their surroundings with flexible strength. Their gift and their challenge are their versatility, charm, and sensitivity.

♈ **Aries** (March 20–April 19): Spring Equinox brings Cardinal Fire Aries to re-invigorate us and get the party started. Brave, direct, vital and alive, Aries energy rebels against the old ways of winter or the culture's clutter, and re-invents our world. Aries wakes us up; our challenge is to now act rather than react.

One born under an Aries Sun is always looking for a better way. Aries people carry this strong and direct, willful, alive, inventive spirit. Do not tell them what to do; share strength and ask for their help instead. Their challenge is to act, not react—to mature but keep the flame alive.

♉ **Taurus** (April 19–May 20): Fixed Earth Taurus encourages us to plant our crops, fertilize new shoots, and grow roots to make it real. Our plans take form and stabilize. Taurus-time also heightens our senses; we smell, taste, feel our world and one another. We're gifted and challenged to honor Spirit imbued in the material world.

Those who are Taurus-born keep the heartbeat; let them move at their own pace, and they help us build, grow, feast and maintain. We can lean on their steady strength, cuddle their sensuality, manifest with their practicality, but we can't push them around. Stubborness and sensuality are their gift and challenge.

♊ **Gemini** (May 20–June 21): Under Mutable Air Gemini we find our wings and cross-pollinate ideas. Like baby animals exploring their new world, we need to investigate, communicate, laugh and go exploring. Our attention-span is shortened but our curiosity is sharpened. Open the eyes, but remember to listen.

Gemini-born people are natural translators; their versatility can find something to share with just about anyone. They run curious, witty, flexible, intelligent electricity through their wires; quick, broad-ranging thinking and adaptability are their gift and challenge.

♋ **Cancer** (June 21–July 22): Summer Solstice initiates Cardinal Water Cancer and calls us home to water our gardens and souls, explore our relationship to homeland. It's time to process family karma. Our lives can ripen with the crops; we want safety to leaf and blossom in peace and may be self-protective in the process.

Cancerians are deep-feeling souls, natural leaders of the interior world who may wear armor to protect their tenderness and sensitivity. They nourish whatever being or work they claim, and can create a warm, safe nest for sanctuary. To swim in deep emotional waters productively is their gift and challenge.

♌ **Leo** (July 22–Aug 22): During Fixed Fire Leo, we dance in the sunshine, gather the first harvest and celebrate the fruits of life. Life is dramatic; creative processes, festivals, demonstrations and romances ripen. We are challenged to balance play with work, and our needs with others.

The Leo-born are natural hearth-fires who warm our lives and light up the room. Big-hearted, stubborn, generous more than empathetic, idealistic, they learn practicality; to live with panache and hold our attention for mutual benefit is their gift and their challenge.

♍ **Virgo** (Aug 22–Sept 22): Mutable Earth Virgo calls in the harvest; we get to work, reap what we've sown and organize for the winter ahead. It's time to evaluate, find allies, throw out waste and make plans. We also need to remember to let summer's kind warmth linger in our hearts.

Virgoan souls are happiest when they love their work and can put their analytical minds together with a quietly compassionate heart for good purpose. They evaluate, diagnose and edit with ease, but need something to chew on. Their strong mind-body connection and ability to see the problem is their gift and challenge.

♎ Libra (Sept 22–Oct 23): When the Fall Equinox brings Cardinal Air Libra, and the days and night equalize, it's time to bring this egalitarian balance to our loves, our politics, and our lives. We crave the beauty way, beauty before us, beauty behind us, beauty within us.

Librans are our natural diplomats; although they'd prefer not to fight, they see both sides of the coin and want to mediate the difference. Aesthetics are not optional for them, they need both bread and roses. To weigh both sides and seek beauty are their gift and challenge.

♏ Scorpio (Oct 23–Nov 22): The Fixed Water sign Scorpio-time calls us to dive deep within, look under rocks and deal with sex, death and the meaning of existence before the winter hits. Scorpio sharpens our attention, but we choose whether we obsess on a problem or focus on solutions.

Those born under Scorpio cut to the chase. Scorpios know where the trouble is, though some step towards, others back. Their x-ray vision sees under the fluff, to the bones beneath. They're passionate about what interests them. Their ability to focus and to look for the root of the problem is their gift and challenge.

♐ Sagittarius (Nov 22–Dec 21): During Mutable Fire sign Sagittarius, we step out of Scorpio's cave, reach for the bigger world, freely speak our truth and celebrate existence. Sagittarius asks us to play, explore gratitude, commune with nature; our challenge is to not lose focus in the process.

Sagittarian people want to know they can explore time, space and ideas at any moment; like a cat with a closed door, they need to feel their options are open before they can relax. They honor the interconnectedness of all life with egalitarian honesty. To speak truth and see the big picture is their gift and challenge.

♑ Capricorn (Dec 21–Jan 19): The Winter Solstice brings Capricorn's Cardinal Earth season and brings us back home to work through karma with our family, traditions, and cultural roots so we can enter the next level of our work. Capricorn asks us to assess responsibility and authority but not be controlling.

If Capricorn-born souls have a dream, they can walk it to the mountaintop with grace, competence and determination. Clear goals keep them on path and help them stay right with the world. To lead, be in control of their own destiny while not controlling others', is their gift and challenge.

Heather Roan Robbins © Mother Tongue Ink 2012
www.roanrobbins.com

MOON SIGNS AND MOON TRANSITS

When the Moon's in: Describes the emotional tone of that day. *One Born Under:* Describes the inner emotional energy, the soul prime directive, instincts, and habits of a person born under that sign of the Moon.

The Occultist © Lisette Costanzo 2010

♒ **Aquarius** When the Moon's in Aquarius it's time to gather. The mood is social, political, open-minded and experimental but stubborn. People want to understand the philosophy behind actions. They notice how they can affect their community, and how their community affects them, but may miss what's going on closer to home. Meetings prosper if kept open-ended. One born under an Aquarius Moon knows group dynamics. She's interested, eccentric, naturally collective and idealistic, and may be more comfortable in her circle than with one-on-one relationships. Her challenges are to become aware of her own feelings and to learn to stay intimately connected.

♓ **Pisces** When the Moon's in Pisces we feel everything. The mood is sensitive, intuitive, permeable, subjective, and imaginative; energy may be low and feelings close to the surface. It is time to be gentle with oneself and others, and put the creative sensitivity to good use. Water both plants and souls, swim in dreamtime. One born under a Pisces Moon has extra layers of awareness. She can be charming, introspective, and compassionate, with prickles when her feelings aren't respected. Her challenges are to discern the difference between imagination and intuition, to manifest her dreams and to find creative uses for her sensitivity.

♈ **Aries** When the Moon's in Aries we feel our life-force, our fire, rise. The mood becomes energized, brash, brusque, direct, independent, rebellious, generous but not empathetic. Moods spike like lightning. It's time to dig the garden, launch projects, initiate action, be honest and real, but stay aware of the consequences of our actions. One born under an Aries Moon has fire at her core. She's brave, generous, independent, outspoken and inherently anti-authoritarian; she listens to her inner direction first and foremost. Her challenges are to move out of reaction and into leadership, and to learn tact and patience.

♉ **Taurus** When the Moon's in Taurus our bodies, our garden and our earthly connections need attention. The mood is stubborn, creative, fertile, and sensual, so slow down, get grounded, put in steady work, tend the body and feed the senses. Nurture rather than push. Plant seeds or ideas.

One born under a Taurus Moon channels earth mother steadiness and comfort, and can lend her strength to others. She knows the worth of things, and knows how to nurture beauty. Her challenges are to stay fluid and flexible, to cherish without being possessive, and to trust in the unseen world.

♊ **Gemini** When the Moon's in Gemini we need to talk it all out. The mood is funny, open-minded, nervous, versatile, restless, and good for multi-tasking, if not for concentration. Cross-pollinate, share information, edit, weed, network, just keep the heart engaged and avoid gossip. One born under a Gemini Moon is a born communicator. She may have eclectic tastes, appreciates diversity and can help disparate people understand one another. While her fast, curious mind can synthesize and scintillate in the broad view, her challenges are to calm her nervous system and to quietly deepen her mind.

♋ **Cancer** When the Moon's in Cancer we connect with our tender sides and process emotional backlog. In response we can either get crabbily defensive, or trust our strength and nurture ourselves and others. It's time to water, plant, fertilize, bathe, cook, and listen to our gut instincts. One born under a Cancer Moon naturally dances with the tides. She's connected to the Great Mother archetype, but may mother communities as well as individuals. Her challenges are to love as an equal, not as a parent or child, and to move past safety and defensiveness into her naturally oceanic understanding.

♌ **Leo** When the Moon's in Leo we'd like to shine in the center of our world. The mood is openhearted, generous, romantic and expressive, if a bit stuck in our personal perspective. We'll be energized when we're emotionally engaged, lazy otherwise. Weed, arrange, design, celebrate, present, reach out and make a grand entrance. One born under a Leo Moon can light up a room. She's generous and stubborn if charismatic; she can hold others' attention and people thrive on hers. Her challenges will be to appreciate quiet, steady effort and to express with drama but without melodrama.

♍ **Virgo** When the Moon's in Virgo our mind and attitude sharpens, our work calls. The mood is thoughtful, sensitive, health-oriented, compassionate and particular; we understand how details create the whole. It is time to edit, weed, critique, analyze, organize, and have faith in the perfection of the whole. One born under a Virgo Moon brings in a soul longing to improve herself and her world. Sensual, connected to the natural world, she is verbal, witty, a natural mystery-seeker and problem solver. Although advice is her way of sharing love, Her challenge is to know when to accept, encourage, and play instead.

♎ Libra When the Moon's in Libra the beauty way calls us to balance our lives and loves. The mood is sociable, friendly, open, diplomatic, romantic, curious, indecisive, and aesthetic. It's time to pursue social justice and negotiate as equals, time to beautify our world and nurture relationships. One born under a Libra Moon is a natural peacemaker. She sees all sides of a problem and can lead the way beyond controversy to a shared perspective. She values fairness, aesthetics, and peaceful surroundings. Her challenges are to know her own mind, to handle conflict smoothly, and to balance relationship with purposeful work.

♏ Scorpio When the Moon's in Scorpio we get focused. The mood broods, deepens, and grows a sultry, investigative, introspective edge. We lose patience with inessentials and are suspicious of inauthenticity; we may deal with primordial feelings, and need boundaries respected. It's time to prune, water, dig, investigate and contemplate. One born under a Scorpio Moon has x-ray vision; she sees through to the roots of a problem. She needs solitude, not isolation. Her feelings are a deep, strong underground river and need healthy expression. Her challenges are to see past suspicion into clarity, and to have breadth of vision as well as depth.

♐ Sagittarius When the Moon's in Sagittarius we grow restless. The mood is exploratory, honest, tactless, restless, outdoorsy, philosophical, playful, international, freedom-loving and optimistic. It's time to drop the attitude and be real, to get moving and connect with the natural world. One born under a Sagittarius Moon is here to explore the world. She's outspoken, eternally youthful and always learning, likes to keep moving and hates to feel hemmed in. She speaks for animals, children, the natural world and all who don't have a voice. Her challenge is to explore the freedom found within commitment.

♑ Capricorn When the Moon's in Capricorn our work beckons. The mood is competitive, task-oriented, managerial, organizational, and serious. It's time to set and achieve short-term goals towards long-term horizons. Focus on one's personal best, set and accomplish clear, achievable short-term goals. Support one another's work, build structure and find the humor within. One born under a Capricorn Moon is a natural organizer. She expresses love through action and may define herself more by what she does than what she is. Her challenges are to manage without manipulation, and to accept herself (and others) holding still, knowing that stillness is worthy.

Moon Crone,
Planning Her
Next Endeavor
© *Kat Beyer 2008*

Heather Roan Robbins © Mother Tongue Ink 2013
www.roanrobbins.com

17

Eclipses: 2014

Solar and Lunar Eclipses occur only when the Earth, Sun and Moon align at the Moon's nodal axis, usually four times a year, during New Moon and Full Moon, respectively. The South (past) and North (future) Nodes symbolize our greater evolutionary path. Eclipses catalyze our destiny's deeper calling. Use eclipse degrees in your birth chart to identify potential release points.

April 15: A total Lunar eclipse at 25° Libra reveals the power of our subconscious desires. Reflect on your inner point of view with curiosity and compassion. **April 28:** This annular Solar Eclipse at 8° Taurus offers us alternative means for communicating. Take liberties with your imagination and spread your views. **October 8:** When the total Lunar Eclipse occurs at 15° Aries, avoid taking extreme positions. Each vantage point offers light to bear on the whole story. **October 23:** A partial Solar Eclipse occurs at 0° Scorpio. Even though interpenetrating energies may complicate our responses, use a direct approach. Honesty speaks volumes.

Mercury Retrograde: 2014

Mercury, planetary muse and mentor of our mental and communicative lives, appears to reverse its course three or four times a year. We may benefit from less stress when it retrogrades by making allowances for a symbolic "sleep cycle." These periods give us permission to pause and go back over familiar territory, reflecting and giving second thoughts to dropped projects or miscommunications. Breakdowns can help us attend to the safety of mechanics and mobility. It's time to "recall the now" of the past and pay attention to underlying issues. Leave matters that lock in future commitments until Mercury goes direct.

Mercury has three retrograde periods this year. During these periods Mercury makes an "inferior conjunction" with the Sun, which can help stimulate our mental circuits, offer flashes of insight and fresh ideas. When Mercury is direct, a "superior conjunction" with the Sun occurs, often a month or two after the retrograde cycle is complete. **February 6–28:** Allow the inferior conjunction with the Sun in Aquarius on February 16th to realize that any art is a process; accept what is incomplete—define and refine goals. **June 7–July 1:** Mercury's inferior conjunction with the Sun in Gemini on June 20th highlights quick wit, fertilizes the imagination and feeds great thinking. Look for potentials. **October 4–25:** Allow Mercury's conjunction to the Sun in Libra on October 17th to offer promise and poise to your communications. Revise and reshape your artistic inclinations.

Sandra Pastorius © Mother Tongue Ink 2013

THE YEAR OF THE HORSE: 2014

Reachable Moon
© *Monika Steinhoff 1999*

The year of the Horse begins on the New Moon of January 30th, 2014.* Horse year is a time of fast victories, unexpected adventure, and surprising romance. Energy is high and production is rewarded. Decisive action, not procrastination, brings success. On a global scale, expect some world economies to become stronger, while others experience economic chaos and collapse. Under Horse's strong influence, there is no middle ground.

Wemoon born in Horse years (2014, 2002, 1990, 1978, 1966, 1954, 1942, 1930, 1918, 1906) are bright, cheerful, popular, and fun loving. A Horse gal finds people and crowds exciting, and she loves parties. Her childish innocence, sunny disposition, and natural charm attract many friends. In general, Horse can enjoy a carefree life. Usually she doesn't need to struggle in order to succeed and obtain the fine things life has to offer.

Horse is a highly intuitive animal, so a Horse wemoon follows her hunches. Her keen judgment and natural intuition often help her make the right decisions throughout her life. Horse will tell you what is on her mind; she is frank and dislikes hidden agendas. Because of her carefree nature, Horse needs ample room for self-expression. When constrained by rules, proud Horse will rebel, refusing to be corralled or tamed.

Powerful Horse has magical qualities, including the ability to fly. A white celestial cloud Horse is sacred to the Chinese Goddess Kwan Yin. Her white Horse flies through the heavens, bringing peace and blessings. The white mare is also sacred to Epona, a Celtic goddess of rebirth. Even Lady Godiva is a form of Horse/wemoon as all-giving fertile Goddess.

Horse year is very fortunate for all Horse wemoon, and for her best friends Tiger, Sheep, and Dog. The spontaneous energy of Horse year brings challenges to the thoughtful Rat who is Horse's opposite. Horse correlates to the western sign Gemini.

* *Chinese New Year begins on the second new Moon after Winter Solstice.*
Susan Levitt © Mother Tongue Ink 2013

19

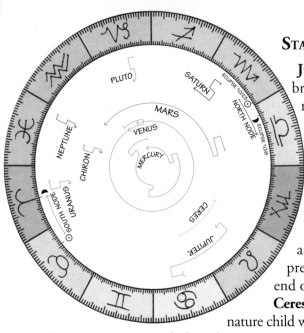

Jupiter's benevolence brings rich emotional nourishment and deeper roots to Cancer until mid-July when it shifts into Leo. Then Leo recieves the gift of Jupiter's "lucky stars," adding to Leo's already flamboyant presence, through the end of the year.

Ceres nurtures the playful nature child within each of us.

Saturn is in its concluding days in Scorpio, offering emotional transformation to the Scorpio part within us, facilitating review and release of ancient, tired stories.

Uranus continues on its sparking, unsettling adventure, jolting awake the bold Aries force—our evolutionary pioneer, our genius so needed when old ways no longer work.

Neptune drifts more deeply into **Pisces**—our dreams, art and music take up the celestial beat, helping us dance the new dance. **Chiron** leads the way through Pisces; increased sensitivity amplifies all sounds and impressions.

Pluto continues its fierce march through Capricorn, and old structures are rattled to the bones, tumbling and crumbling. Experience and wisdom become rich commodities in the new market.

Mars activates Libra through Aquarius, bringing each vitality and courage.

Venus makes a full circle through the zodiac, kissing us all in our own sign. During **Mercury's** three annual retrogrades, it goes back over old ground, inviting review and reconsideration (See p. 18 for more info).

For details, read Year at a Glance *for your Sun and Rising signs, found on the pages listed to the right.*

Gretchen Lawlor © Mother Tongue Ink 2013 www.gretchenlawlor.com

20

Astro-Overview 2014

2014 brings a time of external wild adjustment and internal exploration; let's navigate both with care and hope. Change-agent Uranus and transformative Pluto in Capricorn continue to trigger metamorphic cultural shifts throughout this year and well into next as they complete seven exact squares between 2012 and 2015 (6/12, 9/12, 5/13, 11/13, 4/14, 12/14, and 3/15). We can feel the divergent pulls between the Uranus in Aries call to revolt for free progress, and Pluto's call to reorganize structure and government while remembering the old ways, and finding that true progress comes in the balance of polarity.

We'll see the resurgence of activity in many cultural hot-spots that were triggered the last time these two danced together, when they were conjunct between 1964-67: women's rights, gay rights, racial equality, and longing for an economy based on other vectors than money. A surge of freedom-seeking politics will be met with subsequent efforts to crack down; an apparent split between generations can be breached though collective action. People with planets in mid-degrees of cardinal signs are on the front-lines of the metamorphosis, but we're all in the mix, and all need to stay in there to guide the transformation.

This change is not just political. The last few years have called for some deep personal reorganization and sorting. Saturn in Scorpio continues to challenge us to take this work deep within our souls and do our own homework. From this deep interior work let's develop a personal lighthouse, a lodestar composed of our deepest goals and brightest guiding lights. Keep that lodestar in sight to guide the big decisions and little ones that are urgently demanded as we navigate across the often storm-tossed landscape.

Our ability to adjust, to find our balance in these changing times will be our most essential tool to stay healthy. Although we need to be kind to ourselves and our loved ones, and sympathetic to others in these stressful times, we'll feel drained if we get stuck in self-pity or enabling relationships. Saturn in Scorpio and Neptune in Pisces blur our boundaries while waking up our sense of empathy and connection. Instead, let's work towards a sustainable ecology in the wildness outside, in our flowing economy, and in our personal relationships. Balance the needs of all involved so we can move forward together in healthy interdependence. Expect this lesson to be hammered in; the more stressful the times, the more important this balance will be.

Neptune in Pisces also opens our spiritual hunger to make our connection to the One, hear the Mother's call stronger. If we feel drained it will help to bathe in the collective ocean both literally, as we spend time around water and work towards global water quality, and metaphorically, as we dream and engage spiritual and magical practice. We are not alone.

As 2014 dawns, a conjunction between Pluto, Sun, Moon and Mercury opposes Jupiter and squares both Uranus and Mars, reminding us that we are smack in the transition stage of a societal death and rebirth, and it won't help to fight the changes. Play it safe these first few weeks; own up to unconscious urges and negotiate with them or they may run the show. Feel the wrestling with big forces and make wise long-range, non-reactive decisions. We may ache for what is leaving but use this as inspiration to do our best in the year ahead. Be kind to one another and alert for a sudden, short-term call to service.

Mars spends an unusually long time in Libra (12/9/13–7/28/14) dancing back and forth (retrograde 3/2–5/20) in a grand square with Pluto, Uranus, and Jupiter, calling for major change, but inviting us to dance this revolution. Take a creative, Venusian, heart-centered, egalitarian approach in order to change the paradigm, not just a regime—or just one relationship.

Expansive, abundant, freedom-loving Jupiter in Cancer opposes Pluto and squares Uranus January through June, amping up the speed and depth of change and singing an intense need for personal and political liberation. Mercury also conjuncts Neptune, offering us the creativity to look ahead, but we have to reach for it. Start at home, walk the talk and encourage everyone's evolution, even if it's inconvenient. Relationships need room to breathe now; we need to know we can grow with our beloveds, or the urge for freedom wins.

Spring stays unsettled and blustery, keep in there and keep moving forward; find balance between the wind gusts. The April 15th lunar eclipse and April 28th solar eclipse (seen in the Southern Hemisphere) ratchet our evolution forward, asking us to, once again, let go of what no longer works and embrace new possibilities. As May begins, the Mars, Pluto, Uranus and Jupiter grand square perfects and pushes the creative revolution; feel the wheel of fate turning, see evidence of the changing era.

From May through June, a helpful grand trine between Jupiter, Saturn and Chiron allows us to make headway through unusual alliances; it encourages bi-partisan efforts, strengthens our good judgment, and encourages healthier architecture and economic structures. This aspect does not demand: it offers—we can kick back under its kindness, or use it as an opportunity to make progress.

Jupiter enters Leo July 16th, and can add an element of generous fun to the mix—feeding our creative and romantic efforts—most powerfully as Jupiter and Venus waltz beautifully together in the early morning sky at the beginning of August. Together they can make our hearts long for more love, more time with our muse, but they can also add a melodramatic flare to any conflict. Jupiter trines Uranus in the fall, peaking 9/25, bringing changes we'll be ready for, and supporting all who go back to school or turn their work towards their bliss. Technology can leap forward, leaving us and our equipment feeling out of date. Let's help direct this inventiveness not just towards new toys, but towards environmental solutions. It feeds freedom movements around the globe and here at home.

Make love expansive, not contractive—find that balance between each other's needs, between freedom and connection. Join hands and explore together. If you are not in a relationship, explore and see who else is out there.

Tend to relationships of all kinds in September. Make sure all is on track and that dreams are shared, because the Sun squares Pluto and opposes Uranus 10/3–9, and that, along with a series of eclipses (Moon 10/8, Sun 10/23), can dance on our interpersonal tender spots. Let's do the work together rather than let it wedge us apart. Saturn enters Sagittarius just after Winter Solstice and calls us to take our personal work up and out, into the woods, the schools, the courtroom, and onto the global stage.

Faeth © *Cori Caputo 2005*

Heather Roan Robbins © Mother Tongue Ink 2013
www.roanrobbins.com

Juggling with Paradox

Life is a balancing act! Fortunately, we can look to the Signs of the Zodiac for guidance. Offering us rich symbolism for living the full cycle of life, the Signs illuminate a path of self-actualization for the seeker. This wheel of wisdom is composed of six pairs of opposite and counterbalancing Signs. Each of the six axes represents the interplay of life principles in our quest to live in an integrated, meaningful way. We become skillful "jugglers of paradox" as we face the inevitable dilemmas and contradictions in our experience, and learn to allow other points of view to balance our perspectives and initiate fresh approaches. It is through our struggles to reconcile these polarities that we develop a healthy psyche and a coherency for authentic expression. Mirroring the brain's emphasis on hemispheric synthesis, we learn integration through expressing attributes of both sides. Allow reciprocating dialogues, inner and outer, to expand your awareness. We are hub and spokes on this wheel.

Explore your various positions on each axis. Muse on the reminders below to enchant your journey. Juggling clue: When another "ball" comes into view, relax and connect with the field.

Aries~Libra—Boldly, we come into life through Aries, open and full of fire energy, our "chi." Very early we puzzle: how am I changed by my positions as self/other and subject/object? We are dependent upon the gaze from "another"—to witness, for love, as shadow or as the beloved. Libra symbolizes this mirroring and projecting dynamic. Play "hide and seek." Enjoy being found.

Taurus~Scorpio—Our hunger for growth and regeneration defines us on this axis of embodiment. How do we meet our needs for sustenance both physically and emotionally? What feeds us? How do we feed others? While Taurus retains, Scorpio relinquishes: food, possessions, values, people, life itself.

Gemini~Sagittarius—Our curiosity fuels mental/physical explorations, and stimulates the interplay of learning from, and teaching one another. Gemini loves intellectual connections and values among friends and peers, and a close association with the environment. Sagittarius takes the wide view, allowing opinions and categories to factor into allegiances and philosophies of belief. How can we simultaneously think globally and act locally?

Cancer~Capricorn—Along this axis we develop in kinship groups, growing a sense of belonging in our Cancerian private/home/family space, and in the Capricornian hallways of our public/work/service life. What is our commitment to standing strong on the foundations of our forbearers and the traditions they built? Who decides who belongs? The answers mean everything to the next generation.

Leo~Aquarius—Here the balancing act is between expressing a potency of heart as our unique Self, Leo, and a potency of Mind as a member of a unique group, Aquarius. Does our creativity serve both our sense of personal value and the collective common good? How do we share consciousness?

Virgo~Pisces—Conscious and unconscious motivations can transfix us, and at times hold sway over our freedom of expression. How can Virgo's devotion to order and duty help keep our practical affairs in control, while attending with trust and compassion to the "mysterium tremendum" of Pisces' soulful longings? Hold the other in highest esteem. Serve the sacred.

Sandra Pastorius © Mother Tongue Ink 2013

ASTROLOGY'S ELEMENTAL WEAVE

Nature weaves our reality on every level, from inner to outer space. Astrology attempts to interpret the whole span. The four elements and the three qualities are the warp and woof of the astrological web, weaving unique combinations as they alternate in sequence around the cycle of the year.

4 Elements:
Fire=spirit/transforming energy
Earth=physical/material energy
Air=consciousness/creative energy
Water=emotional, flowing energy

3 Qualities:
Cardinal signs initiate
Fixed signs maintain
Mutable signs dissolve and transform

Understanding the elements and qualities of the signs your planets are in is foundational when learning to navigate your birth chart. You can imagine what the qualities of each sign might be like by building on these key strands. Take the fire signs, for example: Aries—cardinal fire sign—is like kindling wood, a temperament that burns hot and quick; Leo—fixed fire sign—warms with a big steady fire of the heart/hearth; Sagittarius—mutable fire sign—is like the embers that burn long after the flames have gone out, cool and long-lasting. Each quality has both positive and negative manifestations: fixed earth can be loyal and stubborn, fixed water can be deep and stagnant, fixed air can be idealistic and rigid, fixed fire can be radiant and self-centered. Such is the intricate balance of life!

Musawa © Mother Tongue Ink 2007

Dynamic Equilibrium

The natural state of the body is one of dynamic equilibrium. As if by magic, the body knows exactly how much of what mineral to take from the bones to maintain normal heart rhythms. Your heart beats every second of every day your whole life without a conscious thought from you. The food you eat is effortlessly turned to energy for your lifeblood. If the baby of a breastfeeding woman starts to sweat, her milk automatically becomes more watery to ensure the hydration of the babe—Radical Balance.

The eggs you now carry in your ovaries have been with you since you were in your mother's womb. And by turn, the egg which became you was in your mother's ovary when she was in your grandmother's body. We carry the cellular memory of three generations. The wild dandelion greens my grandmother foraged from magnesium-rich soil are part of my diet. The calendula petals I collect for our salads are nutrition for my not-yet-conceived granddaughter—Radical Balance.

Neurotransmitters are chemicals that transmit signals between our nervous system cells, with messages we depend on for survival. Fight or flight. Rest or nurture. Love at first sight. There are as many neurotransmitter receptor sites in your gastro-intestinal tract, as there are in your brain: that gut feeling is the truth. Homeopathy theorizes that in 7 years or less you adopt the strengths and weaknesses of those you spend the most time with. The brain is a muscle. Gratitude and complaint are exercises. Which do you want to build? Use adaptogenic plants (Ashwagandha, Eleuthero, Rhodiola, Schisandra, Reishi) to help our bodies move from stress into balance; nervines (Hawthorne, Motherwort, California Poppy, Lemonbalm, Oat) sooth and tone the nervous system—Radical Balance.

What if we were to hold all our body systems as equally important? Thank our hearts for beating. Chew with intention. Exercise our brain and skeletal muscles with equal gentleness. Breathe clean air deeply. Consciously engage the parasympathetic nervous system before eating. Honor dynamic equilibrium already in place.

What if we got out of our body's way? She is striving for alliance with us, no matter what we do. If instead of drinking coffee every morning, we got enough sleep and were grateful to use the blessed bean only when our sleep was disturbed? If we sipped kombucha with properly nutritious meals?

Too hard? Never. Take every tiny step in the direction of dynamic equilibrium. Eat what you need, move every day, choose your food and herbs wisely, like medicine. Start with a cup of tea. Are you cold? Cinnamon. Hot? Sun-steeped mint. Retiring for the evening? Lavender and chamomile. Grow your own. If you have a windowsill, you can start an herb garden. You're already on your way to Radical Balance.

ASTROLOGICAL TONICS: CELL SALTS AND FLOWER ESSENCES

The 12 cell salts are easily assimilated, nourishing astrological tonics. Use your Sun sign's cell salt in times of stress to rebuild and stabilize your body, mind and spirit. When the stress is more emotional, use your Moon sign's cell salt to reduce anxiety, panic attacks and depression, and to restore emotional resilience.

Wild Flower Mandala
© Maria Silmon 2012

Cell salts are small white, sweet pellets that dissolve easily in the mouth (even children happily take them); they are inexpensive, can be used for extended periods, and are available at most health food stores.

Cell salts are compatible with flower essences and other therapies, and the original Bach flower essences also correlate with specific astrological signs. Some people, and some circumstances, respond better to cell salts, some to essences. Often they are used in conjunction for radical integration.

SIGN	CELL SALT	FLOWER ESSENCE
Aries	Kali Phos.	Impatiens
Taurus	Nat Sulph.	Gentian
Gemini	Kali Mur	Cerato
Cancer	Calc Flour	Clematis
Leo	Mag Phos	Vervain
Virgo	Kali Sulph	Centaury
Libra	Nat Phos	Scleranthuss
Scorpio	Calc Sulph	Chicory
Sagittarius	Silica	Agrimony
Capricorn	Calc Phos	Mimulus
Aquarius	Nat Mur	Water Violet
Pisces	Ferrum Phos	Rock Rose

Two flower essences will be universally supportive in 2014, and can be combined with your Sun or Moon sign essence. Oak (Bach) balances efforts with flexibility and acceptance. Scarlet Monkeyflower (Fes) supports Saturn in Scorpio in clearing away old emotional blocks that keep you from living gracefully in the present.

by Gretchen Lawlor © Mother Tongue Ink 2013 www.gretchenlawlor.com

THE WHEEL OF THE YEAR: HOLY DAYS

The seasonal cycle of the year is created by the tilt of the Earth's axis, leaning toward or away from the Sun, north to south, as the Earth orbits the Sun. Solstices are the extreme points all over the world when days and nights are longest or shortest. On equinoxes, days and nights are equal in all parts of the world. The four cross-quarter days roughly mark the midpoints in between solstices and equinoxes. We commemorate these natural turning points in the Earth's cycle. We use the dates in the ancient Celtic calendar, which closely approximate the eight spokes of the wheel of the year.* We note Lunar Holy Days observed in ancient Celtic practice on the new or full moon closest to what are now date-fixed cross-quarter days. Seasonal celebrations of most cultures cluster around these same natural turning points:

February 2 Imbolc/Mid-Winter: celebration, prophecy, purification, initiation—Candlemas (Christian), New Year (Tibetan, Chinese, Iroquois), Tu Bi-Shevat (Jewish). Goddess Festivals: Brigit, Brighid, Brigid (Celtic).

March 20 Equinox/Spring: rebirth, fertility, eggs—Passover (Jewish), Easter (Christian). Goddess Festivals: Eostare, Ostara, Oestre (German), Astarte (Semite), Persephone (Greek), Flora (Roman).

May 1 Beltane/Mid-Spring: planting, fertility, sexuality—May Day (Euro-American), Walpurgisnacht/Valborg (German and Scandinavian), Root Festival (Yakima), Ching Ming (Chinese), Whitsuntide (Dutch). Goddess Festivals: Aphrodite (Greek), Venus (Roman), Lada (Slavic).

June 21 Solstice/Summer: sun, fire festivals—Niman Kachina (Hopi). Goddess Festivals: Isis (Egyptian), Litha (N. African), Yellow Corn Mother (Taino), Ishtar (Babylonian), Hestia (Greek), Sunna (Norse).

August 2 Lammas/Mid-Summer: first harvest, breaking bread, abundance—Green Corn Ceremony (Creek), Sundance (Lakota). Goddess Festivals: Corn Mother (Hopi), Amaterasu (Japanese), Hatshepsut's Day (Egyptian), Ziva (Ukraine), Habondia (Celtic).

September 22 Equinox/Fall: gather and store, ripeness—Mabon (Euro-American), Goddess Festivals: Tari Pennu (Bengali), Old Woman Who Never Dies (Mandan), Chicomecoatl (Aztec), Black Bean Mother (Taino), Epona (Roman), Demeter (Greek).

October 31 Samhain/Mid-Fall: underworld journey, ancestor spirits—Hallowmas/Halloween (Euro-American), All Souls Day (Christian), Sukkoth (Jewish harvest). Goddess Festivals: Baba Yaga (Russia), Inanna (Sumer), Hecate (Greek).

December 21 Solstice/Winter: returning of the light—Kwanzaa (African-American), Soyal (Hopi), Jul (Scandinavian), Cassave/Dreaming (Taino), Chanukah (Jewish), Christmas (Christian), Festival of Hummingbirds (Quecha). Goddess Festivals: Freya (Norse), Lucia (Italy, Sweden), Sarasvati (India).

* Note: Traditional pagan Celtic / Northern European holy days start earlier than the customary Native / North American ones—they are seen to begin in the embryonic dark phase: e.g., at sunset, the night before the holy day—and the seasons are seen to start on the Cross Quarter days before the Solstices and Equinoxes. In North America, these cardinal points on the wheel of the year are seen to initiate the beginning of each season.

© *Mother Tongue Ink 2003 Sources:* The Grandmother of Time *by Z. Budapest, 1989;* Celestially Auspicious Occasions *by Donna Henes, 1996 and* Songs of Bleeding *by Spider, 1992*

Introduction to the Holy Days

In this time of increasing uncertainty, when climate change and world politics are altering Earth in ways we can barely comprehend, Grandmother Earth cries out for the restoration of Balance, for the interconnection of all that is living, all the Peoples—human, creature, plant, rock—to be honoured, so that the sacred Web of Life

The Sun Bringing Life to the World
◻ *Luz-Maria López 2009*

may continue. It is time to work with her energy, however extreme, aligning ourselves and our communities to the sacred Wheel of the Year: to the Equinoxes and Solstices that follow the dance of sun and earth through light and dark, to the four Fire Festivals that mark the agricultural year and the living and dying of the wild.

As the world turns she spins with her shadow. Learn to see negative and positive in balance; sometimes it is the darkness that shows us her gift, sometimes the light. As we become more and more dependent on the virtual world for our community and relationships, our adventures and realities, so many of us are losing our visceral connections to Gaia. Balance the shift of mind and imagination with the ground beneath your feet.

Go out on the land to feel Gaia's rhythms pulse through your body: take time to be with trees, with shore and sea, with stone. Seek out a singing wolf, a whale, a woodpecker drumming in the dawn like a shaman; let a wild wind unsettle the hair on the back of your neck. Make sure the next generation knows of the beauty of Earth: take children to see how a plant moves through seed, sapling, flower, fruit, husk—how birds live, how stars and moon shine in a sky undimmed by city lights.

Let us use all our senses in wonder at this world, our home and heart, becoming fierce in its protection and restoration, raising our voices loud and strong in passion for Grandmother Earth—She who Changes. This is a new time and requires the risk of new vision to move forward into new balance.

Rose Flint © Mother Tongue Ink 2013

Musings on Evolving We'Moon Themes: The Long View

How do we choose We'Moon's theme each year? We start with the Tarot as oracle—rather than a customary divinatory "reading," we follow the 22 Major Arcana cards in sequence, focusing on the card that corresponds to each datebook year (XIV for We'Moon 2014). The cards map a symbolic journey from zero, the Fool, to XXI, the World, representing archetypes of human potential we encounter as stepping stones in evolving consciousness. Each Major Arcana card signifies a stage in the trajectory of spiritual awakening. We use each year's card as muse, to translate cosmic forces at play, and read the pulse of the times from a We'Moon perspective.

Like a snake biting its tail (the mystical Ouroborus), we circle around and around—recycling lessons of life and spirit as we spiral through the same points in the cycle over time. Since We'Moon has been on this journey for 33 years, we gain perspective by seeing different thematic variations on the same cards as we revisit each step on the path.

This year gives a welcome reprieve from a heavy sequence of Tarot imagery for a tumultuous 5-year period beginning in 2012. We seek the growing edge. With The Hanged One (XII) as our oracle for 2012, we chose to focus on the metaphor of deep inner change in "Chrysalis." The last time around for card XII was *We'Moon '93* (numerologically, 9+3=12), when we named the theme "Invoking Spirit." For 2013 (XIII Death), we explored total transformation from the perspective of "The Other Side"; in *We'Moon '94*, the theme was "Cycles." 2014 re-frames Temperance (XIV) as realignment toward "Radical Balance"; *We'Moon '95*'s theme was "Survivors: the Healer Within." Next year, with *We'Moon 2015*, we encounter The Devil (XV) as "Wild Card"—check out our Call for Contributions (wemoon.ws/call.html). An earlier slant on this card was "Earth Matters" in *We'Moon '96*. The Tower card follows (XVI) for 2016: we feel the rumblings of breakdown, breakthrough, shaking up the patriarchal paradigm. *We'Moon '97* explored "Womyn in Community" as one such transformative force.

In spiritual terms, there are no absolute "good" or "bad" cards dealt in Tarot, as in life. Each card has its flip side: a positive and negative way to go with the energy. Even the most challenging situations can be catalysts for revolutionary change. When consciousness shifts, the rest follows.

In this ancient Mayan greeting the adversarial paradigm is turned on its head. When women join hands and hearts, the upraised fist is transformed into a spiral of cooperation and mutual empowerment that can change the world.

In Lak'ech: I am Another You
Photo and Writing © Musawa 2013

INTRODUCTION TO THE THEME: RADICAL BALANCE

Did someone call a repairperson for the world? Well, yes—desperately—and here she is, on the cover of *We'Moon 2014*! Tools at the ready, in her full power, scoping out the trajectory, holding to Center with a delicate balance among the cosmic whorls of an evolving Space/Time continuum.

This sky-riding woman sets the tone for our 2014 thematic explorations, based on Tarot card XIV, Temperance. The Temperance card is traditionally imaged with an angel pouring Fire and

Temperance
© *Max Dashú 1975*

Water together so they synergize into a marvelously new creation. Pondering that magical blending of extremes to create new reality, we reframed our theme as "Radical Balance": that's what it takes to make synergy, to stay grounded with Source and to right a world spinning with oppositional forces. She-who-balances in the midst of chaos, she-who-tempers, is an alchemist, an artist, a healer—stirring up the old order to invent new substance, stretching and burnishing new possibility, blazing The Middle Path.

How can there be a Middle Way in a world flung far out of balance into war and poverty, violence and misogyny, environmental degradation? Radical Balance is no namby-pamby mollifying stroll between equally powerful adversaries. Imbalance is the given; the Middle Way doesn't necessarily start in the middle.

Building harmony often requires active resistance to the dominant paradigm. Sometimes the people burst out "Stop! Enough!" and the swing toward balance rushes ahead. As I write in the winter of 2013, the horrifics of gun violence entrenched in the US have stirred new waves of mass revulsion. In India, thousands of people are filling the streets to demand the end to an ages-old culture of male violence against women. Mighty efforts are tilting the scales from their long-skewed position. Unfortunately, at a different tipping point of severe planetary imbalance, polar ice melts far faster than predicted.

How does our Alchemist, our Healer navigate these times? *We'Moon 2014* writers and artists go deep into the metaphor of Radical Balance, illuminating layers of creative transformation that both hold steady and spark with daring. We thread through the datebook delightful and evocative images of physical balancing: women on tightropes, on the edge, juggling balls; bird on a fingertip, leopard in a tree. From these balancing centers of exquisite inner peace, a sense of personal wholeness radiates, and committed visions emerge to repair the world. We'Moon contributors affirm synergistic relationships that serve the common good: cooperative earth-friendly practices transforming community life; the holy work of reconciliation, crossing borders, enacting loving-kindness with disparate peoples.

Synergy is no cakewalk. Molecules blend, not always seamlessly. There is the push and pull of relationship, the ever-presence of our Shadow selves. There is the effort to embrace that final union our molecules will complete with the earth, "when flesh and spirit must take separate bows" (excerpt Linda Albert, p. 167).

The heartbeat pulsing through the datebook belongs to Woman as the Temperance icon. Turn to the front cover again and let her balanced power as the Navigator fill you with confidence. Pay devoted feminist attention to Moon VII "Changing Woman," where women's personal and collective triumphs are celebrated. "The dead language shall rise—womanspeak the canary of seasons. . . ." (excerpt Shae Savoy, p. 117).

This year Laadan is one of the four rotating languages naming weekdays in the calendar pages. Laadan was constructed by Suzette Haden Elgin in 1982, for the purpose of expressing the perceptions of women. There is, of course, no unitary Woman with identical experiences across cultures and circumstances. We bring Laadan forward acknowledging women as inventors of culture, whose varied contributions have not been fully appreciated in the dominant discourse. Gerda Lerner (honored as an Ansister on p. 204) was once criticized for establishing Women's History as a separate academic discipline outside the mainstream. She responded, "Give us another 4000 years, and we'll talk about mainstreaming."

Are we there yet? Radical Balance is a work in progress, and our front cover heroine has us well on our way. She lifts us into a fantastical universe of transformation for womankind, and for the Earth—so acutely celebrated in its resourceful depth on the back cover. Welcome to the balancing acts of We'Moon 2014, where we nurture a special home for women's creative brilliance on the edge of unfolding tomorrows.

Bethroot Gwynn © Mother Tongue Ink 2013

On the high wire of these times
Changing Woman dances
surefooted and exuberant.
O Goddess of Radical Alchemy!
Teach us the arts
Of bending with the sway,
Then countering the flow,
Of blending the extremes,
Daring to hold the Middle Way.
Grant us, Kwan Yin,
Your poise in the eye of the storm.
Ground us in your Harmony.
Challenge us with the immeasurable reach
Of your Love.
Pele, Divine Artisan, temper us
In your Great Fire of reconciliation
Where opposites burst into new gold,
Rigidities soften
And the annealed heart can mend.

The Wire

In socks, I pad over, step onto the starting platform.
Give the wire a look.
The ending platform an island with twelve feet of tautness between.
A sliver of place to be.
How I long to dwell there.
One foot on and I am alone.
No one to catch or applaud. No one to clap or console. Just me.
And the wire.
My eyes lock on the ending platform. I have my destination.
My foot down on the wire and further down to the floor,
to the ground below, down to the earth
and further still to the center, where I am not
Alone
where I meet the feet of
Everyone
who stands on the earth wishing for a slim place to call their own.
There, beneath my foot on the wire,
I meet everyone who has ever loved me and everyone who
doesn't know it yet.
I take a second step.
Arms aloft, sending myself
Everywhere.
I am the supporting, catching,
clapping hands.
I am everywhere around the room.
I am supported by everyone below.
I am the joyful tautness between.
I walk step by step across.
Slide my foot to the smooth,
cool flatness of the platform.
Slowly lower my arms. Look around.
Just me. And the wire. And everyone.

◻ *Galloway Quena Crain 2012*

Trust © *Catrina Steffen 2009*

0. AT THE EDGE

Moon 0: December 2–January 1

New Moon in ♐ Saqgittarius Dec. 2; Full Moon in ♊ Gemini Dec. 17; Sun in ♑ Capricorn Dec. 21

Balancing Act
© *Diane Lee Moomey 2012*

December 2013

Adol—Root Month ──── ⟩⟩⟩ Henesháal—East Day

♊   ## Monday
16

☽☍♅ 10:17 am
☿☍♄ 11:02 am

Moon Ring □ *Jennifer Rain Crosby 2012*

──── ♂♂♂ Honesháal—West Day ────

♊
♋   ## Tuesday
17

☉☍☽ 1:28 am v/c
♅D 9:39 am
☽→♋ 10:17 am
☽△♆ 4:07 pm
☽□♂ 8:42 pm

Full Moon in ♊ Gemini 1:28 am PST
Moonrise Time: 5:27 pm PST

──── ☿☿☿ Hunesháal—North Day ────

♋   ## Wednesday
18

☽□♅ 3:32 am
☽☍♇ 7:59 am
☽♂♃ 10:02 pm

──── ♄♄♄ Hanesháal—South Day ────

♋
♌   ## Thursday
19

☽△♄ 12:49 am
☽ApG 3:47 pm
☽☍♀ 8:37 pm v/c
☽→♌ 10:48 pm

──── ♀♀♀ Rayilesháal—Above Day ────

♌   ## Friday
20

☽⚹♂ 11:53 am
☽△♅ 4:11 pm

Today

Be prepared.
There is a lot more
of what never was
to come.

◻ *Janine Canan 2012*

Contemplating Life: Sedona
◻ *Lisa O'Connor 2010*

———————— ᚺᚺᚺ Yilesháal — Below Day ————————

♌ Saturday
21

☉→♑ 9:11 am
♀R 1:53 pm
☽□♄ 2:00 pm

Winter Solstice

Sun in ♑ Capricorn 9:11 am PST

———————— ☉☉☉ Hathamesháal — Center Day ————————

♌
♍ Sunday
22

☽△♅ 5:25 am v/c
☽→♍ 11:19 am
☉△☽ 1:44 pm
☽☍♆ 5:20 pm

December 2013
desamber

Monday
23

♍

☽△♇ 9:09 am
☽⚹♃ 9:19 pm

Tuesday
24

♍
♎

♉→♑ 2:12 am
☽⚹♄ 2:13 am
☉⚹♆ 9:05 am
☽△♀ 7:54 pm v/c
☽→♎ 10:17 pm

Wednesday
25

♎

♂☍♅ 12:33 am
☽□♉ 1:11 am
☿ApG 4:07 am
☉□☽ 5:48 am
☽☍♅ 2:40 pm
☽♂♂ 3:12 pm
☽□♇ 7:15 pm

Waning Half Moon in ♎ Libra 5:48 am PST

Thursday
26

♎

☿⚹♆ 1:03 am
☽□♃ 6:01 am

Friday
27

♎
♏

☽□♀ 3:00 am v/c
☽→♏ 5:58 am
☽△♆ 11:32 am
♂⚹♌ 3:12 pm
☽⚹♉ 4:02 pm
☉⚹☽ 5:25 pm

Equipoise

If it can look like teetering,
if passing through the middle
on my swaying way
counts for balance,
if it can mean
constant course correction—
then I'm extremely
balanced.

The kind that perches steady
isn't mine.
Yet when balance happens—
as after I obsess on love,
and tip into fear,
and spring to right myself again—
I can haul up laughing
and embrace it.

◻ Susa Silvermarie 2012

Transformational Balance
◻ Liz Atticus Ferrie 2008

— ꜛꜛꜛ Šanbe —

♏

Saturday
28

☽⚹♇ 1:35 am
☽△♃ 10:56 am
☽♂♄ 4:58 pm
☉♂♅ 10:27 pm

— ☉☉☉ Yekšanbe —

♏
♐

Sunday
29

☽⚹♀ 5:54 am v/c
☽→♐ 9:37 am
☿□♅ 12:48 pm

☽□♆ 2:52 pm
☉□♅ 9:05 pm
☽△♅ 11:51 pm

Managing a Planet

I can't be the only person
to have this epiphany

how the circus is not an escape at all,
but instead a mirror—

how the ringmasters in flashy suits
are just actors with big voices
who pretend to know how to run these shows

how the clowns with painted tears
who trip over everything
and chase around in circles have a familiar ring

how the animals might roar for a reason
how they could escape their bars
and trample us, shake off their riders
and stampede

how the ladies in leotards
who fly through the air above us
might not be caught one day
by the men with bulging biceps
hanging upside down and backwards

how all of us are doing
this high wire act
without a net together
how all of us could fall

how we might only be able
to swallow so many swords, juggle
so many balls, jump though
so many hoops of fire
before the greatest show
on earth
runs out of encores

how even at age four I felt disquiet
at the circus
how the cotton candy
has been a bribe to distract us—

how the tickets don't come with
money back guarantees.

I. REWORKING THE WORLD

Moon I: January 1–January 30

New Moon in ♑ Capricorn Jan. 1; Full Moon in ♋ Cancer Jan. 15; Sun in ♒ Aquarius Jan. 19

The world calls us to rise in enormous flocks
to reshape the landscape with cattailpuffs and passionjoy
to dance our collective rhythm—peepers and snow geese,
wavecrash and brookgurgle—re-toning the world,
shedding territories, tongues and tribal boundaries
like worn shoes that have grown too tight,
courting our ancient wisdom to spark us bright.

> Let's work together, you and I,
> alongside earthsongbeat,
> heartfirst, handtouch
> souldance.
> please.

excerpt ¤ Holly Wilkinson 2012

(top) **Sacred Sisters (1994)** *&* *(bottom)* **Moonsisters (1993)**
¤ *Ann-Rosemary Conway / Stonewoman*

Dec. 2013 /Jan. 2014
diciembre / enero

— ☽☽☽ lunes —

Monday
30

☽✶♂ 3:36 am v/c
☿✶♄ 7:47 am
♂□♇ 5:22 pm

— ♂♂♂ martes —

Tuesday
31

☿♂♇ 3:26 am
☉✶♄ 3:36 am
☿□♂ 6:59 am
☽→♑ 10:01 am
☽✶♆ 3:06 pm
☽□♅ 11:40 pm

— ☿☿☿ miércoles —

Wednesday
1

☉♂☽ 3:14 am   ☉♂♇ 10:57 am
☽♂♇ 3:44 am   ☽☍♃ 11:09 am
☽□♂ 4:41 am   ☽PrG 1:11 pm
☽♂☿ 6:32 am   ☽✶♄ 6:06 pm

January 2014

New Moon in ♑ Capricorn 3:14 am PST
Moonrise Time: 6:57 am PST

— ♃♃♃ jueves —

Thursday
2

☽♂♀ 3:12 am v/c
☽→♒ 9:03 am
☉□♂ 4:14 pm
☽✶♅ 10:46 pm
☿☍♃ 11:10 pm

— ♀♀♀ viernes —

Friday
3

☽△♂ 5:12 am
♇ApG 10:16 am
☽□♄ 5:46 pm v/c

ALL ASPECTS IN PACIFIC STANDARD TIME; ADD 3 HOURS FOR EST; ADD 8 HOURS FOR GMT

Carmageddon

One morning dawned
with all the cars gone.
Trucks too, vans, SUVs.
The only things left
were buses and trains and these
had lost their ability to idle.
Weeping and wailing ensued.
There was no more road rage.
True, people drank and cycled,
but there were hardly any deaths.
In the forests, waters,
meadows and skies,
endless rejoicing.

¤ *Christine Lowther 2010*

Storm *© Monika Steinhoff 2012*

ᚻᚻᚻ sábado

Saturday
4

☽→♓ 8:58 am
♃PrG 9:46 am
☽☌♆ 2:26 pm

☉☉☉ domingo

Sunday
5

☽⚹♇ 3:52 am
☉⚹☽ 10:30 am
☽△♃ 10:43 am

☉☌♃ 1:11 pm
☽⚹♅ 7:10 pm
☽△♄ 7:48 pm

January
yī yuè

 ))) xī qī yī

♓︎
♈︎

☿⚹♄ 12:51 am
)⚹♀ 1:44 am v/c
)→♈︎ 11:45 am

Monday
6

♂♂♂ xī qī èr

♈︎

)♂♅ 3:20 am
)□♇ 8:13 am
)☍♂ 1:54 pm
☿♂♀ 2:01 pm
)□♃ 2:55 pm
☉□) 7:39 pm

Tuesday
7

Waxing Half Moon in ♈︎Aries 7:39 pm PST

☿☿☿ xī qī sān

♈︎
♉︎

)□♀ 5:19 am
)□☿ 8:22 am v/c
♂□♃ 2:35 pm
)→♉︎ 6:24 pm

Wednesday
8

♃♃♃ xī qī sì

♉︎

)⚹♆ 12:56 am
)△♇ 4:27 pm
)⚹♃ 10:48 pm

Thursday
9

♀♀♀ xī qī w

♉︎

☉△) 9:34 am
)☍♄ 11:07 am
♀PrG 11:41 am
)△♀ 11:57 am

Friday
10

ALL ASPECTS IN PACIFIC STANDARD TIME; ADD 3 HOURS FOR EST; ADD 8 HOURS FOR GMT

The Times We're Living In

It is not so easy to see what is birthing
Beneath the surface of the world,
Getting ready to emerge
Like a newborn crowning

As old ways of domination and violation
Fight to hold sway,
A great birthing has begun,
The birth of a new way
Of being in the world
A way of re-connection and shared power,
A way of cooperation and love

We are flowering out of the mud
Of our darkest time of separation
Evolving from the time of *me*
To the time of *we*
This time is difficult, yes
But it is also juicy and joyous.
It is not easy to soar through mud
But mud is rich and fertile
And out of mud
The lotus blooms.

excerpt ¤ Robin Rose Bennett 2011

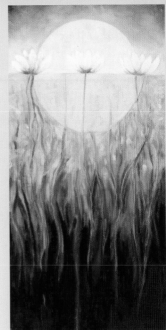

Healing Room
© Beth Lenco 2011

ꜙꜙꜙ xī qī lĩù

♉
♊ ◖ Saturday
11

♀⚹♄ 2:44 am
☽△♅ 2:58 am v/c
☉♂♅ 4:24 am
☽→♊ 4:26 am

☉⚹♄ 5:38 am
☽□♆ 11:25 am
♉→♒ 1:35 pm
☽⚹♅ 10:02 pm

⊙⊙⊙ lD bàī rì

♊ ◖ Sunday
12

☽△♂ 1:33 pm v/c

January
Alel—Seaweed Month

◻ *Bridget Reynolds 2009*

Balance

—————— ⟫⟫⟫ Heneshál—East Day ——————

♊
♋

Monday
13

☽→♋ 4:25 pm
☽△♆ 11:41 pm

—————— ♂♂♂ Honeshál—West Day ——————

♋

Tuesday
14

☽□♅ 10:25 am
☽☍♇ 4:07 pm
☽☌♃ 9:06 pm

—————— ☿☿☿ Huneshál—North Day ——————

♋

Wednesday
15

☽□♂ 4:03 am
☽☍♀ 6:16 am
☽△♄ 11:59 am
☽ApG 5:58 pm
☉☍☽ 8:52 pm v/c

Moonrise Time: 5:06 pm PST
Full Moon in ♋ Cancer 8:52 pm PST

—————— ♃♃♃ Haneshál—South Day ——————

♋
♌

Thursday
16

☽→♌ 5:00 am
♀□♂ 9:13 am
☿⚹♅ 10:25 pm
☽△♅ 11:09 pm
☽☍☿ 11:16 pm

—————— ♀♀♀ Rayileshál—Above Day ——————

♌

Friday
17

☽⚹♂ 6:33 pm

ALL ASPECTS IN PACIFIC STANDARD TIME; ADD 3 HOURS FOR EST; ADD 8 HOURS FOR GMT

2014 Year at a Glance for ♒ Aquarius (Jan. 19–Feb. 18)

By 2014 you are ahead of the pack during this 2012–15 evolutionary portal. Aquarius is a leading voice in out-of-the-box thinking. Your brilliant, zany spin is often far ahead of the times; in 2014 revel in the respect your timely originality garners.

You work well in teams, bringing together diverse voices for electrifying dialogue. You zip here and there, facilitating connections that others would never have dared. You have the ability to stand back, constantly assessing who is capable of what and where the group is heading.

For young Aquarians, a more conservative, hard working façade this year helps you gain position and respect. Your fears of not having what it takes to succeed are resolved with your tenacity and discipline. You begin to understand that you are manifesting some family member's dream.

Mid-2013 to mid-2014 you thrive in a good work setting, with mentors who inspire your methods, practices and routines. As your efficiency and precision grow stronger, you may want to seek new employment. You will be surprised at the enthusiastic response from generous new allies. Be discerning about highly speculative endeavors; financial gains are likely to be elusive in such circumstances.

Special people arrive like gifts into your life the second half of the year. These folks really understand you; they open up your horizons. Aquarians prefer spacious relationships, where they are free to roam and return without being rejected. For anyone wanting to be in relationship with an Aquarian, it's especially important to respect this truth in 2014.

Gretchen Lawlor © Mother Tongue Ink 2013

Life Balance © Modupe 2012

ħħħ Yilesháal —Below Day

♌
♍ ◐ **Saturday**
        18

☽□ħ   12:51 am v/c
☽→♍   5:23 pm

⊙⊙⊙ Hathamesháal —Center Day

♍ ◐ **Sunday**
        19

☽☌♆   12:55 am
♂☌♃   5:03 pm
☽△♇   5:09 pm
⊙→♒   7:51 pm
☽✶♃   8:26 pm

Sun in ♒ Aquarius 7:51 pm PST

January
zhanvīch

© Katheryn M. Trenshaw 2004

Sacred Feet

━━━ ꒯꒯꒯ Dōsanbe ━━━

♍

Monday
20

☽△♀ 1:42 am
☽⚹♄ 12:55 pm v/c

━━━ ♂♂♂ Sešanbe ━━━

♍
♎

Tuesday
21

☽→♎ 4:43 am
☉△☽ 7:40 am
☽☍♅ 10:22 pm

━━━ ☿☿☿ Cahâršanbe ━━━

♎

Wednesday
22

☽□♇ 3:53 am
☽□♃ 6:20 am
☽□♀ 10:06 am
☽△☿ 4:00 pm
☽♂♂ 7:50 pm v/c

━━━ ♃♃♃ Panjšanbe ━━━

♎
♏

Thursday
23

☽→♏ 1:43 pm
☽△♆ 8:56 pm
☉□☽ 9:19 pm

Waning Half Moon in ♏ Scorpio 9:19 pm PST

━━━ ♀♀♀ Jom'e ━━━

♏

Friday
24

☿△♂ 6:57 am
☽⚹♇ 11:43 am
☽△♃ 1:23 pm
☽⚹♀ 4:06 pm

ALL ASPECTS IN PACIFIC STANDARD TIME; ADD 3 HOURS FOR EST; ADD 8 HOURS FOR GMT

Blue Blue Hearts   © *Cori Caputo 2002*

The Earth kisses the soles
of my feet
With each step, I bless her,
promise her healing
© *Giita Priebe 2012*

———— ♄♄♄ Šanbe ————

♏
♐

Saturday
25

☿□♄   3:55 am
☽♂♄   5:42 am
☽□♅   5:55 am v/c
☽→♐   7:12 pm

———— ☉☉☉ Yekšanbe ————

♐

Sunday
26

☽□♆   2:03 am
☉✶☽   6:23 am
☽△♅   10:58 am

Ventriloquy

Essence the marrow the bone structure cheek
pillow jumbalaya—we're all jumbled and mixed, atoms
melting and moving—harmony of the spheres—what is
really inanimate? Who animates? What is animation but
movement of still-life pictures, pulling strings puppet jaws
clacking ventriloquist. Something is speaking through me.
The current runs and hums like the high buzz of fluorescent
lighting which becomes more audible with each extra ounce
of attention I pay—I'm measuring my coins in the offering.
I'm counting my blessings in the offing. My gratitude list
spools and turns like ticker tape, ever-growing, ever-
evolving. When you and I touch, our molecules
blend. See, there is no separation, there are no
easy boundaries or definition. To define is
to limit. There are no hard and fast
lines to draw in the sand.
¤ *Shae Savoy 2011*

All We Are © *Modupe 2012*

Symbiotic Dance   © *Kay Kemp 2012*

January
enero / febrero

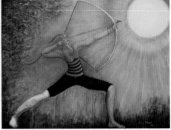

Taking Aim *© Eleanor Ruckman 2010*

———— ☽☽☽ lunes ————

Monday
27

☋
♑

☽✶♂	7:52 am
☽✶♉	2:02 pm v/c
☽→♑	9:04 pm

———— ♂♂♂ martes ————

♑

Tuesday
28

☽✶♆	3:37 am
☽□♅	12:00 pm
☽☌♇	4:35 pm
☽☍♃	5:06 pm
☽☌♀	6:57 pm

———— ☿☿☿ miércoles ————

♑
♒

Wednesday
29

☉✶♅	12:33 am
☽✶♄	8:43 am
☽□♂	8:47 am v/c
☽→♒	8:33 pm

———— ♃♃♃ jueves ————

♒

Thursday
30

Lunar Imbolc

☽PrG	1:55 am
☽✶♅	11:16 am
☉☌☽	1:38 pm

Moonrise Time: 6:23 am PST
New Moon in ♒ Aquarius 1:38 pm PST

———— ♀♀♀ viernes ————

♒
♓

Friday
31

♃☍♇	1:16 am	♀D	12:49 pm
♅→♓	6:29 am	☽→♓	7:44 pm
☽□♄	7:56 am	☉⚼♃	8:05 pm
☽△♂	8:45 am v/c	☽☌♅	8:38 pm

———————————————————

Imbolc

All along the riverbanks swan-clans have gathered together. They wait patiently, their white feathers frosted with crystal; they know Brigit is coming. Black water knows. Furled buds on the sycamore know. Ewes know and let down their milk; frozen acres know as hidden seeds begin to push. *The Serpent is come from her hole*—so chanted the ancient Gaels, in praise of Brigit bringing the end of Winter, the return of Spring.

Great Goddess of Earth, Triple Goddess of Fire—of healing, of smithcraft, of poetry. I see her wild, red-haired, stepping across the skies in brightness. She is Fiery Arrow, the leather-skirted smith striking sparks from the iron anvil of earth, healing the hurt of all winters, lighting the green fuse. Whatever is frozen will warm; whatever is grieved will know joy; whatever bliss is unmade will come into being.

We sit in darkness until light enters—the Maiden, carrying a candle, the flame of hope renewing land and peoples. We pray the light into our hearts and communities. We give ourselves to her transformative fire.

Rose Flint © Mother Tongue Ink 2013

Healing Hand ¤ rain crowe 2009

Synthesis © Mara Berendt Friedman and Trinity Harris 2010

The Importance of Being Initiated

Initiation is not just standing in a coven circle waiting to be admitted; it is not just learning particular forms and speaking ancient words. Initiation is the day you were told you couldn't have children. It is the death of your best friend; it is being made redundant, going bankrupt, miscarriage, devastating illness, being dumped and leaving your coven. Initiation is the event which changes you, marking the death of your old self and heralding the birth of the new you—a changed you, another evolution in your journey. Another part of who you are, absorbed into your self.

excerpt ¤ Becky Annison 2011

One By One

One by one, in tiny increments,
candle by candle, gesture by effort,
wish by prayer, concern by care,
we feed the life-fires of the soul
and light the infinite universe,
little by little from within.

© Mama Donna Henes 2008

Prayers ¤ *Pi Luna 2012*

─── ♄♄♄ sábado ───

| ♓ | | Saturday 1 | February |

D☌Ψ 2:29 am
D△♃ 3:16 pm
D⚹♇ 3:36 pm
D⚹♀ 5:38 pm

─── ☉☉☉ domingo ───

| ♓ ♈ | | Sunday 2 | Imbolc/Candlemas |

D△♄ 8:34 am v/c
D→♈ 8:54 pm

February
èr yuè

Power is She
© *Janine Jackson 2010*

————)))) xī qī yī ————

♈ Monday
3

) ☌ ♅ 1:17 pm
) □ ♃ 5:25 pm
) □ ♇ 6:16 pm
) □ ♀ 8:40 pm
☉ ✶) 11:31 pm

———— ♂♂♂ xī qī èr ————

♈ Tuesday
4

) ☍ ♂ 3:14 pm v/c

———— ☿☿☿ xī qī sān ————

♈
♉ Wednesday
5

) → ♉ 1:46 am
) ✶ ♅ 7:39 am
) ✶ ♆ 9:50 am
♃ △ ♋ 11:53 am
) ✶ ♃ 11:35 pm

———— ♃♃♃ xī qī sì ————

♉ Thursday
6

) △ ♇ 1:00 am
) △ ♀ 4:13 am
☉ □) 11:22 am
☿ R 1:43 pm
) ☍ ♄ 8:49 pm v/c

Waxing Half Moon in ♉ Taurus 11:22 am PST

———— ♀♀♀ xī qī W ————

♉
♊ Friday
7

) → ♊ 10:44 am
) □ ♉ 5:03 pm
) □ ♆ 7:29 pm

ALL ASPECTS IN PACIFIC STANDARD TIME; ADD 3 HOURS FOR EST; ADD 8 HOURS FOR GMT

Awakening

Down, down
deep into the well
that is my own
true source,
deeper and deeper,
emerging
on the other side—
a woman, alive
with her hands
full of gold.

¤ *e.g. wise 2012*

Breaking Through Old Patterns
© *Denise Kester 2005*

ᚾᚾᚾ xī qī līù

♊

☽ ✶ ♅   5:56 am

Saturday
♉

⊙⊙⊙ ID bàī rì

♊
♋

⊙ △ ☽   3:42 am
☽ △ ♂   1:08 pm v/c
☽ → ♋   10:33 pm

Sunday
9

February

Ayáanin—Tree Month

———— ☽☽☽ Henesháal—East Day ————

♋

Monday
10

☽△☿ 2:59 am
☽△♆ 7:44 am
☽□♅ 6:27 pm
☽☌♃ 9:27 pm

———— ♂♂♂ Honesháal—West Day ————

♋

Tuesday
11

☽☍♇ 12:05 am
☽☍♀ 6:19 am
☉□♄ 11:57 am
☽△♄ 9:09 pm
☽ApG 9:10 pm

———— ☿☿☿ Hunesháal—North Day ————

♋
♌

Wednesday
12

☽□♂ 2:51 am v/c
☽→♌ 11:15 am
☿→♒ 7:29 pm

———— ♃♃♃ Hanesháal—South Day ————

♌

Thursday
13

☽△♅ 7:19 am

———— ♀♀♀ Rayilesháal—Above Day ————

♌
♍

Friday
14

☽□♄ 9:41 am
☉☍☽ 3:53 pm
☽⚹♂ 4:02 pm
☉△♂ 6:05 pm
☽☍♅ 7:13 pm v/c
☽→♍ 11:25 pm

Full Moon in ♌ Leo 3:53 pm PST
Moonrise Time: 5:42 pm PST

ALL ASPECTS IN PACIFIC STANDARD TIME; ADD 3 HOURS FOR EST; ADD 8 HOURS FOR GMT

My home, ambitiously called the Planet Repair Institute, is a hub of permaculture demonstration, natural building, and place-making—an abundant nook in the city where fruit trees grow, children play, and empowered humans stand up every day to reclaim the commons for all.

The positive influences we help foster within our local ecology—hosting annual Permaculture Design Courses, neighborhood potlucks, planting seeds to feed our community—ripple

© *Stephanie Wilson 2011*

through the city and across the nation against the grain of the imposed urban grid. We act with the understanding that each of us will thrive only in the context of collective abundance—that connecting both our resources and energetic flow with those around us will result in spontaneous beauty—an earthen poetry post, a neighborhood cold storage cellar, branches hung heavy with fruit to harvest.

Living in community at the Planet Repair Institute empowers my every decision in the name of love—to paint the street with a song on my lips, to earn right livelihood by weaving together books of reclaimed materials, to build and grow with the earth that lies beneath our feet. I understand, now, a truth: the repair of the planet will happen first in my own heart, in my relationships with others, and in the home I continue to build and tend.

¤ *Jane Gray 2012*

―――――――― ♄♄♄ Yileshául—Below Day ―――――――――

♍ Saturday
15

☽☌♆ 8:50 am
☉♂♉ 12:22 pm
☽✳♃ 9:11 pm

―――――――― ☉☉☉ Hathameshául—Center Day ―――――――――

♍ Sunday
16

♉△♂ 12:19 am
☽△♇ 12:40 am
☽△♀ 11:08 am
☽✳♄ 9:04 pm v/c

February
fevrīeh

♍︎
♎︎

Monday
17

☽→♎︎ 10:22 am
☿PrG 7:27 pm

Meeting

© *Deborah Koff-Chapin 2000*

♎︎

Tuesday
18

☽☍♅ 6:00 am
☽□♃ 7:18 am
☉→♓︎ 9:59 am
☽□♇ 11:04 am
☿□♄ 11:11 pm
☽□♀ 11:45 pm

 ♓︎

Sun in ♓︎ Pisces 9:59 am PST

♎︎
♏︎

Wednesday
19

☽△♅ 6:13 am
☽☌♂ 1:52 pm v/c
☽→♏︎ 7:33 pm
☉△☽ 10:24 pm

♏︎

Thursday
20

☽△♆ 4:42 am
☽△♃ 3:26 pm
☽⚹♇ 7:22 pm

♏︎

Friday
21

☽□♅ 9:58 am
☽⚹♀ 10:03 am
☽☌♄ 2:09 pm v/c

ALL ASPECTS IN PACIFIC STANDARD TIME; ADD 3 HOURS FOR EST; ADD 8 HOURS FOR GMT

2014 Year at a Glance for ♓ Pisces (Feb. 18–March 20)

2012–15 is an evolutionary portal held open by a fierce Feminine conscience. We're becoming more entwined, more related—all the people, animals, plants of this precious rare green Earth.

Hearing more, seeing more, knowing more: the cacophony of impressions we can no longer keep out can be overwhelming. Pisces live with this hyper-awareness all the time, and we all need Piscean gentle guidance to manage ourselves.

Pisces is so much happier with a cause, something to utterly surrender into. Your 2014 mission is to show us how to cope, how to shield.

Tell us stories of what you use to stay buoyant in the midst of so many changes. Lift us with your artistic brilliance. Teach us how to dream in healthy ways and to dream good dreams for each other. The maps you make for us are becoming more detailed. Teach or write—your perspectives lift us from despair to ingenuity.

This call to service may come more easily for older Pisceans. If you feel unprepared, look for/pray for teachers this year. Seek the wisdom of mystics, shamans, the sensitives who are present in every faith and spiritual tradition. Be curious, and be also cautious about who and what you expose yourself to.

Friends are laser surgeons who refine and refocus your visions. Lovers and playmates are abundant, dazzled by your gifts. You feel confident that all will be well, no matter the outcome of your efforts. Because of this trust, many opportunities will come your way this year.

Gretchen Lawlor © Mother Tongue Ink 2013

Yemanya © Kit Skeoch 2011

ᚻᚻᚻ Šanbe

♏ ⚰ Saturday
♐ 22

☽→♐ 2:11 am
☉□☽ 9:15 am
☽□♅ 11:02 am
☽△♅ 8:26 pm

Waning Half Moon in ♐ Sagittarius 9:15 am PST

☉☉☉ Yekšanbe

♐ ⚰ Sunday
23

☉☌♆ 10:11 am
☽⚹☿ 12:04 pm

February / March

febrero / marzo

 lunes

Monday
24

☽✳♂ 1:25 am v/c
ΨApG 3:05 am
☽→♑ 5:50 am
☽✳Ψ 2:19 pm

☉✳☽ 4:20 pm
♀✳♄ 8:50 pm
☽☐♅ 11:15 pm
☽☊♃ 11:23 pm

σσσ martes

Tuesday
25

☽σ♇ 3:20 am
♇✳♂ 2:34 pm
☽✳♄ 8:07 pm
☽σ♀ 9:17 pm
♃☐♅ 11:29 pm

☿☿☿ miércoles

Wednesday
26

☽☐♂ 2:51 am v/c
☽→♒ 6:55 am
☽✳♅ 11:54 pm

♃♃♃ jueves

Thursday
27

☽PrG 12:01 pm
☽σ♅ 12:01 pm
☽☐♄ 8:11 pm

♀♀♀ viernes

Friday
28

☽△♂ 2:55 am v/c
♅D 6:00 am
☽→♓ 6:52 am
☽σΨ 3:17 pm
☉△♃ 8:05 pm
☽△♃ 11:44 pm

ALL ASPECTS IN PACIFIC STANDARD TIME; ADD 3 HOURS FOR EST; ADD 8 HOURS FOR GMT

I, Wonder, say to you truly
all that we are
is just one motion of breath and divinity
rushing together—to fill the great lungs of life.
Let me stir in your body, this mystical cauldron,
where matter and spirit meet for a moment—
the one long moment—of your life.

excerpt © Renée Hummel 2006

Arati © Meganne Forbes 1996

━━━ ♄♄♄ sábado ━━━

 ♓

Saturday
1

⊙♂☽ 12:00 am
☽⚹♇ 3:55 am
♂R 8:23 am
☽△♄ 8:37 pm

March

New Moon in ♓ Pisces 12:00 am PST
Moonrise: 6:22 am PST

━━━ ⊙⊙⊙ domingo ━━━

♓
♈

Sunday
2

☽⚹♀ 3:04 am v/c
☽→♈ 7:40 am
♄R 8:19 am
♀□♂ 12:03 pm

Balanced Rock

Atop the hill She watches;
She eats, sleeps, and stretches out into the ethers,
into the coolness of the night
and catches falling stars
sprinkles them with the moon's dust
as moonlight strolls to the other side
then She eats them for breakfast.
Just before day breaks
and catches a glimpse of Her moving,
settling back into Her hilltop,
sandstone, red earthen clay throne
adorned with sage and scrub brush,
rabbits and ravens and rolling stones
moved about by winds and weather,
sunbathing and soaking in Silence and Space,
She looks across the endlessness of blue sky,
across to other Deities,
and gives Them a knowing wink.
Keeping Their secrets.
She settles in to receive guests,
to listen to their hearts and feel their joys and sorrows
to hold them in Her field of gravity and heal them.
In Her majesty this Red Rock Madonna teaches balance.
There are no "what if"s or "if only you knew"s
only balance, and that requires letting go.
Feel balance in the wind, in space and time
feel balance in the Mystery,
that is, after all, what is left and when *we* find It
we usually adorn It with stuff that is familiar—feels safe,
keeps us in illusion—weighs us down, keeps us from Her until
we let it all go again to greet the Mystery once more,
to unfold an unfamiliar path a little farther this time.
To balance.

◻ *Purple Moose 2012*

III. NATURE BALANCES

Moon III: March 1–March 30

New Moon in ♓ Pisces March 1; Full Moon in ♍ Virgo March 16; Sun in ♈ Aries March 20

Balance

¤ *Jeanette M. French 2010*

March
sān yuè

♈

Monday
3

☽□♃	1:14 am
☽♂♅	1:50 am
☽□♇	5:47 am
☉⚹♇	11:15 am
☽⚹♉	3:28 pm
☉♂♄	5:26 pm

♈
♉

Tuesday
4

☽☍♂	6:44 am
☽□♀	9:31 am v/c
☽→♉	11:12 am
☽⚹♆	8:53 pm

♉

Wednesday
5

☽⚹♃	6:02 am
☽△♇	11:02 am
♀→♒	1:03 pm
☉⚹☽	2:56 pm
☽□♅	11:17 pm

♉
♊

Thursday
6

♃D	2:42 am
☽☍♄	5:55 am v/c
☽→♊	6:37 pm
☽△♀	8:45 pm

♊

Friday
7

☽□♆	5:11 am
♄ApG	2:19 pm
☽⚹♅	4:00 pm

Of Sand

When we gather our grains,
I am sea glass,
a softened shard of aquamarine
tumbling and coming to rest,
edges etched with the collected whispers
of waves, white air, and rain,
me and the sea both sky-formed.

We are shore-born.
Where things meet is where we are made
and the elements add their consent.

excerpt © Teresa Honey Youngblood 2012

Daily Cycles: Earth　　　　　　　　© *Barb Levine 1996*

ᏆᏆᏆ x̄ī q̄ī l̄ìū

♊ **Saturday**
ठ

☉□☽　5:27 am
☽△♅　12:19 pm
☽△♂　11:53 pm v/c

Waxing Half Moon in ♊ Gemini 5:27 am PST

○○○ ᛁᗪ ᑲề̄ì r̀ì

♊
♋ **Sunday**
9

☽→♋　6:33 am
☽△♆　5:46 pm

Daylight Saving Time Begins 2:00 am

March
Ahesh—Grass Month

♋

Monday
10

☽☌♃	3:37 am
☽□♅	5:04 am
☽☍♇	9:16 am
☿□♄	11:14 pm

♋
♌

Tuesday
11

☉△☽	12:11 am
☽△♄	5:29 am
☽□♂	12:50 pm v/c
☽ApG	12:52 pm
☽→♌	7:08 pm

♌

Wednesday
12

| ☽☍♀ | 6:57 am |
| ☽△♅ | 6:00 pm |

♌

Thursday
13

☉△♄	2:15 pm
☽□♄	5:48 pm
☽☍☿	11:27 pm

♌
♍

Friday
14

☽⚹♂	12:24 am v/c
☽→♍	7:17 am
☿△♂	9:17 am
☽☍♆	6:41 pm

ALL ASPECTS IN PACIFIC DAYLIGHT TIME; ADD 3 HOURS FOR EDT; ADD 7 HOURS FOR GMT

Here Mother Speak

I have heard Mother speaking to us
When Moon dogs channel the Sun
Stars kiss the Earth
Oceans make Waves
Winds stir the Trees
Animal Eyes look into our Eyes
Fire lashes her sharp tongue
Snow and ice crackle
Water flows over

But how can we hear her speaking
When we have
Three TVs going 12 hours a day
Two computers going 24 hours a day
Cell phones attached to our bodies ringing incessantly
Cars with windows rolled up that we drive unnecessarily
Ear buds stuffed in our heads
Radio waves, video waves, cell phone waves, satellite waves
Filling the air
How can we hear her?
How do you here her?

¤ *Karen Clarke 2012*

Intuition
© *Krista Lynn Brown 1995*

ᚻᚻᚻ Yilesháal—Below Day

♍ ○ **Saturday**
15

☽✳♃ 4:07 am
☽△♇ 9:32 am

☉☉☉ Hathamesháal—Center Day

♍ ○ **Sunday**
♎ **16**

☽✳♄ 4:36 am
☉☍☽ 10:08 am v/c
☉⚻♂ 11:38 am
☽→♎ 5:46 pm

Full Moon in ♍ Virgo 10:08 am PDT
Moonrise Time: 7:21 pm PDT

Spring Equinox

Now is the Brightening. It seems as if the sky is hanging equal to land for this one moment before night gives way to longer days. Wild winds sweep through old dreams to clear the way for new rising energy of light, entering our waking senses and the hearts of primroses and daffodils. Earth is breathing faster, working the sunfire that flares warmth to lift our spirits. Eostre gives all beginnings: first green shoots, lettuce, lambs, eggs, babies—all potential. What will you plan and hatch, bring into being this year? Let the freshening thaw dissolve inertia. As hare and wildcat come alert, so we all shiver like horses at the race's tense beginning—and this is the race against time that Grandmother Earth requires us to win. In the determination of Spring there is strength to overcome unimaginably great difficulties. For love we can move mountains or keep them whole. The extra effort of womankind can be the flower that breaks through concrete to become a forest, the garden that changes the world.

Rose Flint © Mother Tongue Ink 2013

Keeping Watch
© Denise Kester 2008

Lightning Path © *Cathy McClelland 2009*

Ponies in the Rain

Spring rains came
as a shock
the wood-stove stood cold
and the winter wheat
blazed green
cardinals twisted on
bare branches
and the ponies stood with
heads down
and tails to the wind.
The creeks became dangerous
and I paced indoors
watching the songbirds
gather at my feeder
knocking seeds to the ground.

This interlude is all that
separates me
from days of endless light

coaxing muscles
back into service
crouching over
crumbling fertility
performing the same ritual
the compost
the winter wheat
the sun warming to my touch
the brown silk
that will consume every seed
and crack open to
green
that rears sunward.

What blur of summer
can contain the ferocious
bounty that exists
silent in a seed.

¤ *Linda Brunner 2012*

March
mars

Monday
17

♎︎

♀⚹♄♃ 11:01 am
☽□♃ 2:03 pm
☽△♀ 2:17 pm
☿→♓︎ 3:24 pm
☽☍♅ 3:50 pm
☽□♇ 7:12 pm

© *Sandra Stanton 2004*

Tuesday
18

♎︎

♀⚹♅ 12:00 pm
☽♂♂ 6:07 pm v/c

Wednesday
19

♎︎
♏︎

☽→♏︎ 2:13 am
☽△☿ 5:41 am
☽△♆ 1:10 pm
☽△♃ 9:57 pm

Thursday
20

♏︎

☽□♀ 2:24 am
☽⚹♇ 2:48 am
☉→♈︎ 9:57 am
☽♂♄ 8:11 pm v/c

Spring Equinox

Sun in ♈︎Aries 9:57 am PDT

Friday
21

♏︎
♐︎

☽→♐︎ 8:39 am
☉△☽ 10:27 am
☽□♅ 5:29 pm
☽□♆ 7:19 pm

ALL ASPECTS IN PACIFIC DAYLIGHT TIME; ADD 3 HOURS FOR EDT; ADD 7 HOURS FOR GMT

2014 Year at a Glance for ♈ Aries (March 20–April 19)

You're an electrifying force wherever you go these days, and you're ready to set the world on fire. For several years a new you has been emerging, wrestling free from your past and the limiting expectations of those close to you. And you're going to be even bolder in 2014.

Delighting in a new capacity to ignite others, you are best received in progressive crowds and innovative movements. If you are stuck in a lifeless career, something extraordinary is about to happen, especially from July on. Investigate your options. Use your emotions and feelings as well as objective analysis to guide your success.

Lessons regarding power complexities appear as you look to make changes in the world. People in powerful positions, feeling threatened, may resort to underhanded means to keep you hobbled. Challenges just make you more determined, though you will do best if you are empowering, not overpowering. Ethical behavior is essential, or you could tumble from grace in an awkwardly public manner.

2014 is a good year for love, Aries-born. Casual or unconscious interactions are less satisfying than deeper, purposeful, even tantric intimacy. Your passionate playfulness may also attract souls just waiting to incarnate; be warned—you are fertile ground.

Changes in the life of someone close to you bring up ancient emotions, long buried, to be cleared away. Aries does best discharging old stuff through physical activity; try deep housecleaning or anything that builds up a good sweat.

Gretchen Lawlor © Mother Tongue Ink 2013

I am a Rainbow © Cori Caputo 2005

ኡኡኡ Šanbe

♐

Saturday
22

☽△♅ 5:35 am
☽⚹♀ 12:03 pm
♀☌♆ 1:15 pm

☉☉☉ Yekšanbe

♐
♑

Sunday
23

☽⚹♂ 3:40 am v/c
☽→♑ 1:03 pm
☉□☽ 6:46 pm
☽⚹♆ 11:28 pm

Waning Half Moon in ♑ Capricorn 6:46 pm PDT

March
marzo

Monday
24

♑

D⚹♉ 2:56 am
D☍♃ 7:44 am
D□♅ 9:26 am
D☌♇ 11:57 am

Loki *© Jaymie Johnson 2012*

Tuesday
25

♑
♒

D⚹♄ 3:47 am
D□♂ 5:34 am v/c
D→♒ 3:39 pm

Wednesday
26

♒

☉⚹D 12:54 am
♉△♃ 6:11 am
D⚹♅ 11:41 am

Thursday
27

♒
♓

D☌♀ 12:52 am
D□♄ 5:20 am
D△♂ 6:13 am v/c
DPrG 11:40 am
D→♓ 5:10 pm
☿⚹♇ 10:32 pm

Friday
28

♓

D☌♆ 3:27 am
D△♃ 11:42 am
D⚹♇ 3:26 pm
D☌♉ 5:20 pm
☿☌⚷ 10:08 pm

I Stand Tall

The true story,
the one that resonates most,
is that I stand
on good ground,
on solid ground.
I stand rooted
in truth
and love
and light
and wellness.
May I hold my arms out wide
and my head up high
and stand tall
like a tree upon this earth
while the stories of fear
and false beliefs
flow past me
like leaves
being carried
in the wind.

¤ *e.g.wise 2011*

Love is Eternal © Danielle Helen Ray Dickson 2011

♓
♈

Saturday
29

☽△♄   6:44 am v/c
♀△♂   12:05 pm
♀□♄   2:14 pm
☽→♈   6:53 pm

♈

Sunday
30

☉☌☽   11:45 am
☽□♃   2:08 pm
☽☌♅   3:45 pm
☽□♇   5:47 pm

Moonrise Time: 6:33 am PDT
New Moon in ♈Aries 11:45 am PDT

Remember Who We Are

As the earth moves beneath our feet
and new mountains emerge from the depths of the sea,
All that was hidden must now be revealed.
With nothing left to cling to
and no one to blame,
We are at last alone with ourselves,
immersed in the ocean within,
diving below the surface
again and again
while it all rises up to meet us.
And so we learn to breathe
into the turbulent waters of our emotions
To find the inner anchor that holds still
as the winds of change and uncertainty
blow through our minds, our homes, our World.
Nowhere left to run
Right here, Right now, Open, Ready
It is time to return to Wholeness
To Remember Who We Are.

¤ *Melissa Myers 2012*

Second Chakra © *Beth Lenco 2000*

IV. INNER BALANCE

Moon IV: March 30–April 28

New Moon in ♈Aries March 30; Full Moon in ♎ Libra April 15; Sun in ♉ Taurus April 19

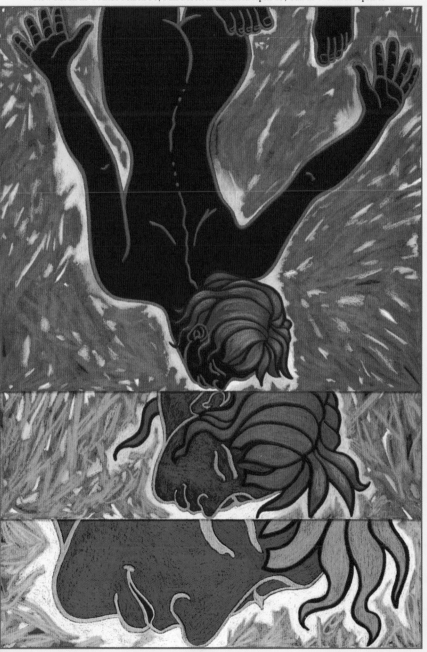

Point of Balance

March / April

sān yuè / sì yuè

 ⟩⟩⟩ xī qī yī

♈︎
♉︎

Monday
31

☽☌♂ 8:21 am
☽⚹♀ 1:07 pm v/c
☽→♉︎ 10:20 pm

♂♂♂ xī qī èr

♉︎

Tuesday
1

⊙□♃ 12:39 am
☽⚹♆ 9:38 am
☽⚹♃ 6:55 pm
☽△♇ 10:29 pm

April

☿☿☿ xī qī sān

♉︎

Wednesday
2

⊙☌♅ 12:08 am
☿⚻♂ 2:44 am
☽⚹♅ 2:09 pm
☽☍♄ 2:54 pm

♅ApG 6:28 pm
☿△♄ 8:02 pm
☽□♀ 11:43 pm v/c

♃♃♃ xī qī sì

♉︎
♊︎

Thursday
3

⊙□♇ 2:22 am
☽→♊︎ 4:48 am
☽□♆ 4:58 am

♀♀♀ xī qī w

♊︎

Friday
4

☽⚹♅ 4:42 am
⊙⚹☽ 8:57 am
☽△♂ 7:45 pm

ALL ASPECTS IN PACIFIC DAYLIGHT TIME; ADD 3 HOURS FOR EDT; ADD 7 HOURS FOR GMT

Blessing

Grace meets you between two heartbeats.
In a blink, pulse, shift of breeze rippling cat's fur, all is changed.
All.
And the world, which leaned into its negative pole, glances,
fascinated by the positive, all
before breakfast, before the day's first tasks.
The great longing lifts
like a voice, like wings, and soars
effortlessly, splendidly, a thing of such joy
the birds stop singing and the animals
come out to listen. All the people put down their masks and
tools and stand awash in the moment. What
will we tell the children? How remember the instant
we glimpsed grace and knew true peace like
stars at night, water in the desert, the first great
breath on surfacing.

© Patrice Haan 2010

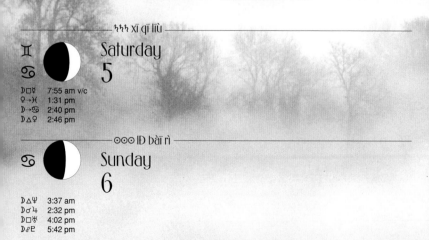

ꜗꜗꜗ xī qī liù

♊
♋

Saturday
5

☽□☿ 7:55 am v/c
♀→⧓ 1:31 pm
☽→♋ 2:40 pm
☽△♀ 2:46 pm

☉☉☉ lD bàī rì

♋

Sunday
6

☽△♆ 3:37 am
☽♂♃ 2:32 pm
☽□♅ 4:02 pm
☽☍♇ 5:42 pm

Mist Playing Amongst Trees
© Barbara Manzi-Fe 2006

April

Athil—Vine Month

──── ꝒꝒꝒ Henesháal—East Day ────

Monday
7

☉□☽ 1:31 am
☽□♂ 5:34 am
☿→♈ 8:35 am
☽△♄ 11:14 am v/c

Waxing Half Moon in ♋ Cancer 1:31 am PDT

──── ♂♂♂ Honesháal—West Day ────

Tuesday
8

☽→♌ 2:50 am
☽△♅ 5:56 am
☽ApG 7:55 am
☉☍♂ 2:03 pm

──── ☿☿☿ Hunesháal—North Day ────

Wednesday
9

☽△♅ 4:50 am
☽✳♂ 4:12 pm
☉△☽ 7:28 pm
☽□♄ 11:26 pm v/c

──── ♃♃♃ Hanesháal—South Day ────

Thursday
10

☽→♍ 3:07 pm

──── ♀♀♀ Rayilesháal—Above Day ────

Friday
11

☽☍♀ 2:55 am
☽☍♆ 4:20 am
☽✳♃ 3:46 pm
☉⚻♄ 5:23 pm
☽△♇ 5:53 pm
♀☌♆ 7:23 pm

Shunyata

© *Meganne Forbes 2011*

ᛣᛣᛣ Yilesháal—Below Day

♍

Saturday
12

☽✶♄ 10:12 am v/c

☉☉☉ Hathamesháal—Center Day

♍
♎

Sunday
13

☽→♎ 1:33 am

April
avril

Monday
14

♎

☽⚹♀ 12:01 am
☽□♄ 1:37 am
☽⚹♅ 2:20 am
☽□♇ 3:08 am
♂PrG 5:58 am

☽♂♂ 8:59 am
♀□♃ 11:32 am
♀♂♅ 4:15 pm
♀R 4:47 pm
♀□♇ 9:13 pm

© Modupe 2012

**She is Making Art
Each Moment**

Tuesday
15

♎
♏

☉♂☽ 12:42 am v/c
☽→♏ 9:20 am
☽△♆ 9:39 pm

Full Moon in ♎ Libra 12:42 am PDT
Total Lunar Eclipse 12:47 am PDT*
Moonrise Time: 8:08 pm PDT

Wednesday
16

♏

☿♂♂ 4:15 am
☽△♀ 6:08 am
☽△♃ 8:47 am
☽⚹♇ 9:45 am
♂⚻♆ 10:04 am

Thursday
17

♏
♐

☽♂♄ 12:09 am v/c
☽→♐ 2:44 pm
♀△♃ 6:19 pm

Friday
18

♐

♀⚹♇ 2:26 am
☽□♆ 2:42 am
☽△♅ 2:00 pm
☽□♀ 3:19 pm
☽⚹♂ 4:59 pm
☿⚻♄ 11:31 pm

* Eclipse visible from Australia, the Pacific, and the Americas

2014 Year at a Glance for ♉ Taurus (April 19–May 20)

A burning fury at unhealthy agendas influencing education, politics or spirituality nudges Taurus to subversive action in 2014. Your perfect setting may be a prison, hospital or church—somewhere that's in need of your seditious efforts. Go where people are curious about you.

Your most excellent cohorts these days are visionaries and artists, dreamers and invisible people. In mystical collective experiences with kindred spirits, Taurus contributes an earthy spirituality, a deep connection with plants and animals and places. This rich loamy brew of pragmatism and otherworldliness is the perfect medium for nourishing a better future for us all.

Some innovative seed will choose Taurus as the most fertile place to take root. Literally or figuratively you are gestating new life. Ground your inspirations and live them first; let them reorganize you at a cellular level in private. Lie on the ground and let the Earth Spirits dream into you. If there's no dream there whispering at you, go wandering; your roots may need a fresh land.

Relationships are at a tipping point in 2014. Recent challenges from mates, clients and cohorts nudge critical review of interpersonal dynamics. Pay attention to who shares your dreams and visions of the future. Who really values you? Who will work hard to keep your connection vital? Have important conversations early in the year.

Taurus becomes even more potent through partnering with accomplished souls this year. Hang out with wise people who know the ropes, whose credibility embellishes your own.

Gretchen Lawlor © Mother Tongue Ink 2013

——— ℏℏℏ Šanbe ———

♐
♑

Saturday
19

☽△♅	4:48 am
♀⊼♂	7:31 am
☉△☽	6:17 pm v/c
☽→♑	6:28 pm
☉→♉	8:55 pm

Sun in ♉ Taurus 8:55 pm PDT

——— ☉☉☉ Yekšanbe ———

♑

Sunday
20

♃□♅	12:29 am	☽♂♇	5:32 pm
☽✶♆	6:15 am	☽☍♃	5:32 pm
♀♂♄	10:40 am	☽□♂	6:56 pm
♃☍♇	4:26 pm	☽✶♀	10:53 pm
☽□♅	5:27 pm		

April

abril

♑︎
♒︎

Monday
21

☽⚹♄ 6:48 am
♅□♇ 12:21 pm
☽□♅ 4:20 pm v/c
☽→♒︎ 9:18 pm

My temple of gravity
directs my mind to stillness.
If only I could love enough
To lay my judgement down.
What would become of me?
excerpt © Amanda Tuttle 2012

♒︎

Tuesday
22

☉□☽ 12:52 am
♂□♃ 12:28 pm
☽PrG 5:30 pm
☽⚹♅ 8:18 pm
☽△♂ 8:24 pm
☿ApG 10:13 pm

Waning Half Moon in ♒︎ Aquarius 12:52 am PDT

♒︎
♓︎

Wednesday
23

♂☍♅ 12:08 am
☿→♉ 2:16 am
♂□♇ 6:38 am
☽□♄ 9:10 am v/c
☽→♓︎ 11:55 pm

♓︎

Thursday
24

☽⚹☿ 3:41 am
☉⚹☽ 7:14 am
☽♂♆ 11:49 am
♀△♄ 10:15 pm
☽⚹♇ 10:54 pm
☽△♃ 11:54 pm

♓︎

Friday
25

☽△♄ 11:48 am
☽♂♀ 1:03 pm v/c
☉♂☿ 8:27 pm

Out on a Limb

© *Jayme Dee 2000*

ㅤㅤ ꙮꙮꙮ sábado ㅤㅤ

♓
♈

Saturday
26

☽→♈ ㅤ3:01 am
☿✶♆ ㅤ10:26 am

ㅤㅤ ☉☉☉ domingo ㅤㅤ

♈

Sunday
27

☽☍♂ ㅤ12:28 am
☽□♇ ㅤ2:26 am
☽♂♅ ㅤ3:01 am
☉✶♆ ㅤ3:34 am
☽□♃ ㅤ4:01 am v/c

MOON IV - April ㅤㅤㅤㅤㅤㅤ 85

Bootings

I wave, but Alice doesn't wave back. We have known one another for decades, have lived together, shared meals, sat in morning meditation—so her not waving back now means we must both walk past one another in an ear-breaking, mind-messing, blood-rushing silence of knowing we aren't going to be friends again today.

I lower my eyes to the ground. My eyes watch her boots come level with mine. Both sets of boots are far more similar than they are different—both encrusted with mud, both fiercely functional, waterproof, shit-kicker style boots. Boots that say "we don't care what people think about our footwear, what people think women like us are like." Our boots come side by side now like family members, sharing paths as well as treads, treads as well as traits, traits which are busy with metaphoring how strong we show ourselves to the outside world.

How deliberately innocent we are of that world's expectations. How coherently we choose to ignore those ridiculous, dangerous expectations; ignoring them is our sign to each other of how capable we are to choose for ourselves good footwear: safe, strong, easy-to-run-in shoes that will take us as far as we need to go. Far and away from the people who demean us. These not-nice-girl shoes stride us through fields, clamber with us over ditches and beyond sexism, beyond patriarchy to these valleys of our remote women-only space, out of harm's way in a place to repair our wounds, where we can rest, rest and find our feet again.

Our feet that have walked us so far away from the traps and prisons kept ready for us, feet armored in strong, solid, reliable boots that we proudly bought and paid for by ourselves. So proud that somehow we have out-prouded one another, used our boots to keep on walking, keep walking even now, away from one another.

Alice turns and her boots disappear. Boots once used to walk towards one another as home, now stomp away, leaving me to hold tightly silent to my thumping heart. I try not to feel it. I try to pull myself together by some handy bootstraps to remain a militant believer in Alice's freedom to walk on by, even in the face of how hard it is for me to bear the loss of smiles and waves and looks, from the lips and hands and eyes of a long loved, now greatly missed—even when she is only a few feet away—good friend.

◻ Maj Ikle 2011

V. BETWEEN US

Moon V: April 28–May 28

New Moon in ♉ Taurus April 28; Full Moon in ♏ Scorpio May 14; Sun in ♊ Gemini May 20

Badger Knows All Things in the Earth;
Hawk Knows All Things in the Sky ▫ *Sophia Kelly Schultz 2012*

Medicine Wheel

Stepping slowly around the Wheel,
how I love each Self there, my other Me,
each Sister on the other side,
played out each day in my one soul.
We reach for each other, Sisters all,
me and me, and me and me,
and make one whole.

excerpt © Annelinde Metzner 2012

April / May
sì yuè / wŭ yuèi

Fool For Love
© *Sophia Rosenberg 2006*

 ◁◁◁ xī qī yī

 ♈
♉

Monday
28

D→♉   7:23 am
☿⚹♂   4:44 pm
D⚹♆   8:07 pm
☉♂D   11:14 pm

Moonrise Time: 5:46 am PDT
Annular Solar Eclipse 11:04 pm PDT*
New Moon in ♉ Taurus 11:14 pm PDT

♂♂♂ xī qī èr

 ♉

Tuesday
29

D♂☿   7:07 am
D△♇   7:40 am
D⚹♃   9:56 am
☿△♇   10:30 am
D☍♄   8:56 pm

☿☿☿ xī qī sān

 ♉
♊

Wednesday
30

☿⚹♃   1:32 am
D⚹♀   8:53 am v/c
D→♊   1:56 pm
☿⚹♄   9:22 pm

♃♃♃ xī qī sì

 ♊

Thursday
1

D□♆   3:23 am
☉⚹♂   9:55 am
D△♂   11:02 am
D⚹♅   4:32 pm v/c

May
May Day/Beltane

♀♀♀ xī qī w

 ♊
♋

Friday
2

☿☍♄   5:56 pm
♀→♈   6:21 pm
D→♋   11:13 pm
D□♀   11:43 pm

---

*Eclipse visible from S. Indian Ocean, Australia, and Antarctica

Beltane

Sun sinks into crimson—and dark hills leap into answering flame as Beltane Fires welcome the rising, fiery, sappy uprush of the year. Fire dancers spin and sparkle, crackling with energy, giving vision to the wild joy that pours through the land in fertility: luscious green vines pushing and twining, trees blazing with green-gold fire. From garden to mountain, life shouts and parades its will to continue in Beauty. And we are part of this earthy wildness, we are Earth, urgent to live. We leap the fire to open our souls to rituals of pleasure, to deep creative power that surges forward, wave after wave, as Rhiannon rides her white horses into our dreams. We are kin with all creatures—fully alive in every precious second. Earth enchants us. We brim with elixirs of passion; leaves form under our skin. Our hair is electric in the thunder of our naked dance, in love and lust. Spirit surges in free sexuality. The Universe drums with the heartbeat of the Goddess held in our own sacred bodies.

Rose Flint © Mother Tongue Ink 2013

Dream Teller   ¤ *Gretchen Butler 2005*

The Woman I Love

The woman I love
Is cardamom spicy
Mango curry sweet
Sashays resolutely
All up and down the street
On wide, confident,
Unladylike
Feet.

The woman I love
Has hair more silver than black
Taught me to never,
Ever turn back. . .
Unless there's a loved one
(And we are all loved ones)
Reaching out their hand.

La mujer que amo
Has curvas for days
Logros for miles
A laugh you can hear
Del otro la'o del mundo
She smiles
And roars
And smiles

The woman I love
Flies
On the backs of iron birds
Ever returning
To her families
To her homelands
To her lovers
To me.

The woman I love
Has freckles on her shoulders
Hair that whispers from its bun
Stands tall
Speaks plain
Eyes that crinkle
No shame.

The woman I love
Sends me pictures
From her homes in faraway lands
Calling me to join her:
Palestine, Senegal,
Ohio, Japan

The woman I love plays guitar
Bateria piano and bass
She dances absolutely
All over the place
She cries with my sorrow
She laughs with my pain
She offers her shoulder
To carry my strain.

La mujer que amo
Thinks with her heart
Always has a fat book
In her purse
And in her car.
Wears glittery glasses
Dreams in Dr. Who
Strawberry cherry
Summersweet lips
Technicolor tattoos.

excerpt © Liliana Darwin López 2012

Union

© *Autumn Skye Morrison 2011*

♋

Saturday
3

☽△♆ 1:25 pm
☉△♇ 5:37 pm
☽□♂ 8:16 pm

♋

Sunday
4

☽☌♇ 1:50 am
☉⚹☽ 2:33 am
☽□♅ 3:20 am
☽☌♃ 5:51 am
☽△♄ 3:44 pm

May
Amahína—Flower Month

♋
♌

Monday
5

☽✶♀ 1:46 am v/c
☽→♌ 10:55 am
☽△♀ 5:45 pm

♌

Tuesday
6

☉✶♃ 2:54 am
☽ApG 3:21 am
☽✶♂ 7:32 am
☽△♅ 3:56 pm
☉□☽ 8:15 pm

Waxing Half Moon in ♌ Leo 8:15 pm PDT

♌
♍

Wednesday
7

☽□♄ 3:50 am v/c
☉✶♇ 6:03 am
☿→♊ 7:56 am
☽→♍ 11:24 pm

♍

Thursday
8

☽□♅ 2:25 am
☽☍♆ 2:00 pm

♍

Friday
9

☽△♇ 2:06 am
☽✶♃ 7:47 am
☉△☽ 1:16 pm
☽✶♄ 3:08 pm v/c

ALL ASPECTS IN PACIFIC DAYLIGHT TIME; ADD 3 HOURS FOR EDT; ADD 7 HOURS FOR GMT

Falling and Flying with You

To my past, present and future Teen Youth Ambassadors.

Before there was you, I did my work, and it was good work, alone. I looked out a window to the sun, typing

Line Dance © *Donna Coleman 2011*

and listening to NPR, and few people knew my name. Before there was you, I knew myself—sweet and passionate. Balanced, a lover of tree climbing. I kept a clean refrigerator. Before there was you, I had hope, sure. A calm brightness leading me along the paved stones of my path. I seldom stumbled, never fell.

And then there was you, erupting into my life in groups of thirty, seventy-seven, and last summer's twelve who stole my heart. Pulling me out of my office chair to the tight-rope of togetherness.

For you, I facilitated dialogue. I did nightly bed checks; I led workshops on oppression, liberation, project sustainability. I learned all the words to this season's pop songs. I lost my balance and fell into bed exhausted, night after night and woke up excited and eager to do it all again. Whole meals went bad in my fridge.

With you my hope has a name: Luis. Yurixy. Ismael. Alice. Caio.

And now I stumble often, so often it feels like normal. So often it feels like life. When you first begin to fly, you may only see how far you have to fall. But how can I not get up again and again with all of you shouting, and laughing, and calling my name.

¤ *Galloway Quena Crain 2012*

ᚻᚻᚻ Yilesháal—Below Day

♍︎
♎︎
Saturday
10

☽ ⚹⚹ ♎︎ 10:19 am
☉ ⚹ ♄ 11:28 am
♄PrG 12:37 pm
☽ △ ☿ 11:28 pm

☉☉☉ Hathamesháal—Center Day

♎︎
Sunday
11

♀ ☍ ♂ 2:27 am
☽ ☌ ♂ 4:22 am
☽ ☍ ♀ 4:34 am
☿ □ ♆ 5:34 am

☽ □ ♇ 11:40 am
☽ ☍ ♅ 1:55 pm
☽ □ ♃ 5:51 pm v/c

May
meh

ᴅᴅᴅ Dŏsanbe

The quarrels that endure
are with the self.
excerpt © Joanne Rocky Delaplaine 2001

♎ ♏

Monday 12

☿△♂ 9:02 am
☽→♏ 6:07 pm

♂♂♂ Sešanbe

♏

Tuesday 13

☽△♆ 7:21 am
☽⚹♇ 5:55 pm

☿☿☿ Cahâršanbe

♏ ♐

Wednesday 14

Lunar Beltane

☽△♃ 12:28 am
♃△⚷ 4:35 am
☽☌♄ 5:02 am
♀□♇ 10:50 am
☉☍☽ 12:16 pm v/c
☿⊼♇ 6:18 pm
☽→♐ 10:43 pm

Full Moon in ♏ Scorpio 12:16 pm PDT
Moonrise Time: 7:58 pm PDT

♃♃♃ Panjšanbe

♐

Thursday 15

☽□♆ 11:22 am
☽⚹♂ 2:16 pm
☿⚹♀ 2:55 pm
☿⚹♅ 4:22 pm
♀☌♅ 4:54 pm
☽△♅ 11:50 pm

♀♀♀ Jom'e

♐

Friday 16

☽△♀ 12:26 am
☽☍☿ 12:43 am v/c

A Ritual for Finding Balance

Find a friend, lover, sister, mother, daughter, colleague. Ask her to sit in a comfortable seated position back-to-back with you. If she'll go first, ask her to push her spine powerfully against yours. Let yourself be pushed over. Stay in that position long enough for both of you to experience that energetic state, pusher or pushed-over. Come up. Change roles. Second round, ask her to push against you. This time, you will resist with all your might, not give an inch. Change roles. Third round, both of you will push with all your might and resist being pushed over. Fourth round, press just enough so that each of you feels backed up and energized. Enjoy this feeling. Slowly disengage from your partner while internalizing you partner's support. Thank your partner and give yourselves time to debrief the experience verbally. What was it like to push, to resist, to be pushed over, to come into balance? Know that you're doing the most difficult yoga of all: the yoga of relationship.

© Joanne Rocky Delaplaine 2012

Point of Contact
© *Sandra Ure Griffin 2008*

ᚨᚾᚾ Šanbe

♐
♑

Saturday
17

☽→♑ 1:12 am
☿□♂ 7:14 am
☽⚹♆ 1:34 pm
☽□♂ 4:13 pm
☽♂♇ 11:17 pm

☉☉☉ Yekšanbe

♑

Sunday
18

☽□♅ 1:57 am
☽PrG 4:57 am
☽□♀ 6:42 am
☽☍♃ 6:49 am

♀□♃ 8:31 am
☽⚹♄ 9:25 am
☿☌♄ 7:58 pm

May
mayo

© Lupen Grainne 2009

Jewel in the Heart

♑
≈

Monday
19

⊙△☽ 12:02 am v/c
☽→≈ 2:58 am
♀⊼♄ 2:50 pm
☽△♂ 6:00 pm
♂D 6:31 pm

♂♂♂ martes

≈

Tuesday
20

☽⚹♅ 4:01 am
☽□♄ 11:11 am
☽⚹♀ 1:05 pm
☽△♅ 3:21 pm v/c
⊙→♊ 7:59 pm

Sun in ♊ Gemini 7:59 pm PDT

☿☿☿ miércoles

≈
♓

Wednesday
21

☽→♓ 5:18 am
⊙□☽ 5:59 am
☽☌♆ 6:05 pm

Waning Half Moon in ♓ Pisces 5:59 am PDT

♃♃♃ jueves

♓

Thursday
22

☽⚹♇ 3:56 am
☽△♃ 1:14 pm
☽△♄ 2:05 pm
☽□♅ 11:25 pm v/c

♀♀♀ viernes

♓
♈

Friday
23

☽→♈ 9:01 am
⊙⚹☽ 1:38 pm

ALL ASPECTS IN PACIFIC DAYLIGHT TIME; ADD 3 HOURS FOR EDT; ADD 7 HOURS FOR GMT

2014 Year at a Glance for ♊ Gemini (May 20–June 21)

Some transcendent experiences happened to Gemini in these last two years, the voltage of which continues to hurtle through your system in 2014. An extreme moment, an illumination or a loss deepened your appreciation for life or inspired you, setting you off on a quest.

Your body is an excellent compass for this quest. It's easy for Gemini to overlook having a body (mental gymnastics being much more interesting). To let an inspiration live through you, you must 1. inhabit your body and 2. clear away distractive mental and physical clutter.

You are midway in a cycle most auspicious for confronting destructive habits and implementing healthier patterns. Your work environment improves as you develop new tools/techniques to take your inspirational self out into the world. Apprentice yourself to a superior craftsperson or healer, someone who is already living your dream.

Future plans continue to be unsteady, with unexpected interruptions and redirections that repeatedly drop you into new communities. Why? To radicalize your perspective, and to be a lightning bolt of inspiration wherever you show up. Your ideas spread like wildfire this year.

Gemini hates being jammed into one suit, one option, one voice. Don't limit yourself by expecting anything to be a perfect fit. Revel in the fact that you of all the signs, really can bilocate, be of two minds, carry on two lives at once. Wow! A hobby that feeds your spirit might free up the day job to be simply the thing that pays the bills.

Gretchen Lawlor © Mother Tongue Ink 2013

Red Earth, Blue Mountains
© Toni Truesdale 2005

—————— ♄♄♄ sábado ——————

♈

Saturday
24

☽☍♂	1:07 am
☽□♇	8:20 am
♃△♄	10:47 am
☽♂♅	11:52 am
☽□♃	6:44 pm

—————— ☉☉☉ domingo ——————

♈
♉

Sunday
25

☽♂♀	7:06 am
☽⚹♅	8:57 am v/c
☽→♉	2:27 pm

A-rise

There is a crumbling grandeur to Havana. I do not often voice this, as scenes of warp and decay are too many, too vivid and multiply almost daily here. Apartment-filled buildings literally fall to pieces, release a fine dust, sweeping and swirling through the *baches*[1] and into the faces of passengers in cars with no windows. The ground-down remains of walls which once held lives together, now stick to sweat-coated skin. What remains are *huecos*[2], gaping holes in the face of the street, with jutting-out ledges of concrete appearing like veins in a cadaver, plotting out where rooms had once been, spaces that life once occupied.

I see a new tribe of visionaries emerging from the ranks of the peoples—artists dedicated to the use of the city's remains as their creative material, and the deteriorated places as their galleries. They birth new life into the deadened places, dignify the debris of their city with images of hope and humour. They see life-sized canvas in the *huecos* and fill in the gaps with new and colourful life-blood. They often paint the faces of the people onto the walls left vacant by the collapse of their contents—not some "other" to look up to, as with the statues and billboards of national heroes, orators and generals—but people who remind passers-by of their own Selves, their own majesty, beauty and strength, even amidst the ruined places of their lives.

The passage of time acts on this city, its streets, its decision-makers, as the insistency of the waves acts on a cliff-ledged coastline—grinding away at its hardened density, percolating, dissolving and ultimately sweeping away what once appeared so insoluble and impenetrable. The new visionaries encourage the people to look up to themselves, to look into the debris with eyes of creative re-visioning and know that they embody the new life that will flesh out their city once more.

[1] *Potholes* [2] *Holes*

◻ *Alyson McEvoy 2012*

VI. RECONCILIATION

Moon VI: May 28-June 27

New Moon in ♊ Gemini May 28; Full Moon in ♐ Sagittarius June 12; Sun in ♋ Cancer June 21

◘ *Ginger Salkowski 2006*

Reclaiming Waste for Renewal

The reconciliation of communal and environmental ideals within the hustle and ever-expanding infrastructure of city life is modeled in this beautifully sculpted cob wall—made of clay, sand and straw—the grand entrance to the Portland Rebuilding Center. Over four million pounds of reusable building materials are salvaged here every year. Progress can mean stepping with ever-lighter footprints when we use a synergistic mix of inspiration, creativity and cooperation to transform refuse into resource.

◘ *Barbara Dickinson 2012*

May / June

wŏ yuè / liù yuè

♉

Monday
26

☽⚹♆   4:11 am
☽△♇   2:30 pm

♉
♊

Tuesday
27

☽☍♄   12:54 am
☽⚹♃   2:10 am v/c
☽→♊   9:47 pm

♊

Wednesday
28

☿⚹♀   6:58 am
☉☌☽   11:40 am
☽□♆   12:03 pm
☽△♂   3:46 pm
☉□♆   4:43 pm
♀→♉   6:45 pm

Moonrise Time: 5:51 am PDT
New Moon in ♊ Gemini 11:40 am PDT

♊

Thursday
29

☿→♋   2:11 am
☽⚹♅   2:59 am v/c

♊
♋

Friday
30

☽→♋   7:13 am
☽☌♉   8:49 am
☽⚹♀   11:03 am
☽△♆   10:03 pm

Queen of the Night © Diana Rivers 1986

Wind Prayer

I am every blade of grass and I am alone.
I walk the sharp edge between worlds and see far and wide.
Where is the middle? I ask. The Wind Mother speaks,
"You could not see both ends if you were not in the middle."

excerpt ¤ Lynn Flory 2012

--- ᚺᚾᚾ xī qī līù ---

♋

Saturday
31

☉△♂ 1:01 am
☽□♂ 2:29 am
☽☊♇ 8:56 am

☽□♅ 1:42 pm
☽△♄ 7:39 pm
☽☌♃ 11:32 pm v/c

--- ☉☉☉ ID bāī rì ---

♋
♌

Sunday
1

☽→♌ 6:43 pm

June

June
Athesh—Herb Month

 ♌

Monday
2

ꝺ□♀	5:10 am
ꝺ⚹♂	3:17 pm
☉⚹ꝺ	7:54 pm
ꝺApG	9:20 pm

♌

Tuesday
3

ꝺ△♅	2:10 am
ꝺ□♄	7:41 am v/c
☉⚼♇	9:18 am

♌
♍

Wednesday
4

♀⚹♆	6:15 am
ꝺ→♍	7:20 am
ꝺ⚹☿	1:10 pm
ꝺ☍♆	10:37 pm

♍

Thursday
5

ꝺ△♀	12:23 am
ꝺ△♇	9:24 am
☉□ꝺ	1:39 pm
ꝺ⚹♄	7:42 pm

Waxing Half Moon in ♍ Virgo 1:39 pm PDT

♍
♎

Friday
6

ꝺ⚹♃	2:13 am v/c
☉⚹♅	4:20 am
ꝺ→♎	7:01 pm

Loving Kindness

Loving Kindness   I soften at her name
Hello, come sit beside me
She curves into the hard seat
quietly   alert
with gratitude for wide open
sky   cool water
newly mown grass
Loving Kindness—
what a mush she is
a naive
pushover   but still   wise
you can't stop
watching her
moment to moment
helping cheerfully
babbling slightly
She laughs at all our jokes
We love hearing her
relax around her   put our
heads in her lap   our hearts in her
hands

Held by Mother Earth © Petra LeFaye 2005

© *Claire Blotter 2011*

—————— ᚻᚻᚻ Yilesháal—Below Day ——————

♎

Saturday
7

☽□☿	1:10 am
☿R	4:56 am
♀⊼♂	5:10 am
☽♂♂	4:31 pm
☽□♇	7:52 pm

—————— ⊙⊙⊙ Hathamesháal—Center Day ——————

♎

Sunday
8

☽♂♅	1:13 am		☽□♃	12:47 pm v/c
⊙△☽	4:44 am		⊙⊼♄	1:53 pm
⊙□♁	6:36 am		♀△♇	6:40 pm

June
zhūīn

Hestia

—))) Dōsanbe —

Monday
9

♎︎
♏︎ ☽

☽→♏︎ 3:38 am
☽△♀ 9:04 am
♆R 12:50 pm
☽△♆ 5:21 pm

— ♂♂♂ Sešanbe —

Tuesday
10

♏︎ ☽

☽⚹♇ 2:43 am
☽☍♀ 5:49 am
☽♂♄ 11:30 am
☽△♃ 7:21 pm v/c

— ☿☿☿ Cahâršanbe —

Wednesday
11

♏︎
♐︎ ☽

☽→♐︎ 8:23 am
☽□♆ 9:11 pm

— ♃♃♃ Panjšanbe —

Thursday
12

♐︎ ☽

☽⚹♂ 4:56 am
☽△♅ 10:59 am
♀⚹♅ 9:05 pm
♀☍♄ 9:09 pm
☉☍☽ 9:11 pm v/c
♄△♅ 10:23 pm

Moonrise Time: 7:46 pm PDT
Full Moon in ♐︎ Sagittarius 9:11 pm PDT

— ♀♀♀ Jom'e —

Friday
13

♐︎
♑︎ ☽

☽→♑︎ 10:04 am
☽☍♅ 12:56 pm
☽⚹♆ 10:22 pm

ALL ASPECTS IN PACIFIC DAYLIGHT TIME; ADD 3 HOURS FOR EDT; ADD 7 HOURS FOR GMT

CODE PINK Women Cross the Line

"Don't go to Pakistan," all our relatives said.
"They hate Americans; they hate women; they are so violent."
We went anyway.   We did find violence—
violence of the Taliban,   violence against women,
and violence of our drones.
We went to apologize for U.S. killer drone attacks.

We found sisterhood,   open arms,
appreciation and much wisdom.

"You can't stop the Taliban, that's our job,"
the Pakistani women told us.
"But you can stop your own government's remote-controlled,
high-tech, sophisticated killer drones that feed the cycle of violence."

We held hands and said, in English and Urdu,
"We will not raise our children to kill other women's children."*
We returned home invigorated, educated, reinforced,
and deeply committed to our Pakistani sisters—
to our work for peace and justice.

This is how to plant the seed of reconciliation.
We cross borders. We push past our fear.
We shed tears together.
And we refuse to be enemies.

¤ *Medea Benjamin & Rae Abileah 2012*

**Inspired by Julia Ward Howe's Mother's Day Proclamation, 1870.*

♄♄♄ Šanbe

♑

Saturday
14

♂□♇ 5:43 am
☽☌♇ 6:43 am
☽□♂ 6:44 am
☽□♅ 11:50 am
☽⚹♄ 2:34 pm
☽△♀ 6:17 pm
☽PrG 8:20 pm
☽☍♃ 11:35 pm v/c

☉☉☉ Yekšanbe

♑
♒

Sunday
15

☽→♒ 10:27 am

The Human is The Universe Being © Felicity Nightingale 2010

To Become the Rain

Now, now we must become
the rain,
letting our bodies sink into
the parched earth, filling
every crevice with a listening
so great that flowers
bloom where our bodies lie.

Look up at the sky and shout
prayers of thanksgiving
that cause
the heavens to join in,
raining down sweet mercy.

There is no choice anymore
but to lie still and sink in.

We must moisten the ground
of each other
with our own sweet essence,

showing the rains,
by our example,
what it is to flow down,
gathering strength and unity.

What is it to love one another?
It is to belly down and
become the rain.
That way
the Earth may remember
and so share her own heart
which beats in-sync with
our own.

¤ *Sulis Sarasvati 2011*

Summer Solstice

The sun-drum is high and taut as the wheel lifts to the peak of ascension. Gaia stretches out luxuriously; flowers pour from her, colours, light, heat—time to rest, play, blossom—flowers in our hair and our hearts wide open to celebrate Beauty, Grace of Earth. We gather together, travel and dance, campfires opening like stars on the land as long lovely blue velvet nights wrap us in ease. Yet we have Gaia's work to do: Earth is heating up, strangely, erratically, scorching lands into deserts, setting wild fires. Water, that sweet companion of solace to heat, comes ferocious in floods and storms, or refuses us rain, so we thirst. Our crops are now burnt, now drowned. Earth, Air, Fire and Water spin out of their true integration.

Let each circle be a powerhouse—each drum, each throat open in prayer for Gaia and her continuance to be at the heart of all we do. Our world will only come into balance if we make our own radical shifts, bringing women's wisdom into the centre.

Rose Flint © Mother Tongue Ink 2013

Tree of Life ▫ *Laurie Bauers 2006*

June

junio

≈

Monday
16

☽△♂ 8:06 am
☽✳♅ 12:25 pm
☽□♄ 2:54 pm
☽□♀ 11:09 pm

≈
♓

Tuesday
17

☿→♊ 3:04 am
☉△☽ 5:12 am
☽△♅ 11:07 am v/c
☽→♓ 11:26 am

♓

Wednesday
18

☽☌♆ 12:05 am
♀✳♃ 2:16 am
☿PrG 8:03 am
☽✳♇ 8:41 am
☽△♄ 4:46 pm

♓
♈

Thursday
19

☽△♃ 4:15 am
☽✳♀ 6:15 am
☉□☽ 11:39 am
☽□♅ 12:05 pm v/c
☽→♈ 2:26 pm
☉☌♅ 3:50 pm

Waning Half Moon in ♓ Pisces 11:39 am PDT

♈

Friday
20

♂R 3:39 am
☽□♇ 12:40 pm
☽☍♂ 4:25 pm
☽☌♅ 6:55 pm

ALL ASPECTS IN PACIFIC DAYLIGHT TIME; ADD 3 HOURS FOR EDT; ADD 7 HOURS FOR GMT

2014 Year at a Glance for ♋ Cancer (June 21–July 22)

In 2014 take your newfound/recharged confidence out into the world. Launch a new career or unleash innovative brilliance in your present field. Opportunities that appeared in 2013 benefit from reconsideration in January and February, and implementation from March 2014 onward. A trip becomes a vision quest, bringing vague longings into sharp focus—get going if you haven't already.

Highlighting distinctive talents, you radiate a sense of comfort and hope. People want to support you, attracted to your fresh approach. Scan your periphery to neutralize jealous underhandedness. Flack is unavoidable; challenges provoke ingenuity.

Experiment rather than hold to a predefined trajectory in all matters, as old settings have become stagnant puddles. Love, play and creativity are critical to your wellbeing and need to be prominent on your calendar this year. Any slumbering artistic ambitions will flourish from your devotions.

Relationships are life-changers for Cancers in 2013–14. A love affair may transform into a partnership; a mate going through huge metamorphoses could rock your world. Saturn in Scorpio scours away old shadows that hunkered upon you like an unlovable shell. Freed up pride and self-love encourage you to show up more authentically, or to shed a long-standing entanglement. An associate, personal or professional, may have censored you for too long.

Your family/community increases; subsequent responsibilities offer calm and joy, requiring more discipline, organization than you needed before. Many Cancer-born will have children, or a comforting, family-like community may appear.

Gretchen Lawlor © Mother Tongue Ink 2013

♈
♉

Saturday
21

⊙→♋ 3:51 am
☽□♃ 10:13 am
☽⚹♉ 3:24 pm v/c
☽→♉ 8:03 pm
⊙⚹☽ 9:19 pm

Summer Solstice

Sun in ♋ Cancer 3:51 am PDT

♉

Sunday
22

☽⚹♆ 9:57 am
☽△♇ 7:16 pm

We Are Water

We are Water
Rebuilt
Safe passage to the motherlands and
Even when they took our bodies our hearts pumped watery blood
And even when they tried to unhinge our minds
These memories were the undercurrent still a flood
And even when they plucked the feathers from our wings
We lived in oceans above their sky
Realms where our wings swam through the psychic passage
They couldn't find with just their eyes
And when they took our clothes, we spun linen from sea horse skins
The Ocean floor made offerings to the unborn in out midst and
They cloaked us in effortlessness
And when they took our lands
We retraced the lines on our grandmothers' hands
To barren deserts, we collected grains of sand, one by one,
Carried in baskets we wove the belly of time, carried them home
To recreate the embankment of the sea from sheer memory
Re-Membering recipes for the elixirs of making life
And when they fed us lies, we digested their false prophesies
Vomited the truth back
Into a porcelain chalice filled with star water
And when they poisoned our gardens,
We held seeds between our teeth, got quiet, stood silent,
Dug our way beneath the Earth's surface to pure springs
Cleansing the soul of every place stained with their disgrace,
We Water transformed without a trace

No matter what the obstacle, We are Water
Our nature can transcend any landscape,
Crest on changes and break free when we are captured,
Find solace in the crevice and take back the ground from every captor
We can transform any place we must take shape
We can transmute any memory, make it a birthplace
We can transcribe the essence and get pregnant with the remnants

We are Water
Clear, soothing, bloody, putrid, shapeless, formless, fluid, roaming,
Undercover, in caverns growing, weightless, the void, cleansing, breaking
Lovers' fluids, moon milk white, making ruins, nourish the wounded,
Capture the ruthless, storming rapture, nature's benefactor

We are Water

River Breath Life

June
liù yuè

♉ ## Monday
23

☽☍♄ 3:59 am
♀→Ⅱ 5:33 am
☽⚹♃ 6:49 pm v/c

♉
Ⅱ ## Tuesday
24

☽→Ⅱ 4:05 am
☽☌♀ 6:26 am
☽□♆ 6:29 pm

Ⅱ ## Wednesday
25

♂☍♅ 1:26 am
☽⚹♅ 11:15 am
☽△♂ 11:31 am

Ⅱ
♋ ## Thursday
26

☽☌☿ 4:56 am v/c
☽→♋ 2:05 pm

♋ ## Friday
27

☉☌☽ 1:08 am
☽△♆ 4:53 am
☽☍♇ 2:39 pm
☽□♅ 10:16 pm
☽△♄ 11:48 pm

New Moon in ♋ Cancer 1:08 am PDT
Moonrise Time: 6:14 am PDT

ALL ASPECTS IN PACIFIC DAYLIGHT TIME; ADD 3 HOURS FOR EDT; ADD 7 HOURS FOR GMT

Climacteric Changes

Some days
I can melt ice in the freezer
at a distance of 15 meters.
I can turn a hotel ballroom
into a sauna.
I can wash the kitchen floor
with my own sweat.

My unstable atmosphere
spins cataclysmic storms.

I never thought
I would learn to love winter,
its dark and frozen days,
but now I am drawn
to the silence of heavy snow
and my thoughts sing there
like power lines at 40 below.

excerpt © Janice Lore 2010

Prometheus
© Eleanor Ruckman 2002

ካካካ xī ɑ̄ ı̄ū

♋

Saturday
28

☽□♂ 12:19 am
☽♂♃ 6:02 pm v/c

☉☉☉ ıᗞ ɓāī ɾ̀ı

♋
♌

Sunday
29

☉△♇ 12:22 am
☽→♌ 1:43 am
♂⊼♇ 2:10 am
♀□♇ 12:31 pm
☽⚹♀ 5:16 pm

June / July

Athesh—Herb Month / Ameda—Vegetable Month

Wisdom © Jakki Moore 2012

☽☽☽ Henesháal—East Day ─────────────

♌

Monday
30

☽△♅ 10:40 am
☽□♄ 11:58 am
☽ApG 12:11 pm
☽⚹♂ 2:42 pm

♂♂♂ Honesháal—West Day ─────────────

♌
♍

Tuesday
1

July

☽⚹♀ 3:00 am v/c
♀D 5:50 am
☽→♍ 2:23 pm
♇PrG 11:47 pm

☿☿☿ Hunesháal—North Day ─────────────

♍

Wednesday
2

☽☍♆ 5:30 am
☉⚹☽ 12:19 pm
☽□♀ 12:50 pm
☽△♇ 3:20 pm

♃♃♃ Hanesháal—South Day ─────────────

♍

Thursday
3

☽⚹♄ 12:32 am
♀⚻♇ 1:15 pm
☽□♀ 4:01 pm
☽⚹♃ 9:21 pm v/c

♀♀♀ Rayilesháal—Above Day ─────────────

♍
♎

Friday
4

☉☍♇ 1:03 am
☽→♎ 2:43 am

ALL ASPECTS IN PACIFIC DAYLIGHT TIME; ADD 3 HOURS FOR EDT; ADD 7 HOURS FOR GMT

Our Ladies of Produce

Goddess in the grocery store,
head gracious above the purple plums,
daughter tugging at sleeve, young son in stroller
not ready to walk

To kneel down in worship
would have embarrassed us both
so I smiled and bowed my gray head
above the deep-hued fruit.
fingers testing for ripeness, searching smooth skin
for the fullness of time,
glorying in depth of color
even here beneath harsh fluorescent white

Bag half full, I looked up and they were gone,
the goddess and her children

In her place, a spike-haired teen in bomber jacket
and short, tight skirt,
who smiled when she beheld me,
and bowed her gracious head
above the fruit

¤ *Deborah Wiese 2012*

ᚺᚺᚺ Yileshául—Below Day

 ♎

Saturday
5

☽□♇ 2:47 am
☉□☽ 4:59 am
☽△♀ 6:52 am
☽☍♅ 10:46 am
☽☌♂ 6:31 pm

Waxing Half Moon in ♎ Libra 4:59 am PDT

☉☉☉ Hathameshául—Center Day

♎
♏

Sunday
6

☽△♉ 3:52 am
☽□♃ 8:31 am v/c
☽→♏ 12:33 pm
♀⚹♅ 11:49 pm

July
zhūyīeh

Monday
7

☽△♆	2:14 am
♀⊼♄	7:08 am
☽⚹♇	10:59 am
☉△☽	5:27 pm
☽♂♄	7:11 pm
♀□⚷	11:47 pm

**Demeter Talks Through
The Crop Circles**
© *Lindy Kehoe 2012*

Tuesday
8

☉□♅	9:23 am
☽△♃	3:32 pm v/c
☉△♄	5:28 pm
☽→♐	6:24 pm

Wednesday
9

☽□♆	7:00 am
☉△⚷	2:26 pm
☽△♅	10:13 pm

Thursday
10

☽☍♀	4:30 am
☽⚹♂	8:07 am
☽☍♅	5:19 pm v/c
☽→♑	8:24 pm

Friday
11

☽⚹♆	8:12 am
☽♂♇	3:48 pm
☽□♅	10:45 pm
☽⚹♄	11:07 pm

A Dead Language

My tongue forks
a dead language,
one of owl.
My fragments
have hidden
feathers
in broom closets
in the face
of Academy,
The War,
still.
Old ball and cannon,
what's allowed
into this canon,
the precious words
of women
before,
yanked from the stacks.

The Bird Girls © *Denise Kester 2012*

The dead language shall rise—womanspeak the canary of seasons,
a land folding in on itself, creatrix—repairing the split.

excerpt ¤ Shae Savoy 2012

ᚠᚠᚠ Šanbe

♑
≈≈

Saturday
12

⊙☍☽ 4:25 am
☽□♂ 9:41 am
☽☍♃ 6:56 pm v/c
☽→≈ 8:07 pm
☿→♋ 9:44 pm

Full Moon in ♑ Capricorn 4:25 am PDT
Moonrise Time: 8:18 pm PDT

⊙⊙⊙ Yekšanbe

≈≈

Sunday
13

☽PrG 1:21 am
♀△♂ 1:22 am
☽⚹♅ 10:07 pm
☽□♄ 10:26 pm

July
julio

♒︎
♓︎

Monday
14

☽△♂ 10:37 am
☽△♀ 12:23 pm v/c
☽→♓ 7:40 pm
☽△♅ 11:07 pm

I Know Why

□ *Teresa Gagné 2012*

♓︎

Tuesday
15

☽♂♆ 7:25 am
☽✳︎♇ 3:08 pm
☽△♄ 10:47 pm

♓︎
♈︎

Wednesday
16

♃→♌ 3:30 am
☉△☽ 11:13 am
☽□♀ 5:57 pm v/c
☽→♈ 9:07 pm
☽△♃ 9:23 pm

♈︎

Thursday
17

☽□♅ 5:25 am
☽□♇ 5:39 pm

♈︎

Friday
18

☽♂♅ 1:37 am
♀→♋ 7:06 am
☉□☽ 7:08 pm
☽♂♂ 7:18 pm v/c
☿△♆ 10:36 pm
☉□♂ 11:32 pm

Waning Half Moon in ♈Aries 7:08 pm PDT

ALL ASPECTS IN PACIFIC DAYLIGHT TIME; ADD 3 HOURS FOR EDT; ADD 7 HOURS FOR GMT

Don't Sit Still

Don't sit still!
Let your inner being pulse with the wings of a bird
rising and falling with the breath.
Let the wild thing inside you soar beyond its cage
unseen by the keepers of the classroom or the office
who would have you stay motionless,
dying within your skin.

Don't sit still!
As though your teeming energy submitted to these chains.
Let the waters of your body roar,
churning oceans in a seashell.
Let the rhythmic snake inside climb the tree unseen.
Let the tips of your fingers open, curiously, each one
the eye of some wild creature.

Don't sit still!
Let your inner being venture out into the wildest terrain,
tasting the fruits that flourish there, tasting the fresh unsheltered sky.
Deftly seek the motion that you may find in stillness,
for there is a current of life inside you, strong enough to lift
your pinioned feathers into flight.

© Renée Hummel 2006

ħħħ sábado

♈
♉

Saturday
19

☽→♉ 1:42 am
☽□♃ 2:54 am
☽⚹♀ 3:34 am

☽⚹♅ 2:49 pm
☽⚹♀ 4:52 pm
☽△♇ 11:31 pm

☉☉☉ domingo

♉

Sunday
20

☽☍ħ 8:21 am
ħ☽ 1:35 pm

July
qī yuè

□ Wolfsong 2009

Watching Spirits

♉
♊

Monday
21

☉⚹☽ 7:12 am v/c
☽→♊ 9:36 am
☽⚹♃ 11:52 am
♅R 7:53 pm
☽□♆ 11:19 pm
⚵⚹♇ 11:49 pm

♊

Tuesday
22

☉→♌ 2:41 pm
☽⚹♅ 5:29 pm

Sun in ♌ Leo 2:41 pm PDT

♊
♋

Wednesday
23

☽△♂ 5:52 pm v/c
☽→♋ 7:59 pm

♋

Thursday
24

♀△♆ 4:09 am
☽△♆ 10:03 am
☽♂♀ 10:43 am
☉♂♃ 1:43 pm
⚵□♅ 5:07 pm
☿△♄ 7:11 pm
☽♊♇ 7:23 pm

♋

Friday
25

☿△⚵ 2:42 am
☽□♅ 4:49 am
☽△♄ 5:08 am
☽♂⚵ 6:53 am v/c
♂→♏ 7:25 pm
♃ApG 8:48 pm

ALL ASPECTS IN PACIFIC DAYLIGHT TIME; ADD 3 HOURS FOR EDT; ADD 7 HOURS FOR GMT

2014 Year at a Glance for ♌ Leo (July 22 – August 22)

Leo strides into 2014 already well into life-changing personal and psychological improvements. Building solid foundations for future success and stability, most of your progress has involved completion and resolution. Starting this year, in July, generous Jupiter lifts your spirits and brings fortune, protection and blessings.

In the first months of the year, deep healing modalities scour away old family scripts/attitudes that have impeded your progress. Support clearing through physical detox (fasting, sweats). Guardian angels/ancestors cluster around you, keeping you safe, sweeping in with last minute miracles. Watch for some golden thread appearing from the past to guide and steady your future: a legacy (gifts of spiritual insight, a trait, or financial inheritance).

You may relocate to a richer environment or commence a course of study (as teacher or student) in 2014. It's a good year for retraining or specializing in your field (especially beneficial for releasing you from a toxic work environment). Cultivate your electronic presence. Keep in contact with inspiring people or groups you encountered in 2012-13; they carry some key to your future. Seek a new stage—new endeavors have an excellent chance of success. People will cheer you on; they have been holding doors open, ones you couldn't step through until you finished old business.

Start simply, no need to expand too fast. Weigh all opportunities—do they honor your personal and intimate life, provide peace and tranquility? You are at the beginning of a new era, seeding rich possibilities for years to come.

Gretchen Lawlor © Mother Tongue Ink 2013

───── ᚺᚺᚺ XT ᚲᛏ ᛗᚢ ─────

Queen Urraca of Spain and Lion
▢ June Boe 2010

<table>
<tr><td>♋
♌</td><td>●</td><td>Saturday
26</td></tr>
</table>

☽→♌ 7:55 am
☽□♂ 8:29 am
☽♂♃ 12:33 pm
☉♂☽ 3:42 pm

Moonrise Time: 5:54 am PDT
New Moon in ♌ Leo 3:42 pm PDT

───── ☉☉☉ ᛁᛚ ᛒᛖᛏ ᚱᛁ ─────

<table>
<tr><td>♌</td><td>●</td><td>Sunday
27</td></tr>
</table>

☽△♅ 5:14 pm
☽□♄ 5:37 pm v/c
☽ApG 8:30 pm
♀♂♇ 11:39 pm

I wear my nightgown to the garden, and the hem rakes the leaves. Like a kid whose unwashed face has the day's treats painted on, the colors I've wiped on my thighs tell a streaky story of my morning: raspberry patch, blood and red juice; dug horseradish, yellow sprinklings of pollen. My hands are black from rooting in the soil. I smell of warm animal.

In my rubberbooted gait, I'm trundling wheelbarrows, slopping watering cans to minister to squash or loll-headed sunflowers, wading through anarchist kale plants. Kneeling into earth, a compliant pew, eye level with pea tendrils whose single vine spine supports a whirled fist, a bursting bud, a spiralling cosmos, a complete and perfect slice of a complete and perfect universe. Nature sings one clear note inside of me.

Gardening is not big revolutionary work. It is about stakes and plants, and being in the moment. Meanwhile I, humanly, stubbornly, am impatient with my own clumsy hands. I have a schedule and a to-do list that work like a grappling hook to yank me out of "now" and into "next."

Sidestepping nettles, I unhook a crooked gate and pass into the coop of the crooning chickens. A row of blinking featherballs sit on rafters, flapping and flustering. I pour grain into chicken silos; the air fills with dust and the noise of typewriters as beaks hit metal in a frenzy of feeding. I fold eggs, warm, in the crook of my arm. Perfectly contained materials for life, unfertilized, like a dream woken up from too early. I am mother bringer of sustenance, full bellymaker. I am a thief making brute exchange. I go inside to make breakfast.

Grapes pour over the roof, leaves like green faces clamoring for a better view. The fir tree sends a subtle current of its once-upon-a time wildness through me as I move across the wooden floor. Inside, a reversal of the garden's equation: human things wink at me and nature's in a frame. Time to change into town clothes, check email. From out of the garden where I am just a midwife, I step into My Invented Life.

Circling overhead is death, ready to pick me off as I ripen. I light up altars: I fill hummingbird feeder, place gleaming mugs on shelves, clean. These offerings are vulnerable as berries at creekside while crows assemble, conspiracies of ravenous night, gossiping away in broad daylight.

I break the egg, for a moment, a perfect sun singing in the pan. Then, like a kid scribbling, I scramble what it meant by arranging itself just so.

this poem is a grace, for every living thing that I displace
and an appeal to all that lives and courses within me:
may all my daily deeds be worthy, of all the lives that make me.

□ *Andrea Palframan 2011*

VIII. SUSTENANCE

Moon VIII: July 26 – August 25

New Moon in ♌ Leo July 26; Full Moon in ♒ Aquarius Aug. 10; Sun in ♍ Virgo Aug. 22

Grandmother Corn

© *Marla Faith 2007*

July / August

Ameda—Vegetable Month

Wholeness © Gáia Orion 2012

⋙ Henesháal—East Day

♌
♍

☽→♍ 8:37 pm

Monday
28

♂♂♂ Honesháal—West Day

♍

Tuesday
29

☽⚹♂ 12:02 am
☽☍♆ 10:46 am
☽△♇   8:15 pm
☉⚻♆   9:44 pm

☿☿☿ Hunesháal—North Day

♍

Wednesday
30

☽⚹♀ 1:26 am
☽⚹♄ 6:28 am

♃♃♃ Hanesháal—South Day

♍
♎

Thursday
31

☽⚹♅ 7:47 am v/c
☽→♎ 9:09 am
♅→♌   3:46 pm
☽⚹♃   4:02 pm
♀□♅   9:43 pm

♀♀♀ Rayilesháal—Above Day

♎

Friday
1

August

☉⚹☽ 3:16 am
♀△♄ 3:22 am
♀△♅ 8:05 am
☽□♇   8:14 am
♂□♃   3:46 pm
☽☍♅   5:45 pm
☽□♀   7:58 pm v/c

ALL ASPECTS IN PACIFIC DAYLIGHT TIME; ADD 3 HOURS FOR EDT; ADD 7 HOURS FOR GMT

Lammas

Earth ripples alive in her golden skin as wheat ripens under summer sun, pulses to fullness fattened by rain and wild airs. Bronze rods of barley brushed by the weather, shimmer in fields of light as Corn Mother moves amongst us. Her fertile body is swollen with grain, sheaf after sheaf—enough to bring bread to the whole planet, even to famine, if we work with the climate, tend our fields as holy places, share with those who lack as an act of Compassion. Her belly is big with promise, with miracles, wonders, but our shadows stretch long on the harvest acres as we eat up the land. At the heart of the Eleusinian mysteries lay a single grain of wheat—sun-energy so small, holding the future. Women everywhere engage with the sacred alchemy of making bread: grain, water, fire, to feed their families and those who are in need. Loaves and flatbreads, chapattis, sour rye unite us in simple ritual: May we break bread in peace with all nations, in the name of Goddess.

Rose Flint © Mother Tongue Ink 2013

Sisters of Abundance © Mara Berendt Friedman 1998

We are creatures born to thrive on beauty, art, human warmth—in a world that overstimulates all of these. Our senses are inundated.

My mother has been saving salad dressing, olive oil, vinegar, and wine bottles for about six years. I notice them when I caretake for my sister, Cully, who is autistic. I've been living in Austin for two years now, and it's my weekly routine to spend a quiet evening with Cully in the warm hippy home where I was raised. I find the bottles everywhere, mostly stashed in concealed spaces, sometimes left on the kitchen counter, as if they contained a few more drops. Sometimes I reach over to recycle them, but then think twice about it. Would doing so disrespect the ways of my mother? (And oh, how she has her ways!) Her meticulous storage of empty glass containers is something I don't understand. She's older and wiser than I, and knows things I cannot yet fathom.

The chapters in my mother's creative, circular life have undulated through four children, the creation of two Montessouri schools, one macrobiotic restaurant, several country homesteads, all while keeping Cully healthy and beautiful. My mother's a diva. She listens to Democracy Now! every morning. She drives her biodiesel Mercedes to the Farmer's Market early every Saturday and returns home to make brunch for her communal neighbors. She builds cobb homes, keeps chickens and stashes empty bottles like it's her job.

I'm moving back home at the end of the month, adding one more daughter to the household. I desperately need to feel rooted again. I've had a rough few years, feel bruised from the fast whirl of the city and a fallen relationship, and am tired of doing things that I don't support—driving superfluously, paying a mythical landlord most of my earnings. I'm moving home because I'm lonely, over-stimulated, slightly lost. My equilibrium needs mending.

In these few evenings that I have left before I become a permanent resident here, I'm tempted to start recycling the glass bottles that fill every nook. In some areas, the bottles are stored so skillfully—hidden under stairwells, holding up mattresses, stored in boxes in the attic. You can *feel* their presence around us, collecting dust and filling the space with noise. I hear my mother's voice in my head. "Lilly, when you recycle the bottles, they just go somewhere else. So why not keep them here?" Why not? My mother's nurturing ways cultivate balance. . .in everyone, and everything she touches.

excerpt ¤ Lilly Rose 2012

Make Bread Not War © Sandra Ure Griffin 2011

Blessed are the fierce,
the outraged, as they rise
like fast fermentation.

excerpt ¤ Earthdancer 2010

ᛉᛉᛉ Yilesháal—Below Day

♎︎
♏︎

♉︎☌♃ 12:33 pm
☿□♂ 5:01 pm
☽→♏︎ 7:57 pm

Saturday
2

Lammas

☉☉☉ Hathamesháal—Center Day

♏︎

☽□♃ 3:33 am
☽☌♂ 4:31 am
☽□♉︎ 6:11 am
☽△♆ 8:58 am

☉⚻♇ 4:59 pm
☽⚹♇ 5:46 pm
☉□☽ 5:50 pm
☿⚻♆ 11:01 pm

Sunday
3

Waxing Half Moon in ♏︎ Scorpio 5:50 pm PDT

MOON VIII - August

August
ūt

Between Moments

☾☾☾ Došanbe

♏︎

Monday
4

☾☌♄ 3:29 am
☾△♀ 10:43 am v/c

♂♂♂ Sešanbe

♏︎
♐︎

Tuesday
5

☾→♐︎ 3:18 am
♄△⚴ 9:09 am
☾△♃ 11:17 am
☾□♆ 3:18 pm
☾△⚥ 10:33 pm

☿☿☿ Cahâršanbe

♐︎

Wednesday
6

☉△☾ 3:34 am
☿⚻♇ 4:43 am
☾△♅ 7:52 am v/c

♃♃♃ Panjšanbe

♐︎
♑︎

Thursday
7

♂△♆ 5:13 am
☾→♑︎ 6:38 am
☾⚹♆ 5:43 pm
☾⚹♂ 6:14 pm

♀♀♀ Jom'e

♑︎

Friday
8

☾☌♇ 1:22 am   ⚴△♅ 1:14 pm
☾□♅ 9:15 am   ☿⚻⚴ 5:12 pm
☉☌⚥ 9:21 am   ☉△♅ 5:36 pm
☾⚹♄ 10:08 am   ☿□♄ 7:49 pm

Hope

. . . is what brought you here
why you stay, why you love
why you plant seeds
hope never turns away
even if you do
it flows like a waterfall
or rises like a geyser
just when you need it to
hope is a flavor for
your morning cereal
and to stir in your coffee
it's your vitamin and
benediction
it's the garment you wear
sun shining through leaves
dolphins alive despite the oil
despite human greed
hope retypes the novel
fixes the leaky pipe
raises our children
better than we do
it is in the mailbox
hidden behind bills
with a rare stamp on it
from someone you never expected
to hear from again
hope leaps over the fence
to find you
hope knows your quirks
it has translated your life already
into three languages
body mind spirit
hope lifts us, hope cradles us
it springs from our forehead
and out our fingertips
and moves up our spine
and laughs out loud
hope writes poems
and makes salads
and laces the iced coffee
with cinnamon
hope never says goodbye
but always stays near you
closer than a shadow
singing in the shower
strewing rose petals in your path

excerpt ¤ Katya Sabaroff Taylor 2010

— ᚻᚻᚻ Šanbe —

♑
♒

Saturday
9

☽☌♀	1:09 am v/c	☉☐♄	8:10 am
☉⚹♇	1:49 am	☽☍♃	3:24 pm
☽→♒	6:52 am	☽☐♂	7:51 pm

— ☉☉☉ Yekšanbe —

♒

Sunday
10

Lunar Lammas

☽⚹♅	8:31 am
☽☐♄	9:31 am
☽PrG	10:51 am
☉☍☽	11:09 am
☽☍☿	3:11 pm v/c

Full Moon in ♒ Aquarius 11:09 am PDT
Moonrise Time: 7:40 pm PDT

August
agosto

Monday
11

☽→♓   5:55 am
☽☌♆   4:26 pm
☽△♂   8:51 am
☽⚹♇   11:58 pm

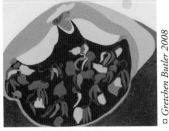

Big Mom's Beans

© *Gretchen Butler 2008*

Tuesday
12

♀→♌   12:23 am
☽△♄   9:01 am v/c
☿ApG 10:08 pm

♓
♈

Wednesday
13

☽→♈   6:00 am
☽△♀   8:43 am
☽△♃   4:26 pm

♈

Thursday
14

☽□♇   12:54 am
☽☌♅   9:14 am
☉△☽   7:22 pm
♃⚼♆   9:12 pm

♈
♉

Friday
15

♂⚹♇   2:29 am
☽△☿   8:50 am v/c
☽→♉   8:58 am
☿→♍   9:44 am
☽□♀   4:57 pm
☽⚹♆   8:35 pm
☽□♃   9:01 pm

Plant four seeds
One for the worm
One for the crow
one to rot and
One to grow

Plant Four Seeds © *Tessa Helweg-Larsen 2009*

Wild Seed

Some souls are born with seeds of the wild carried in their pouches, seeking to plant where the pavement cracks, seeking to split apart the deadness, seeking to bring the wild fruit back, to feed all hungry souls.

excerpt © Renée Hummel 2001

ħħħ sábado

♉

☽△♇	5:11 am
☽☍♂	6:28 am
☽☍♄	3:56 pm

Saturday
16

☉☉☉ domingo

♉
♊

☉□☽	5:26 am v/c
♀⚼♆	8:08 am
☽→♊	3:41 pm
♀☌♃	10:21 pm

Sunday
17

Waning Half Moon in ♉ Taurus 5:26 am PDT

August
bā yuè

□ Marysia Miernowska 2006

Life Force

Monday
18

☽□♂	1:06 am
☽□♆	4:00 am
☽✳♃	5:33 am
☽✳♀	6:11 am
♂☍♆	8:40 pm
☽✳♅	10:41 pm

Tuesday
19

☉✳☽	7:54 pm v/c

Wednesday
20

☽→♋	1:45 am
☽△♆	2:29 pm
☽✳☿	9:59 pm

Thursday
21

☽☍♇	12:07 am
♀⊼♇	4:52 am
☽△♂	7:48 am
☽□♅	9:55 am
☿△♇	12:20 pm
☽△♄	12:34 pm v/c

Friday
22

☽→♌	1:49 pm
☉→♍	9:46 pm
♂⊼♅	11:32 pm

Sun in ♍ Virgo 9:46 pm PDT

ALL ASPECTS IN PACIFIC DAYLIGHT TIME; ADD 3 HOURS FOR EDT; ADD 7 HOURS FOR GMT

2014 Year at a Glance for ♍ Virgo (August 22–Sept. 22)

Inspiring people light up your life in 2014. With these new allies, especially during the first half of the year, you'll come across some brilliant new options for your future.

You now realize it's time to release some long-standing involvements and communities that no longer hold your interest. Give yourself time for this work of undoing. Appropriate grief and mourning honor gifts received from this old life, eventually freeing tremendous energy to invest in your new life. Virgos are consummate ceremonialists; soulful, ritualized gratitude brings completion to the deepest levels of your being.

Important, perhaps difficult conversations need to happen, even with those who are no longer physically present. A letter written and witnessed by someone helps you regain a part of yourself, with profound impact in places you may not realize.

An excellent year to write, study, teach—these devotions strengthen your voice of authority. Honing skills with tools of communication allows more people to know about your services, your gifts.

Virgos are privately quite earthy, sensual creatures, with an innate understanding of the impact of intimate engagement. This may place you in the forefront of a current collective sexual awakening. Saturn into Scorpio (late 2012 through 2014) focuses our attention on conscious and intentional intimacy. We need your understanding of the power of daily devotions, of settings and foods. Children born to Virgo out of this passionate time will be exceptional in some way, and change your life forever.

Gretchen Lawlor © Mother Tongue Ink 2013

Peaceful Warrior
¤ *Beverly Naidus 2002*

♄♄♄ XT ɋT ÑÙ

♌

Saturday 23

♂△⚷ 12:14 am
☽☌♃ 6:47 am
☽☌♀ 7:01 pm
☽△♅ 10:21 pm
☽ApG 11:11 pm
☽□♂ 11:40 pm

⊙⊙⊙ ID bàĭ rì

♌

Sunday 24

☽□♄ 1:25 am v/c
☿☍⚷ 6:55 am
☿⚻♅ 7:01 am

Longevity

You cannot say this at the beginning.
You cannot know how long it will last
or when it will end. You just know it will.
Cold and hunger, grief and rot
have already impressed you
with their power. They sit at the door
waiting to enter. You go
to the Farmer's Market early
grab whatever catches your eye:
purple fingerling potatoes, chorizo, Palisade peaches
a dozen duck eggs, goat cheese with dill
a braid of fresh garlic, two skeins
of handspun yarn, one dyed with walnut hull,
the other with onion skin. That afternoon
you crochet lunar yellow with nut brown
making a warm scarf for coming winter. You
imagine how lovely it will look
tucked beneath
her chin against the glow
of her mahogany skin.
You perfume the kitchen
with garlic
simmering in the cast iron
making Sunday dinner
to share.
All day you make
because delight is in
the making.
You make because
by making
love comes in.

© Ann Filemyr 2012

Hearts Reflection
© Mary Ruff- Gentle Doe 2011

IX. CREATE

Moon IX: August 25–September 23

New Moon in ♍ Virgo Aug. 25; Full Moon in ♓ Pisces Sept. 8; Sun in ♎ Libra Sept. 22

Melancholy Journey
© *Betty LaDuke 2010*

Art transforms the creator, the viewer, the performer and the listener: art transforms us all.

excerpt © Lisa Noble 2011

August
Adaletham—Berry Month

© Lisette Costanzo 20[...]

♌
♍

Monday
25

☿✶♂	1:46 am
♀⊼♄	2:12 am
☽→♍	2:33 am
♀△♅	2:38 am

☿✶♄	5:29 am
☉☌☽	7:13 am
♂☌♄	12:30 pm
☽☍♆	3:15 pm

Moonrise Time: 6:29 am PDT
New Moon in ♍ Virgo 7:13 am PDT

♍

Tuesday
26

☽△♇	1:08 am
♀□♄	11:22 am
☽✶♄	2:20 pm
☽✶♂	3:37 pm
☽☌☿	7:29 pm v/c

♍
♎

Wednesday
27

♀□♂	8:46 am
☽→♎	2:54 pm

♎

Thursday
28

☽✶♃	9:44 am
☽□♇	1:03 pm
♆PrG	2:47 pm
☽☍♅	10:30 pm

♎

Friday
29

☉☍♆	7:33 am
☽✶♀	9:00 am v/c

ALL ASPECTS IN PACIFIC DAYLIGHT TIME; ADD 3 HOURS FOR EDT; ADD 7 HOURS FOR GMT

Transmuting Anger

I grapple with my own grit.
I contain my anger in the centering of pen on page,
choosing words that don't sting.
In strokes sweeping out from the center,

creating circles
on a new page.
Can I turn reactive
flames
to creative motion?
Anger falls away
to reveal
what can be born
through transmutation.
Less I bite, grip, judge,
regret and close,
More I open
to what creates
inside me.

© Amanda Tuttle 2010

Daily Drawing ¤ *Rachel Kaiser 2005*

ㅌㅌㅌ Yileshaál—Below Day

Saturday
30

☽→♏ 1:53 am
☽△♆ 1:41 pm
☉⚹☽ 4:16 pm
☽□♃ 9:00 pm
☽⚹♇ 11:09 pm

◉◉◉ Hathameshaál—Center Day

Sunday
31

☽♂♄ 12:10 pm
☽♂♂ 6:51 pm

September

---- ꒰꒰꒰ Dŏsanbe ----

Monday
1

☽□♀ 12:17 am
☽⚹☿ 8:39 am v/c
☽→♐ 10:17 am
☽□♆ 9:19 pm
☿→♎ 10:38 pm

---- ♂♂♂ Sešanbe ----

Tuesday
2

☉□☽ 4:11 am
☽△♃ 5:10 am
☽△♅ 2:38 pm

Waxing Half Moon in ♐ Sagittarius 4:11 am PDT

---- ☿☿☿ Cahâršanbe ----

Wednesday
3

☉△♇ 9:10 am
☽△♀ 11:06 am v/c
☽→♑ 3:15 pm
☽□♅ 8:04 pm

---- ♃♃♃ Panjšanbe ----

Thursday
4

☽⚹♆ 1:28 am
♅PrG 9:10 am
☽☌♇ 9:56 am
☉△☽ 11:44 am
☽□♅ 5:41 pm
☽⚹♄ 9:57 pm

---- ♀♀♀ Jom'e ----

Friday
5

♃⊼♇ 3:23 am
☽⚹♂ 8:08 am v/c
♀→♍ 10:07 am
☽→♒ 4:59 pm

I stepped on the polished stones in the stream, noting that the water was slipping away from the winter rush, half way towards the summer trickle. I reached up under the long moss covered roots of an old stump hanging over the small bank.

I thought of sacred caves, earliest peoples and rituals as I dug the clay out with my fingers. It was wet, dark and smelled of fertile earth, the goddess and magic-making. When I had a good handful, I thanked all the elements for giving me this precious gift, one I could fashion into vessels for carrying water and food, or just a small figure, something molded from my own hands, a talisman, like ancient women once made to remind them of the fecundity of the female spirit.

¤ *Amarah Gabriel 2012*

Baobab
© *Kit Skeoch 2012*

ኁኁኁ Šanbe

♒ ☽ **Saturday**
6

☿⚷Ψ 12:01 am
☽△♅ 2:52 am
☽☍♃ 11:11 am
☽⚹♅ 6:05 pm
☽□♄ 10:32 pm

☉☉☉ Yekšanbe

♒ ☽ **Sunday**
♓ **7**

☽□♂ 10:19 am v/c
☽→♓ 4:47 pm
☉☍♃ 7:43 pm
☽PrG 8:20 pm
☽☍♀ 9:38 pm

September
septiembre

☽☽☽ lunes

♓

Monday
8

☉⊼♅ 1:47 am
☽☌♆ 2:08 am
☽✶♇ 10:16 am
☉☍☽ 6:38 pm
☽△♄ 10:18 pm

Full Moon in ♓ Pisces 6:38 pm PDT
Moonrise Time: 6:55 pm PDT

♂♂♂ martes

♓
♈

Tuesday
9

☽△♂ 12:09 pm v/c
☿□♇ 3:40 pm
☽→♈ 4:33 pm

☿☿☿ miércoles

♈

Wednesday
10

♀☍♆ 3:50 am
☽□♇ 10:31 am
☿✶♃ 11:37 am
☽△♃ 12:22 pm
☽☍♅ 12:25 pm
☽☌♅ 5:58 pm v/c

♃♃♃ jueves

♈
♉

Thursday
11

☉✶♄ 8:03 am
☽→♉ 6:17 pm

♀♀♀ viernes

♉

Friday
12

☽✶♆ 4:16 am
☽△♀ 9:09 am
☽△♇ 1:22 pm
☽□♃ 4:06 pm
☿⊼♇ 7:26 pm

ALL ASPECTS IN PACIFIC DAYLIGHT TIME; ADD 3 HOURS FOR EDT; ADD 7 HOURS FOR GMT

Mother-Child Song © Amy L. Alley 2009

Saturday
13

1:16 am
3:24 am
6:31 am v/c

♂→♐ 2:57 pm
☽→♊ 11:26 pm
☽☍♂ 11:53 pm

Sunday
14

7:35 am
10:04 am
9:16 pm
11:44 pm

September
jiǔ yuè

---──))) xī qī yī ─────────────────────────

♊

Monday
15

☽⚹♅ 4:13 am
☽△♉ 9:52 am
☉□☽ 7:05 pm v/c

---── ♂♂♂ xī qī èr ────

Waning Half Moon in ♊ Gemini 7:05 pm PDT

♊
♋

Tuesday
16

☽→♋ 8:24 am
☽△♆ 7:34 pm

---── ☿☿☿ xī qī sān ─────────────────────

♋

Wednesday
17

☽☍♇ 6:05 am
♀☍♄ 11:31 am
☽⚹♀ 2:12 pm
☽□♅ 2:38 pm
♀⚻♅ 6:20 pm
☽△♄ 10:43 pm

---── ♃♃♃ xī qī sì ──────────────────────

♋
♌

Thursday
18

☽□☿ 3:00 am
☉⚹☽ 11:38 am v/c
☽→♌ 8:10 pm

---── ♀♀♀ xī qī wǔ ──────────────────────

♌

Friday
19

☽△♂ 3:41 am

---

respond

tides

neap tides the water is so high
fish lay eggs by the moon
up in the safest reaches
in sedge forest nurseries.
a woman must keep some things
only for those reaches
safe until the next moon.

tide in

produce produce produce
reflect the beauty of the world,
prime it, marinate it
so it may be easily digested.
sing, soar, teach,
make people laugh,
feed them cinnamon,
and beet muffins.
write.

tide out

stretch those milky limbs,
oh stretch out beneath the window
wool blankets.
crocheted shadows;
quilted hills.
sleep, dream, love.
edit.

but wherever the tide lies:
dance.

¤ *J.ellen Cooper 2012*

Rendezvous
¤ *Gretchen Butler 2007*

᚜ xī qī liù ᚛

| ♌ | | Saturday |
| | | 20 |

☽☌♃ 12:29 am
☽△♅ 2:57 am
☽ApG 7:23 am
☽□♄ 11:46 am
☽⚹☿ 9:33 pm v/c

᚜ ☉☉☉ ID bảī rì ᚛

| ♌ ♍ | | Sunday |
| | | 21 |

♀⚹♄ 6:03 am
☽→♍ 8:54 am
☽□♂ 8:05 pm
☽☍♆ 8:07 pm
♂□♆ 8:39 pm

Blanket of Miracles

I stand on a blanket of miracles.

I am strange stuff and dark magic:
broken bones and black feathers,
chants, fire, wood and
so many tears.
Tears like drops of moonlight
along an evergreen path.

I am soft kisses and slick touch,
heavy and round,
like my grandmother.
I arch,
reciting fever prayers
to old forest gods,
breathing the rhythm,
and giving birth to the world.

This is no spell.

I am deep memories and
lies long forgiven.
With tongue and teeth,
skin and spirit,
I drum.

I stand on my blanket of
miracles
and dance, singing

I am
the blood of my mothers,
dangerous knowledge,
fire and water and
salted bread.

I come to this place
to remember my beginning.
I come to this place
to honor my end.

Then I curl up
on my blanket of miracles,
exhausted,
to dream my daughters
into being.

□ *Katharine Saunders 2012*

X. RITUAL

Moon X: September 23–October 23

New Moon in ♎ Libra Sept. 23; Full Moon in ♈ Aries Oct. 8; Sun in ♏ Scorpio Oct. 23

With Soul

© *Melissa Harris 2010*

Share This Day

Fall Equinox

Leaves blaze tawny and russet with bright beauty in this last fall of light. Seedpods thicken on wild grasses, elderberries shake fistfuls of dark rain, quinces shine treasure brighter than coin. We give thanks for Gaia's storehouse of plenty, for this true wealth, as she gives and gives of her body: berries, squashes, beans—more and more we request and receive. Eat, she says, to all creaturely life—this is your being. Honour Gaia's nature by refusing to squander or disrespect her. Learn to need less and waste nothing; find ways to create sustainability and safeguard the magnificent diversity that is the body of the Goddess. We are living in the Sixth Great Extinction, losing our beloved creatures and plants. Take time to care for something that is other, and in need; from garden bird to snow leopard, all ecology is linked directly to our hearts. We may grieve for the lost summer of the world but change is our certainty: the balance of all future abundance is in our hands.

Rose Flint © Mother Tongue Ink 2013

In the Neighborwives' Garden

In the twilight
The highway's rhythm a few blocks away
Creates a lulling to cradle the occasional barking dog, crying child
And basketball dribbled down
The center of the street
Streetlights overtake the stars in the city,
Punctuated with flashing lights from the police in the distance

Deep in this city
On a good block in a not-that-good neighborhood
Lives the Neighborwives' garden

On this night,
Womyn assemble and invoke air, fire, water, earth and great mother
To awaken the collective and individual goddess

Teenagers roam the street talking loud
Cats hold stand-offs under porches
Except for the calico who practices witchcraft

Swaying, praying, chanting, dancing womyn
Deign this place holy
Hot red power
Shoots up from the fire
Raining back down
And infusing

Sacred tomato plants
With green fruit
And lily-scented breaths
Bear witness

To magic

◻ *Tari Muñiz 2012*

Prayer Meeting
◻ *Jennifer Rain Crosby 1999*

September

Ahede—Grain Month

 ♍

Monday
22

Fall Equinox

☽△♇ 7:04 am
♇☽ 5:36 pm
☉→♎ 7:29 pm

Sun in ♎ Libra 7:29 pm PDT

♍
♎

Tuesday
23

☽⚹♄ 12:41 am
☽☌♀ 5:15 am v/c
♃⊼♂ 3:04 pm
☽→♎ 8:59 pm
☉☌☽ 11:14 pm

Moonrise Time: 6:11 am PDT
New Moon in ♎ Libra 11:14 pm PDT

♎

Wednesday
24

☽⚹♂ 11:30 am
☽□♇ 6:39 pm

♎

Thursday
25

☽⚹♃ 2:20 am
☽☍♅ 2:30 am
♃△♅ 11:19 am

♎
♏

Friday
26

☽☌♉ 5:38 am v/c
☽→♏ 7:29 am
☽△♆ 5:53 pm

2014 Year at a Glance for ♎ Libra (Sept. 22–October 23)

In 2014 you leap forward in your life when you are wildly adventurous with your resources and talents. Taking responsibility for material circumstances improves your sense of self-worth. It is a good year for building solid foundations and clarifying your material priorities.

Innovative ventures or careers flourish as people notice and are inspired by your electrifying originality. You have a gift for making environments elegant and harmonious in simple ways (home, school, shop or office). You effortlessly create situations where connections between people happen easily. This ability will be appreciated, bringing respect and professional advancement.

Into this 2012–15 Uranus/Pluto portal, Librans carry the banner of radical, experimental relationships, new ways of joining forces. You have a deep understanding that none of us can afford the emotional or material resources to maintain lonely, independent lives. People really notice how you are bringing more freedom, honesty, integrity and consciousness into your most intimate alliances.

In 2014 friendships are favored, with special opportunities appearing through spiritual, artistic or foreign companions. A sense of belonging comes through organizations and communities devoted to instigating reforms.

You continue to clear deeply buried inherited patterns that have subtly dictated your life. This process requires solitude and periodically pulls you away from others. Cathartic therapies scour away deep childhood attachments, facilitating core changes. Freed up to take charge of your own destiny, you surprise even yourself with your choices.

Gretchen Lawlor © Mother Tongue Ink 2013

Equilibra © Modupe 2012

———— ♄♄♄ Yilesháal—Below Day ————

 ♏ Saturday 27

D✶♇ 4:25 am
D□♃ 12:39 pm
☿→♏ 3:39 pm
D♂♄ 9:46 pm

———— ☉☉☉ Hathamesháal—Center Day ————

 ♏ Sunday 28
♐

☉⊼♆ 7:52 am
D✶♀ 1:30 pm v/c
D→♐ 3:50 pm

September / October

septamber / aktober

ᗡᗡᗡ Dŏsanbe ─────────────────────────────

Monday
29

☽□♇ 1:42 am
☉⚹☽ 3:10 am
☽♂♂ 11:34 am
♀→♎ 1:52 pm
☽△♅ 6:46 pm
☽△♃ 8:29 pm v/c

───────────── ♂♂♂ Sešanbe ─────────────────────

Tuesday
30

☽→♑ 9:41 pm

───────────── ☿☿☿ Cahâršanbe ─────────────────────

Wednesday
1

October

☽⚹☿ 12:37 am
☽□♀ 12:51 am
☽⚹♇ 6:59 am
☉□☽ 12:32 pm
☽♂♇ 4:48 pm
☽□♅ 11:11 pm

Waxing Half Moon in ♑ Capricorn 12:32 pm PDT

───────────── ♃♃♃ Panjšanbe ─────────────────────

Thursday
2

☽⚹♄ 9:18 am v/c

───────────── ♀♀♀ Jom'e ─────────────────────

Friday
3

☽→♒ 1:00 am
☽□♅ 4:43 am
☽△♀ 8:53 am
☉△☽ 6:55 pm
♀⚹♄ 7:35 pm

ALL ASPECTS IN PACIFIC DAYLIGHT TIME; ADD 3 HOURS FOR EDT; ADD 7 HOURS FOR GMT

The Power of Magic

It is within your power to make your life more magical. Let yourself think magically. Symbolically. Metaphorically. Loosen up and let the boundaries between mundane and magical living become thinner. Invite yourself to see like an artist, to think like a poet.

Love Spell © *Kara Tosto 2004*

This is not about making stuff up and disconnecting from reality. It's about expansiveness, cultivating an openness to discover the magic and synchronicity that's already here. The more you are open to magic, the more magic happens. The more such things happen, the more magical life becomes. Ritual opens doorways. Create your own simple rituals of healing and reconnection. Meaningful rituals speak to the child-self within us as well as to our ancient souls, and these ritual experiences reverberate into our daily lives. Magic changes everything.

¤ *Robin Rose Bennett 2012*

— ሰሰሰ Šanbe —

≈
♓

Saturday
4

☽✶♂ 12:14 am	♂□♃ 7:16 am
☉□♇ 1:05 am	☿R 10:02 am
☽✶♅ 1:18 am	☽□♄ 11:32 am v/c
☽☍♃ 4:22 am	♂△♅ 9:18 pm

— ☉☉☉ Yekšanbe —

≈
♓

Sunday
5

☽→♓ 2:24 am
☽△♉ 6:06 am
☽☌♆ 10:56 am
☽✶♇ 8:20 pm

October
octubre

♓ ## Monday
6

D PrG 2:36 am
D □ ♂ 3:35 am
D △ ♄ 12:38 pm v/c
♅ PrG 9:11 pm

Angel © *Beth Lenco 2012*

━━━ ♂♂♂ martes ━━━

♓
♈ ## Tuesday
7

D → ♈ 3:07 am
☉ ⊼ ♏ 3:50 am
☉ ♂ ♅ 1:58 pm
D ♂ ♀ 7:58 pm
D □ ♇ 9:12 pm

━━━ ☿☿☿ miércoles ━━━

♈ ## Wednesday
♉

D ♂ ♅ 2:52 am
☉ ♂ D 3:51 am
D △ ♂ 7:05 am
D △ ♃ 7:20 am v/c
♀ □ ♇ 10:33 am
♂ △ ♃ 1:43 pm

Full Moon in Aries 3:51 am PDT
Moonrise Time: 6:49 pm PDT
Total Lunar Eclipse 3:56 am PDT*

━━━ ♃♃♃ jueves ━━━

♈
♉ ## Thursday
9

D → ♉ 4:44 am
D ♂ ♅ 6:08 am
D ✳ ♆ 1:30 pm
D △ ♇ 11:36 pm

━━━ ♀♀♀ viernes ━━━

♉ ## Friday
10

☿ → ♎ 10:27 am
D □ ♃ 10:48 am
☉ ✳ ♃ 4:17 pm
D ♂ ♄ 5:49 pm v/c
♀ ⊼ ♅ 6:17 pm

---

*Eclipse visible from Asia, Australia, the Pacific and the Americas

Setting a Cup for Shadow

For times of heart and mind meetings, conflict transformations,
mediations, visioning or accountability processes and so forth.

When coming to circle: participants check in by saying a few words of what energy each is holding as they come into the gather.

A cup of water is set on the table for Shadow, by which that stealthy entity may be checked in, and the invisible given visibility—to be clear, Shadow is not invoked, it is simply acknowledged as already being in the room. It is the neglected or repressed parts of our being, which are both our essential, consistent places of struggle, and our magnificent, en-ripened, un-picked potential.

We can ignore these parts, to our detriment. For then, their presence moves only through the cracks given, unintentionally, as we inter-relate without full consciousness. Seeping or banging their way into the room with exaggerated visibility, they can hold us hostage at inconvenient or painful moments. Or we can set a cup for the Shadow parts of ourselves and our groups, to honor them as maps for how to heal, step into our power, and live well in these times.

When Shadow presents in the room, we can look at the cup, be reminded to honor Shadow, and step towards vulnerability and compassion, with insight as our ally. We can become mirrors to ourselves and for each other, energizing prayers for releasing those patterns and creating new neural pathways in the minds of our beings and our togetherness. Changing behaviors, changes the mind. Changing the mind, changes the Mind. Changing the Mind, changes the World.

The Alchemy of Revolution is possible in each moment.

¤ *rain crowe 2012*

ᚻᚻᚻ sábado

♉
♊

Saturday
11

♀☌♅ 2:10 am
☽→♊ 8:51 am
☽☐♆ 6:06 pm

☉☉☉ domingo

♊

Sunday
12

☽✶♅ 10:57 am
☽△♀ 2:34 pm
☽✶♃ 5:35 pm
☉△☽ 9:04 pm
☽☍♂ 10:12 pm

October
shí yuè

What Does Peace Look Like
Peace is like the steam
that rises above a tea cup,
swirling in an upward motion
with unknown motives.
excerpt © Asya F. Guillory 2011

——— ☽☽☽ xī qī yī ———

♊
♋

Monday
13

☽△♀ 10:58 am v/c
☽→♋ 4:30 pm

——— ♂♂♂ xī qī èr ———

♋

Tuesday
14

♀⚹♃ 1:33 am
☽△♆ 2:18 am
☽☍♇ 2:02 pm
☽□♅ 8:07 pm
☿PrG 11:35 pm

——— ☿☿☿ xī qī sān ———

♋

Wednesday
15

☉⚹♂ 12:19 am
☽□♀ 6:46 am
☽△♄ 11:35 am
☉□☽ 12:12 pm
☽□☿ 4:27 pm v/c

Waning Half Moon in ♋ Cancer 12:12 pm PDT

——— ♃♃♃ xī qī sì ———

♋
♌

Thursday
16

☽→♌ 3:29 am
☉♂☿ 1:40 pm
☿⚹♂ 6:48 pm

——— ♀♀♀ xī qī w ———

♌

Friday
17

☽△♅ 7:58 am
☿♂♀ 10:55 am
☽♂♃ 5:05 pm
☽ApG 11:01 pm
☽⚹♅ 11:22 pm

deep breath

i will ink a spell
that braids
purpose with plant
i will prescribe the poem
with a tea
and women's voices
will whisper back
the magic
into being

excerpt ▫ J.ellen Cooper 2010

Peace Potion
© *Melissa Ireland 2008*

ᚼᚾᚼ xī qī liù

♌
♍

Saturday
18

☽□♄	12:34 am
☽⚹♀	2:13 am
☽△♂	4:18 am
☉⚹☽	6:10 am v/c
☽→♍	4:08 pm

☉☉☉ īþ bàī rì

♍

Sunday
19

☽☍♆	2:15 am
☽△♇	2:41 pm
♀⚹♂	10:18 pm

---

snatch

if you think it's all going to
hell in a handbasket
imagine meeting a woman
in labor
in the middle of the sidewalk,
water broken,
bellowing—if we didn't
know she was in labor
we'd just think she was crazy,
going to hell
in a handbasket even

instead, trust
that all is somehow well
that we are breaking open
into something capable
of carrying on
life

wombs,
handbaskets,
houses,
tides:
the world, which is a woman
earthen, holy,
dynamic, nurturer
nest, cavern, wholeness
the earth-world
is making more life in the snatch
womb basket house tide
ladle
kangaroopouch
of possibility

remember to stand
close to the teacher
(who's channeling
the future unborn
laden with advice)
as we learn to weave
(how life weaves)
and listen, and
for the sake of life, of earth
do as she guides us
pick up the floss
the straw, the branch
and flex it through
connect, and flex;
weaving things back
together
again

excerpt ¤ marna 2012

Primordial Womb
© cinders gott 2010

XI. CYCLES OF LIFE

Moon XI: October 23–November 22

New Moon in ♏ Scorpio Oct. 23; Full Moon in ♉ Taurus Nov. 6; Sun in ♐ Sagittarius Nov. 22

Forest Madonna   © *Barb Levine 2008*

October
Ayu—Fruit Month

© Abby Mariah Wentworth 2010

---------- ꙏꙏꙏ Henesháal—East Day ----------

 Monday
20

☽✶♄	1:32 pm
☿✶♃	1:38 pm
☽□♂	8:30 pm v/c

Madame Mermaid

---------- ♂♂♂ Honesháal—West Day ----------

 Tuesday
21

☽→♎	4:12 am

---------- ☿☿☿ Hunesháal—North Day ----------

 Wednesday
22

☽□♇	2:09 am
☽☍♅	7:24 am
♀ApG	10:37 am
☽♂♅	2:25 pm

---------- ♃♃♃ Hanesháal—South Day ----------

 Thursday
23

☽✶♃	5:48 pm		☽→♏	2:10 pm
☉→♏	4:57 am		☽♂♀	2:11 pm
☽✶♂	10:22 am v/c		☉♂☽	2:57 pm
♀→♏	1:52 pm		☽△♆	11:28 pm

Lunar Samhain

Sun in ♏ Scorpio 4:57 am PDT
Moonrise Time: 6:50 am PDT
New Moon in ♏ Scorpio 2:57 pm PDT
Partial Solar Eclipse 2:46 pm PDT*

---------- ♀♀♀ Rayilesháal—Above Day ----------

 Friday
24

☽✶♇	11:15 am

*Eclipse visible from the North Pacific and North America

2014 Year at a Glance for ♏ Scorpio (Oct. 23–Nov. 22)

You were a pivotal presence in 2013 when things got lively around you. Calm authority descended upon you, born of your own battles. You knew exactly what to do while others wrestled with their shadows. Keep it up this year, we're all still in this 2012-2015 evolutionary upgrade. We need you, angel of crisis. You thrive in fierce times.

You are at a turning point in your life. Changing circumstances call for new long-term plans. With perseverance comes richer character, depth and potency. You can be microscopic in your personal dissections; take time to play. From this scouring, you re-emerge more capably wielding your powerful presence.

The energy required for inner and outer transformation demands better time management, better boundaries and respect for your own limits. Body challenges/changes may activate a dormant healing gift or artistic talent. Use yourself as a tuning fork to develop innovative tools and techniques. If an existing job restricts your inventiveness, strike for better circumstances or look elsewhere.

The mysteries of intimate exchange, especially of sex, as a way to energize other elements of your life, are important spiritual journeys for Scorpio-born. In increasing number of us are curious about your insights, You may be propelled into teaching or writing about the spirit of passion that flows through you so naturally. Progressive media will be appreciative; don't bother with the mainstream.

Illumination
© Nancy Watterson 2010

Gretchen Lawlor © Mother Tongue Ink 2013

——————— ♄♄♄ Yileshấal—Below Day ———————

Saturday
25

☉♂♀ 12:31 am
☽□♃ 2:44 am
☽♂♄ 9:11 am v/c
♅D 12:17 pm
☽→♐ 9:40 pm

——————— ☉☉☉ Hathameshấal—Center Day ———————

Sunday
26

♂→♑ 3:43 am
☽□♆ 6:33 am
☽△♅ 10:22 pm

October
aktober / novamber

© nancy bolley 2004

Pray Wild

―――― ♌♌♌ Dõsanbe ――――

 ♐

Monday
27

☽⚹♅ 4:10 am
☽△♃ 9:18 am v/c
♀△♆ 11:48 am

―――― ♂♂♂ Sešanbe ――――

♐
♑

Tuesday
28

☉△♆ 2:49 am
☽→♑ 3:03 am
☽♂♂ 5:45 am
☽⚹♆ 11:36 am
☉⚹☽ 12:18 pm
☽⚹♀ 2:00 pm
☽♂♇ 10:47 pm

―――― ☿☿☿ Cahâršanbe ――――

♑

Wednesday
29

☽□♅ 2:50 am
☽□♅ 10:29 am
☽⚹♄ 8:01 pm v/c

―――― ♃♃♃ Panjšanbe ――――

♑
♒

Thursday
30

☽→♒ 6:52 am
☉□☽ 7:48 pm
☽□♀ 10:34 pm

Waxing Half Moon in ♒ Aquarius 7:48 pm PDT

―――― ♀♀♀ Jom'e ――――

♒

Friday
31

☽⚹♅ 5:57 am
☽△♅ 4:41 pm
☽☍♃ 5:29 pm
☽□♄ 11:22 pm v/c

Samhain/Hallowmas

Samhain

Darkness sinks its teeth into day as the year's descent deepens. Shadows fill up the street and cold creeps under our skin. Small valleys are bowls of mist brimmed with endings: bones, leaf-litter, rinds, skins, all the husks that held bright fires of life. This is the hour of the Cauldron of Transformation—from death comes rebirth. Listen for wisdom-voices in the storm: Kali, Crow-Woman, Ceridwen, Hecate—all know the need to cut and cull. In a world where women are disempowered—denied education, raped in war and peace, taught to distrust their own bodies—let the Hag guide you to face down fear. Do not get lost in grief. Ride your power, disturb the air; be the witch, the shocking voice of truthful stories that shatter the status quo. Protest, refuse, fight for a new equality that places the wellbeing of Mother Earth in the centre. The seven generations that will follow us are waiting, crying for a vision. It will come from women working together: sisters weaving magic circles of intent.

Rose Flint © Mother Tongue Ink 2013

Women Friends   *© Johari Harris 1991*

Belonging

Our bodies belong to earth,
our minds to sky.
Nothing, really, belongs to us.
Everything just is,
and teaches. We borrow,
and will give it all back.

One day soon, my mind will fly
back to sky. The birds will sing it.
My body will bleed back into earth.
The ground will drink my reds and browns.
Imagine the relief, not trying
to hold the colors together.

Start now.
It will be easier.
Re-collect the memory shards
from when we were shattered
into existence,
when we came into curled, wet leaves,
howling body bundles
touching down.

Potential

Transcendence *© Carrie Wachter Martinez 2012*

♄♄♄ Šanbe

November

♒ ♓

Saturday 1

☿⚹♃	5:44 am	♂⚹♆	4:43 pm
☽→♓	9:36 am	☽☌♆	5:46 pm
♀⚹♇	4:09 pm	☽⚹♂	5:49 pm

☉☉☉ Yekšanbe

♓

Sunday 2

☉△☽	1:10 am
☽⚹♇	3:45 am
☽△♀	4:56 am
☽PrG	4:21 pm

Daylight Saving Time Ends 2:00 am PST

November
noviembre

—— ☽☽☽ lunes ——

♓
♈ ## Monday
3

☽△♄ 1:05 am v/c
♀△♃ 3:27 am
♀⊼♅ 7:04 am
☽→♈ 10:53 am
☉✶♇ 2:50 pm
☽□♂ 9:52 pm

—— ♂♂♂ martes ——

♈ ## Tuesday
4

☽□♇ 6:07 am
☽♂♅ 9:29 am
☽△♃ 10:01 pm

—— ☿☿☿ miércoles ——

♈
♉ ## Wednesday
5

☽☊☿ 5:25 am v/c
☉△♃ 10:20 am
☽→♉ 1:33 pm
☉⊼♅ 1:59 pm
☽✶♆ 9:49 pm

—— ♃♃♃ jueves ——

♉ ## Thursday
6

☽△♂ 3:39 am
☽△♇ 9:18 am
☉☍☽ 2:23 pm
☽☍♀ 8:31 pm

Full Moon in ♉ Taurus 2:23 pm PST
Moonrise Time 5:06 pm PST

—— ♀♀♀ viernes ——

♉
♊ ## Friday
7

☽□♃ 1:59 am
☽☍♄ 8:17 am v/c
☽→♊ 5:45 pm

© *Hawk Madrone 2011*

———— ♄♄♄ sábado ————

♊  Saturday
♉

♌
☽□♅ 2:21 am
♉→♏ 3:09 pm
☽⚹♅ 5:42 pm

———— ☉☉☉ domingo ————

♊ Sunday
9

☽⚹♃ 8:22 am v/c
♀□♃ 12:41 pm

November

shí yī yuè

Monday
10

Dance Between Possibilities
© *Katja Maria Lewek 2008*

D→♋ 12:38 am
D△♉ 5:05 am
D△Ψ 9:44 am
♂♂♇ 3:06 pm
D☍♇ 10:44 pm
D☍♂ 11:13 pm

Tuesday
11

D□♅ 1:53 am
☉△D 1:55 am
☿△Ψ 7:38 pm
D△♀ 11:38 pm

Wednesday
12

D△♄ 1:16 am v/c
D→♌ 10:44 am
♂⚹♆ 4:37 pm
♀♂♄ 5:02 pm
♂□♅ 5:29 pm
D□☿ 11:57 pm

Thursday
13

D△♅ 1:04 pm
☉□♃ 7:05 pm

Friday
14

D♂♃ 6:18 am
☉□D 7:15 am
D□♄ 2:03 pm
DApG 5:47 pm
D□♀ 6:52 pm v/c
D→♍ 11:08 pm

Waning Half Moon in ♌ Leo 7:15 am PST

ALL ASPECTS IN PACIFIC STANDARD TIME; ADD 3 HOURS FOR EST; ADD 8 HOURS FOR GMT

Talking Myself Down

You know that time at the circus
when the aerialists climb to the tent top;
the audience stills.

That time when she suspends in air—that stunning time
when no one breathes between?

I wonder when we reach the real finale,
when flesh and spirit must take separate bows,
will the daring hurl toward new adventures,
trusting in that time between,
while I lie dizzied on a bed just feet above the floor,
clutching any hand who'll have me,
afraid to go where I have never been?

I want to leave with better grace
than all my hanging onto earth suggests.
I practice when I can on airplanes,
when turbulence and seat belt signs become my own trapeze.

I think about the ones I love; count savings
still unused—the benefit of my untimely
end; picture well attended funerals, console myself
by feeling missed.

I will my muscles to relax, unclench the death grip
on my seat arms; imagine calmly flying free
like spangled girls in leotards

who dare to love the time between.

© Linda Albert 2012

—— ᚺᚺᚺ xī qī liù ——

♍ Saturday
15

☽☌♆   8:52 am
☽⚹☿   9:49 pm
☽△♇ 10:53 pm
♆D   11:05 pm

—— ☉☉☉ lD bāi rì ——

♍ Sunday
16

☿⚹♇   5:57 am
☽△♂   7:18 am
♀→♐ 11:03 am

November
Athon—Seed Month

© Jo Jayson 2012

♍
♎

Monday
17

☉⚹☽	1:26 am
☿⊼♅	2:04 am
☿△♄	2:57 am
☽⚹♄	3:11 am v/c
☽→♎	11:30 am
☽⚹♀	2:19 pm
♄ApG	10:58 pm

♎

Tuesday
18

☉♂♄	12:50 am
☽□♇	10:40 am
☽☍♅	1:03 pm
☽□♂	10:30 pm

♎
♏

Wednesday
19

☽⚹♃	6:25 am v/c
☽→♏	9:31 pm

♏

Thursday
20

☽△♆	6:30 am
♀□♆	6:55 am
☽⚹♇	7:32 pm

♏

Friday
21

☿⚹♂	6:00 am
☽⚹♂	10:02 am
☽♂☿	10:19 am
☽□♃	2:18 pm
☽♂♄	9:53 pm v/c

2014 Year at a Glance for ♐ Sagittarius (Nov. 22–Dec. 21)

Perennial adventurer Sagittarius hits new heights of restlessness in 2014. Tend to old business in the early months. Then off you go: join a circus, sail to exotic ports, seek enlightenment in a Himalayan cave. An old sense of self is unraveling. This is best accomplished in privacy, especially while gazing at inspiring vistas.

You have a deep longing to find a place where you truly belong. Your quest takes you to ancestral lands, back to where you were born. Many Sagittarians will be on the move, literally or metaphorically, though the longing is not easily soothed. Explore without feeling you have to nail things down right away.

You continue to be electrically, playfully creative. You are a frisky mentor, and it is an excellent year to inspire. Consider a sabbatical early in the year to get your work ready for the world, then teach and/or publish. Fertility is high this year; ancestors may return as magical children.

Back to that old business in the early months of the year: you need to leave some draining situation behind, pass something on. Don't invest in an old story, especially on a whim. Some ancient business can be resolved or shed—a family curse, an unlived dream. Yes, there may be some melodrama; your irreverence inspires others to fool with the unstable nature of reality.

Ongoing financial storms challenge your innate optimism, and catalyze serious financial review. Assets require some deep review and redistribution. Reinvest in enduring resources: creativity and art, joy, lovers, the future.

Gretchen Lawlor © Mother Tongue Ink 2013

ħħħ Yileshaal—Below Day

♏︎
♐

Saturday
22

⊙→♐ 1:38 am
☽→♐ 4:19 am
⊙☌☽ 4:32 am

☽□♆ 12:50 pm
☽☌♀ 6:17 pm
♀□♃ 8:43 pm

Sun in ♐ Sagittarius 1:38 am PST
New Moon in ♐ Sagittarius 4:32 am PST
Moonrise Time: 6:35 am PST

⊙⊙⊙ Hathameshaal—Center Day

♐

Sunday
23

☽△♅ 3:02 am
♄D 2:00 pm
☽△♃ 7:16 pm v/c

I will be quiet no longer
now my unleashed voice has ranged
　　like hounds on the scent
　　　　trembling
　　　　　　bouncing
　　　　　　　　barking
　　　baying heart bounding
　　　　　pounding a fierce rhythm
I will be still　　no longer
now my unbound feet have slipped
　　off the curb
　　　　stepping
　　　　　　tapping
　　　　　　　toeing
　　greening soles skipping

O Cinderella, you could have a kingdom for the taking
for forcing your wild dancing feet into
　　this tiny glass sarcophagus
　　　　Run, run for the hills!

I will run and never stop running
run for the sake of my own long legs pumping
　　hair streaming like a maenad
　　　　galloping joyful across fields
　　　　　　circling ecstatic on hilltops
　　chasing through trees like ribbons of moonlight or song
I will not stop till I am exhausted
　　sated　　satisfied
　　　delirious with laughter and star-wine
　　　to laugh loudly　　catch my breath
　　　　tell a story about dogs racing the fences of their small yards
　　　　　howling
　　　　　　begging to join me

XII. CHARTING COURSE

Moon XII: November 22–December 21

New Moon in ♐ Sag. Nov. 22; Full Moon ♊ Gemini Dec. 6; Sun in ♑ Capricorn Dec. 21

Soaring
© Catherine Molland 2009

November
novamber

□ *June Boe 2007*

Bike Woman

─── ⟩⟩⟩ Dōsanbe ───

♐
♑

Monday
24

☽→♑ 8:31 am
☽⚹♆ 4:45 pm
♂⚻♃ 4:55 pm

─── ♂♂♂ Sešanbe ───

♑

Monday image

Tuesday
25

☽☌♇ 4:55 am
☽□♅ 6:25 am
☿☌♄ 6:37 pm

─── ☿☿☿ Cahâršanbe ───

♑
♒

Wednesday
26

☽☌♂ 12:06 am   ♀△♅ 4:22 pm
☽⚹♄ 6:10 am   ☉⚹☽ 7:28 pm
☽⚹♅ 7:30 am v/c   ☉□♆ 8:19 pm
☽→♒ 11:23 am   ♀□♇ 9:33 pm

─── ♃♃♃ Panjšanbe ───

♒

Thursday
27

☽⚹♅ 9:00 am
☽⚹♀ 10:38 am
☽PrG 3:10 pm
☿→♐ 6:26 pm

─── ♀♀♀ Jom'e ───

♒
♓

Friday
28

☽☍♃ 1:16 am
☽□♄ 9:14 am v/c
☽→♓ 2:03 pm
☽□♅ 4:31 pm
☽☌♆ 10:16 pm

─────────────────────────

ALL ASPECTS IN PACIFIC STANDARD TIME; ADD 3 HOURS FOR EST; ADD 8 HOURS FOR GMT

Note on the Castle Door

You are too late.

I have spent 50 years at the casement in this stone tower
that faces the road and river—the ways you might have arrived
on foot or on horseback,
by car or boat, a lone rider or entourage.
And with you would come my freedom,
the one answer to all my dreams.

Finally, this morning,
weary from waiting,
I took my eyes from the road,
turned from the window,
caught sight of myself in the mirror.
I expected to see a plaintive princess.
Instead, I saw a heroine
in full battle dress,
wearing as tokens her own ribbons.

So I am off to find my fortune.
I am not seeking riches, or love,
but my own way.
To weave in the vast world
the bold scenes I had elaborated
on the loom in my chamber:

visions—I recognize that now—

woven while I waited for you.

© Janice Lore 2012

Into the Light © Cori Caputo 2000

ታታታ Šanbe

♓

Saturday
29

⊙□☽ 2:06 am
☽⚹♇ 10:36 am
☽□♀ 6:28 pm

Waxing Half Moon in ♓ Pisces 2:06 am PST

⊙⊙⊙ Yekšanbe

♓
♈

Sunday
30

☽⚹♂ 11:41 am
☽△♄ 12:47 pm v/c
☽→♈ 5:14 pm
♀□♆ 8:26 pm

December
diciembre

She Watches

☽☽☽ lunes
♈

Monday
1

☽△♅	2:15 am
☉△☽	9:30 am
♂⚹♄	11:00 am
☽□♇	2:12 pm
☽♂♅	3:12 pm

♂♂♂ martes
♈
♉

Tuesday
2

☽△♀	3:14 am
☽△♃	8:16 am
☽□♂	6:42 pm v/c
☽→♉	9:15 pm

☿☿☿ miércoles
♉

Wednesday
3

☽⚹♆	5:49 am
☽△♇	6:46 pm

♃♃♃ jueves
♉

Thursday
4

♀△♃	11:11 am
☽□♃	1:12 pm
☉△♅	2:30 pm
♂→♒	3:56 pm
☽☍♄	10:45 pm v/c

♀♀♀ viernes
♉
♊

Friday
5

☉□⚷	1:31 am
☽→♊	2:28 am
☽△♂	3:07 am
☽□♆	11:20 am
☿△♅	7:44 pm

ALL ASPECTS IN PACIFIC STANDARD TIME; ADD 3 HOURS FOR EST; ADD 8 HOURS FOR GMT

Keepers of the Ember

Dream, January 13: In this dream I am in a crowd of people, and I hear a telephone ringing. Someone answers the phone and hands it to me and says, "It's for you." I say "hello," and the person on the other end is a woman, and she says, "I am calling from the Hopi Nation. The ember is in the canoe. The time is now."

The canoe carries precious cargo through flood-high waters in a desert land. The time is upon us and we are in this boat together, grateful that we are not alone.

The keepers are guided by helpers who send signals ahead.
They know the way by how it feels in their bodies.
It is a feeling of resonance that they follow.
The keepers are the guardians of the precious ember.

The ember will spark the imagination, allowing the slow burn of ideas to ignite and become clear harbingers of creative solutions for a troubled land.

Art and Writing © Denise Kester 2011

--- ㅏㅏㅏ sábado ---

♊

Saturday
6

☽⚹♅	1:28 am
☽☌☿	2:15 am
☿□♃	3:18 am
☉□☽	4:27 am
☽⚹♃	7:48 pm

Full Moon in ♊ Gemini 4:27 am PST
Moonrise Time: 5:21 pm PST

--- ⊙⊙⊙ domingo ---

♊
♋

Sunday
7

☽☌♀	1:51 am v/c
☽→♋	9:34 am
☽△♆	6:52 pm
☿ApG	9:43 pm

December
shí yī yuè

♋

Monday
8

☉☌☿	1:51 am
☽☍♇	9:02 am
☽□♅	9:32 am
♃R	12:41 pm

Bear Mandala
© *Diane Lee Moomey 2012*

♂♂♂ xī qī èr

♋
♌

Tuesday
9

☽△♄	4:14 pm v/c
☽→♌	7:14 pm

☿☿☿ xī qī sān

♌

Wednesday
10

☽☍♂	3:38 am
♀→♑	8:42 am
☽△♅	8:16 pm

♃♃♃ xī qī sì

♌

Thursday
11

☉△☽	10:20 am
☽△☿	2:40 pm
☽☌♃	4:21 pm

♀♀♀ xī qī w

♌
♍

Friday
12

☿△♃	3:24 am
☽□♄	4:48 am v/c
☽→♍	7:19 am
☽△♀	12:51 pm
☽ApG	3:10 pm
☽☍♆	5:28 pm

Causes

Maybe you think you are determined
by your genes, or your karma.

Or you think
that childhood experiences
are more important.

Maybe you believe
it's really a matter
of the food you eat.
Or subtle things
like magnetic waves
from phones
and ghosts and planets.

Sinking In ¤ *Pi Luna 2012*

Or you sense how
others' thoughts, words
and actions affect you, even your own!

Maybe you are convinced it's all in the effort you make.
Or—all in God's hands.

Well, She has sent a poet to say: It is *all* of the above—
and below—and beyond.

¤ *Janine Canan 2012*

— 十十十 xī qī liù —

♍ ☽ **Saturday**
13

☽△♇ 8:47 am

— ☉☉☉ 日 bāi rì —

♍ ☽
♎

☉□☽ 4:51 am
☉△♃ 7:56 am
♀⚹♆ 8:54 am
☽□♅ 12:47 pm

☽⚹♄ 6:11 pm v/c
☽→♎ 8:05 pm
♅□♇ 9:14 pm

Waning Half Moon in ♍ Virgo 4:51 am PST

Water Blessing

© Heather Taylor 2009

Winter Solstice

Once more the balance tips;
the scales of the year veer toward the light,
and we pray in that illumination
for peace.

excerpt © Patrice Haan 2008

Winter Solstice

Winter has swallowed us, taken us deep. In the chill of ice, trees stand stark as bones, the land is cold iron, frost slows all movement so Gaia is still as death. Only the brilliant stars in the black sky remember the rhythms of earth as they wheel through the night. All is connected. As stars bloom and die, as flowers fall to seed, as bone becomes nurturing ground, the wheeling universe lives in its Beauty and pattern. We are stardust, born of the Great Goddess, and in her is all hope. Even in the most severe terror of darkness and cold that Kali brings, the Spark flares again to ignite the perfect miracle of life. When all seems lost, the mystery of the universe begins to lift us into light and renewal once more. Women will tend the sacred fires until the voice of Demeter is heard in the Halls of Dis, and Persephone returns, a Queen filled with the knowledge of great mysteries. The pomegranate seed will become again a tree of life.

Rose Flint
© Mother
Tongue
Ink
'13

Favorite Tree © Gaia Orion 2011

December
Adol—Root Month

♎︎

Monday
15

🌓

☽□♀ 8:36 am
☽△♂ 12:56 pm
☽☍♅ 9:07 pm
☽□♇ 9:12 pm

▷▷▷ Henesháal—East Day

if at the crossroads she appears
do not be surprised
when she points in five directions.
know that, whichever chosen,
they all curve home.

excerpt ⌁ marna 2012

——— ♂♂♂ Honesháal—West Day ———

♎︎

Tuesday
16

☽⚹♃ 4:31 pm
☿→♑ 7:53 pm
☉⚹☽ 9:40 pm v/c

——— ☿☿☿ Hunesháal—North Day ———

♎︎
♏︎

Wednesday
17

☽→♏ 6:52 am
☽⚹♅ 8:26 am
☽△♆ 4:29 pm

——— ♃♃♃ Hanesháal—South Day ———

♏︎

Thursday
18

☽⚹♀ 12:59 am
☽□♂ 2:29 am
☽⚹♇ 6:40 am

——— ♀♀♀ Rayilesháal—Above Day ———

♏︎
♐︎

Friday
19

☽□♃ 12:25 am
☽☌♄ 1:11 pm v/c
☽→♐ 1:55 pm
☽□♆ 10:56 pm

ALL ASPECTS IN PACIFIC STANDARD TIME; ADD 3 HOURS FOR EST; ADD 8 HOURS FOR GMT

2014 Year at a Glance for ♑ Capricorn (Dec. 21–Jan. 20)

For the last six years, most extremely 2008–10, you've shed all manner of old identities. In 2014 you fine tune your new list of life priorities and a new identity solidifies around them. Make sure you include time to simply appreciate the present moment; refer to this suggestion at the first signs of excessive seriousness.

In 2013 and 2014, people are quite attracted to this new you. Beneficial alliances appear, increasing your happiness and opportunities for the future. Relationships that begin this year bring joy, sensual delight and enduring good fortune. You are favored in all manner of joint finances, great for receiving loans and grants (especially good for education, travel or transportation).

If you already have a good love, you'll be feeling the urge to spice things up. Remember, Capricorn is one of those sensual earthy signs, known to improve with age. If you are a young Capricorn, give yourself permission to be a bit bawdy; if you are older, revel in it. Travel with a partner or study something new to both of you.

With 2014's laser vision, look for other devoted agents of change. This is not a year for taking the burden exclusively on your own shoulders. You need others with fresh perspectives. Some friendships and groups do not support your new approach to life; you cannot afford their distraction. You may need to start your own movement. A blend of earthy pragmatism and lofty spiritual curiosity will serve you well in 2014.

Gretchen Lawlor © Mother Tongue Ink 2013

Mielycux Hears the Cry of Another Pack
© Kat Beyer 2009

ᚻᚻᚻ Yileshȧal—Below Day

♐

Saturday
20

☿✶♆ 1:30 am	☽△♅ 11:52 am
♀□♅ 9:08 am	♀☌♇ 1:09 pm
☽✶♂ 11:23 am	♂✶♅ 7:47 pm

☉☉☉ Hathameshȧal—Center Day

♐
♑

Sunday
21

♀✶♄ 2:02 am	☉→♑ 3:03 pm
☽△♃ 4:34 am v/c	☽→♑ 5:25 pm
♅D 2:45 pm	☉☌☽ 5:36 pm

Winter Solstice

Moonrise Time: 6:19 am PST
Sun in ♑ Capricorn 3:03 pm PST
New Moon in ♑ Capricorn 5:36 pm PST

Radical Headline

Listen to this news:

Today is the very day
when new connections
are possible
and the unexpected
can occur.

It is the day for living
with an open heart
and wide eyes.

Take everything in.

The gifts of living are
everywhere,

and you
are in the midst
of great wonder.

¤ *e.g. wise 2011*

The Decision © Cynthia Ré Robbins 1994

December
desamber

♑

Monday
22

☽⚹♆ 2:02 am
☽☌☿ 7:57 am
☽□♅ 2:17 pm
☽☌♇ 2:44 pm
☽☌♀ 7:17 pm v/c

━━━ ♂♂♂ Sešanbe ━━━

♑
♒

Tuesday
23

♄→♐ 8:34 am
☽→♒ 6:52 pm
☽⚹♄ 6:57 pm

━━━ ☿☿☿ Cahâršanbe ━━━

♒

Wednesday
24

☽PrG 8:47 am
☽⚹♅ 3:26 pm
☿□♅ 5:31 pm
☽☌♂ 8:36 pm
☿☌♇ 10:53 pm

━━━ ♃♃♃ Panjšanbe ━━━

♒
♓

Thursday
25

☽☍♃ 7:11 am v/c
☿⚹♄ 8:29 am
☽→♓ 8:07 pm
☽□♄ 8:33 pm

━━━ ♀♀♀ Jom'e ━━━

♓

Friday
26

☉⚹☽ 3:46 am
☽☌♆ 4:50 am
☽⚹♇ 5:46 pm
☉⚹♆ 7:10 pm
☽⚹☿ 11:04 pm

Out on a Limb, Jumping In
Forward with Courage
One Step at a Time
and the bridge
will appear.
excerpt © Maya Fink 2005

ALL ASPECTS IN PACIFIC STANDARD TIME; ADD 3 HOURS FOR EST; ADD 8 HOURS FOR GMT

The Climb ◻ *Pi Luna 2011*

♓ ### Saturday
♈ ### 27

☽⚹♀ 7:44 am v/c
♀⚺♃ 9:51 pm
☽→♈ 10:35 pm
☽△♄ 11:25 pm

♈ ### Sunday
28

⊙□☽ 10:31 am
☽♂♅ 8:19 pm
☽□♇ 9:09 pm

Waxing Half Moon in ♈ Aries 10:31 am PST

Dec. 2014/ Jan. 2015

diciembre / enero

♈

Monday
29

D⚹♂ 7:54 am
D□☿ 9:19 am
D△♃ 12:37 pm
D□♀ 4:45 pm v/c

♈
♉

Tuesday
30

D→♉ 2:56 am
D⚹♆ 12:29 pm
☿ㅠ♃ 12:37 pm
☉△D 7:40 pm

♉

Wednesday
31

D△♇ 2:28 am
D□♂ 4:50 pm
D□♃ 6:04 pm
D△☿ 10:18 pm

Trust ¤ *Dorrie Joy 2008*

♉
♊

Thursday
1

January 2015

D△♀ 4:19 am v/c
D→♊ 9:09 am
D☍♄ 10:53 am
♂☍♃ 11:49 am
D□♆ 7:07 pm

♊

Friday
2

D⚹♅ 8:29 am

ALL ASPECTS IN PACIFIC STANDARD TIME; ADD 3 HOURS FOR EST; ADD 8 HOURS FOR GMT

From One Good Year to the Beginning of Another

Gust southeast winds,
   enough to blow away the old year
     and usher in the new.
Slam the door open
and crack chime against window;
   song upon glass,
     confetti on bottle.
Carry my wishes high above the night ravens
   that seek shelter from storm in Yellow Cedar branches,
high above the tempestuous dance of Sitka Spruce tops,
   that rattle their cones in the wind like a rain stick.
Release them into cloud-pocked starscapes
and onto the kite tails of the aurora borealis—
   northern, cold, eerie translucent greens.
Carry my wishes out to sea,
beyond rocky shore and sheltered inlet.
Drop them like sparks of flame
onto the crests of white-capped swells,
   to later become green tourmaline crystals
     delivered to distant shores
      by the wispy wash of sea foam.
Peace, Joy and Prosperity in the year to come.

¤ Kersten Christianson 2011

— ♄♄♄ sábado —

♊
♋

Saturday
3

☉□♅ 12:40 am
☽✶♃ 1:13 am
☽△♂ 3:55 am v/c

♀→♒ 6:48 am
☉☌♇ 3:34 pm
☽→♋ 5:07 pm

— ☉☉☉ domingo —

♋

Sunday
4

☽△♆ 3:32 am
♀✶♄ 6:15 am
☉✶♂ 6:31 am
☿→♒ 5:08 pm

☽□♅ 5:18 pm
☽♂♇ 6:34 pm
☉☍☽ 8:53 pm v/c

Moonrise Time: 4:58 pm PST
Full Moon in ♋ Cancer 8:53 pm PST

We'Moon Evolution: A Community Endeavor

We'Moon is, as always, rooted in womyn's community. The datebook was originally planted as a seed in Europe where it sprouted on women's lands in the early 1980s. Transplanted to the USA in the late '80s, it flourished as a cottage industry on We'Moon Land in Oregon in the '90s and on into the 21st century. It grew in abundance and yielded colorful new fruits: the wall calendar, the notecards, and the datebook in full color with *We'Moon '04*. In 2009, we branched out to publish a children's book by Starhawk with illustrations by Lindy Kehoe: *The Last Wild Witch*, and in 2011, a 30 year Anthology: *In the Spirit of We'Moon*! Mother Tongue Ink, the home-grown company that publishes We'Moon, now supports women in communities in Southern Oregon and the city of Portland, as well, where an inspired new generation continues to produce and distribute it.

The first We'Moon was created as a handwritten, pocket-size diary and handbook in Gaia Rhythms, written in five languages, by womyn living together on land in France. It was self-published as a volunteer "labor of love" for years, publicized mostly by word-of-mouth and sometimes distributed by backpack over national borders. When We'Moon relocated to the US, it changed to a larger, more user-friendly format, as we entered the computer age. Through all the technological changes of the times, we learned by doing, step by step, without much formal training. We also grew into the business of publishing by the seat of our pants, starting with a little seed money that we recycled each year into printing the next year's edition.

By the early '90s, when we could finally afford to pay for our labor, We'Moon Company was incorporated (dba Mother Tongue Ink). Then came the learning process of how to "do business" with employees, staff meetings, labor laws, copyrights, payroll and accounting, timelines and budgets, editing and proofing, marketing to distributors and bookstores, advertising, web sales, etc.—until we became an efficient year-round business supporting nine or ten women living and working on land in community. Whew! It was always exciting, and always a lot more work than anyone ever thought it would be. But we learned how to do what was needed, and *voila*: We'Moon lives! We met and overcame major hurdles along the way that brought us to a new level each time. By now, the publishing industry has transformed, and independent distributors and women's bookstores are in decline. Nonetheless, We'Moon's loyal and growing customer base continues to support our unique womyn-created products, even in difficult economic times.

Every year, We'Moon continues to be created by a vast web of womyn. The Call for Contributions goes out to thousands of women, inviting art and writing on that year's theme (see How to Become a We'Moon Contributor on p. 232). All the original material sent in is reviewed in

Weaving Circles where local area women give feedback. The We'Moon Creatrix then collectively selects, designs, edits, and weaves the material together in the warp and woof of natural cycles through the thirteen Moons of the year. In Final Production, we fine-tune the finished copy and page lay-out through several rounds of contributor correspondence, editing and proofing. Approximately nine months after the Call goes out, the final electronic copy is sent to the printer. All the activity that goes into creating We'Moon is the *inbreath*; everything else we do to get it out into the world and into your hands is the *outbreath* in our annual cycle. To learn more about those in whose hands We'Moon eventually lands, check out our web survey summary at our website.

We'Moon Land and We'Mooniversity are related We'Moon community organizations. We'Moon Land (the original home of the We'Moon datebook in the USA and current home base of We'Mooniversity) is the oldest womyn's land community in Oregon, founded in 1973. We celebrated 40 years as an intentional wemoon's community last year and are in the process of re-inventing a sustainable model for the future (healing sanctuary/co-housing/eco-village/old lesbians' home/We'Mooniversity hub). We envision organically growing into an intergenerational community of earth-and-wemoon loving friends and extended family who live creatively, share a vision of a spirit-centered life on the land, and a home economy of mutual support. wemoonland@wemoon.ws. We'Mooniversity is a We'Moon Community School of Life—online and on the land. It's a 501(C)(3) non-profit organization that sometimes sponsors workshops, retreats and gatherings on the land, and is regenerating as an online network of We'Moon resources. Check out your favorite links and join the We'Moon Community conversation and activities. wmu@wemoon.ws.

Musawa ¤ Mother Tongue Ink 2013

WE'MOON ON THE WEB

At wemoon.ws, you can window shop our products, make purchases, read and submit raves and reviews, and sign up to receive one or both of our email newsletters: We'News—a periodic mailing announcing Mother Tongue Ink releases, specials and events, sent about five times a year—and the Weekly Lunar News—a brief and lovely reminder of upcoming holy days, astrological and lunar events with a weekly art feature. See what We'Moon astrologers are saying on the Starcodes page, and connect to websites of We'Moon artists and writers. You'll find information on We'Moon Land and We'Mooniversity, and on how you can become a contributor to We'Moon. You can also find us on Twitter (twitter.com/wemoonchat) and Facebook (facebook.com/wemoon)—stop in and say hello!

Myshkin ¤ Mother Tongue Ink 2012

STAFF APPRECIATION

Every year we get big appreciation from our We'Moon fans. I want to thank you for the encouragement and inspiration you send our way. We have a fantastic staff, and I'd like to take a moment to recognize each one:

Susie is our steadfast Shipping Coordinator and Promotions Assistant in the Southern Oregon office. She quickly and skillfully sends packages flying out our doors and keeps a We'Moon presence in the social media world.

Sequoia, ever patient with our opinionated Creatrix group, is our Graphic Designer, and web-mistress extraordinaire. She comes up with beautiful graphic highlights that constantly surprise and thrill us all.

Sue is a valiant Co-Manager in our Northern Oregon office. She is point person for promo and wholesale accounts, and keeps our fiscal data in tip top shape.

Ecole is the happy voice on this end of the sales line, helping folks place orders, and answering all manner of questions. She's also been an indispensable Production Assistant throughout the creation of this datebook.

Bethroot is our long-standing Special Editor, lending her wisdom, creative eye and sharp red pen to help make We'Moon the refined and meaningful book you hold in your hands.

Barbara is Co-Manager and Production Coordinator, helping the Southern Oregon office run smoothly and keeping the production scene on track.

Myshkin helps with promotion, brings you weekly inspiration and beauty via the Weekly Lunar News (you can sign up on our website), and is also an important creative consultant in our production office.

Musawa is We'Moon's founding Mother, and we thank her for laying the strong foundation of Mother Tongue Ink, guiding and growing We'Moon through the years.

Jillian was Shipping Assistant during our high tide shipping season, working alongside Susie to get our goodies into your waiting hands.

Elissa was Sue's right hand woman in the Portland office, taking summertime sales orders and assisting with office organization.

Big gratitude to Kalyn, Sandra Pastorius, Eagle Hawk, Marianne, Renée for the indispensable work of fresh eyes proofing and fine tuning.

Barbara Dickinson © Mother Tongue Ink 2013

© Copyrights and Contacting Contributors

Copyrights for most of the work published in We'Moon belong to each individual contributor. Please honor the copyrights: © means: <u>do not reproduce without the express permission of the artist, author, publisher or Mother Tongue Ink,</u> depending on whose name follows the copyright sign. Some we'moon prefer to free the copyright on their work: ¤ means: <u>this work may be passed on among women who wish to reprint it "in the spirit of We'Moon."</u> In all cases, give credit to the author/artist and to We'Moon, and send each a copy. If the artist has given permission, We'Moon may release contact information. Please email inquiries to mothertongue@wemoon.ws or contact contributors directly.

Contributor Bylines and Index

Autumn Skye Morrison (Powell River, BC, Canada) I aim to share honesty and faith in our blessed awakening, celebrate this incredible adventure, inspire and be inspired. Each canvas takes me on a journey, and as my paintbrush follows, I am led back to my center. autumnskyemorrison.com **p. 91**

Barb Levine (Corvallis, OR) is painting on wood these days as she renovates a very old, shabby house. Her paintings celebrate nature and strong, nurturing women as natural conduits for bringing peace, beauty and healing into the world. **p. 67, 157**

Barbara Dickinson (Sunny Valley, OR) Living, loving and learning more, every day. May the Muse be with you. **p. 99**

Barbara Manzi-Fe (Haresfield, UK) I enjoy it when my photos encourage people to look differently at what is around them—discovering the magic in the landscape and the flowers, looking further afield and very close. barbaramanzi-fe.co.uk **p. 79**

Beate Metz (1959–2009, Berlin, Germany) An astrologer, feminist, translator who was a mainstay of We'Moon's German edition and the European astrological community. **p. 204**

Becky Annison (Middlesex, UK) **p. 54**

Beth Lenco (Chester, NS) is a painter searching for truth and beauty in all things, focusing on being bigger and louder about it. starflower.ca **p. 45, 76, 152**

Bethroot Gwynn (Myrtle Creek, OR) marks her 18th year as We'Moon's Special Editor. At Fly Away Home women's land for 38 years, she writes, grows food, theater and ritual. FFI re: spiritual gatherings, working visits, possible residency, SASE to POB 593, Myrtle Creek, OR 97457. **p. 31, 33**

Betty LaDuke (Ashland, OR) Through my art, publications, and work in the academic world, I honor and illuminate international women artists who have inspired my work. *Dreaming Cows* is a book depicting a 100-foot mural created in collaboration with Heifer International. Art Photography by Robert Jaffe. bettyladuke.com **p. 135**

Beverly Naidus (Burton, WA) Activist, artist, subversive educator and dreamer, is the author of *Arts for Change: Teaching Outside the Frame*. Her work explores and confronts contemporary social issues with reconstructive visions of the future. artsforchange.org & beverlynaidus.net **p. 133**

Bonnie Morrissey (Hinesburg, VT) has the privilege of being claimed by fertile landscape—gardens, fruit trees, ponds, beehives, mountains. She is as a psychologist in private practice, writes, and teaches Authentic Movement, a body-based meditative discipline. bmorrissey@madriver.com **p. 162**

Bridget Reynolds (Ashland, OR) Deityarts.com, bridgetthebrit@aol.com **p. 46**

Carrie Wachter Martinez (Redway, CA) is a self-taught artist and designer, creative business entrepreneur, mama of two little creative souls, lover of nature and spirit, lucid dreamer and tarot reader. CaraMiaBella.com **p. 163**

Catherine Molland (Sante Fe, NM) is an artist, organic farmer, hairstylist/shop owner and mother of an artist son. Lots of opportunities to create joy and beauty! catherinemolland.com **p. 171**

Cathy McClelland (Kings Beach, CA) paints from her heart and imagination. Her art reflects her love for nature, cross-cultural mythical subjects, magical and sacred places and symbols. Her hope is that her artwork inspires viewers to see and feel the magic life has to offer each of us. cathymcclelland.com **p. 71**

Catrina Steffen (Potsdam, Germany) I am an artist and mother of three children. Through art, I praise the beauty of mother earth and the miracle of life, encourage people to realize that we are all creators of our realities. catrinasteffen.de **p. 34**

Christine Lowther (Tofino, BC, Canada) is a published poet and nonfiction author on Vancouver Island. A list of her books can be perused at christinelowther. blogspot.com **p. 43**

cinders gott (Ashland, OR) M.F.A., is an expressionist visual/performance artist, melding eco-feminism with mysticism, a priestess of Arachne Circles, a wild woods witch, and love-shamaness in training. She taught interdisciplinary arts in 50+ schools. cinderswitch@hotmail.com **p. 156**

Claire Blotter (Sausalito, CA) a Marin performance poet, teaches poetry writing for children of all ages. Her chapbook, *Moment in the Moment House*, is forthcoming from Finishing Line Press. Her video documentary, *WAKE-UP CALL: Saving the Songbirds*, is distributed by Video Project. **p. 103**

Cori Caputo (Nottingham, NH) works primarily with watercolor. I love to create pictures that allow the viewer to journey to enchanted lands and uncharted islands. You are invited to step inside my world and find the painting that speaks to your heart. coricaputo.com **p. 23, 49, 73, 173**

Cynthia Ré Robbins (Tavernier, FL) Her paintings emanate tranquility, magic and mystery. They inspire others to give their loving care to the seas and springs. See more paintings of the Spirits of the Springs and Mystical Mermaids at art4spirit.com **p. 183**

Dana Logan (Boise, ID) is an acupuncturist, ayurvedic medicine practitioner and artist. 3dana@live.com or facebook "Dana Logan, artist" **back cover**

Danielle Helen Ray Dickson (Nanaimo, BC, Canada) I consider art to have the power to change lives, heal people, unite them, spread love and shed light & love into the world. My artistic purpose is to inspire reflection and in turn be inspired. Blessings & Bliss. danielledickson.com **p. 75**

Deborah Koff-Chapin (Langley, WA) Deborah's evocative images are created through the process of Touch Drawing, which she has been developing since discovering it in '74. She is creator of *Soul Cards 1 & 2* and author of *Drawing Out Your Soul*. She teaches internationally. touchdrawing.com **p. 60**

Deborah Wiese (Port Townsend, WA) is a poet, playwright and novelist growing food, producing solar power and creating a more fun and resilient culture alongside her partner of thirty years, Tudi Haasl. dwiess55@yahoo.com **p. 115**

Denise Kester (Ashland, OR) is a mixed media print-making artist and renowned teacher, and founder/artistic director of Drawing on the Dream, an art distribution company, specializing in original art, prints, cards. Workshops, teaching and presentations: drawingonthedream.com **p. 57, 70, 117, 175**

Diana Rivers (Fayetteville, AR) is an artist and writer living on women's land. She writes books about the Hadra—women with powers—as well as poetry and short stories. She has helped organize several venues for women in the arts. Website: thehadra.com, Email: Rivers5524@aol.com **p. 101**

Diane Lee Moomey (El Granada, CA) Sculptor, painter and writer Diane has exhibited in California and Canada. Her current work is a large series of watercolors entitled "Paths, Portals and Elements." dianeleemoomeyart.com **p. 1, 35, 176**

Donna Coleman (Oberlin, OH) is a painter, art teacher, and visiting Art Professor. She has happily adapted to the open spaces of the Midwest. She studied painting at Rhode Island School of Design and Brooklyn College, and lives with her husband, a composer, and her teenage daughter. **p. 93**

Dorrie Joy (Dartmoor, UK) is an artist and craftswoman, creating with the land. Commissions welcome. dorriejoy.com **p. 186**

e.g. wise (Seattle, WA) loves truth and truth-seeking and is committed to learning her heart's song. gloryspress.com **p. 57, 75, 182**

Earthdancer (Elizabethtown, IL) lives in her handmade solar powered fairy cottage in the Shawnee National forest, spending her days homeschooling her wild child, running Dancing Spirit Herbs and Crystals with her wonderful herbalist partner, growing food, and snuggling kitties. Love blessings! Facebook: DancingSpiritHerbs **p. 127**

Eleanor Ruckman (Berkeley, CA) When I envision and create art, divine spirit flows through me to manifest as an image. Sharing with receptive community completes the cycle. As an art therapist, I help people experience wholeness, wellness through creative process: artgiveshope.com. **p. 52, 113**

Elizabeth Diamond Gabriel (Garden Valley, MN) is a professional artist, illustrator and teacher—since 1975. She holds private art sessions and small group classes involving the discovery/recovery of the Divine Creative Self. She enjoys immersing herself in long walking meditations along her beloved Minnesota lakes and woodlands. sites.google.com/site/edgstudioarts **p. 162**

Emelie Hebert and Deborah Wyatt (Madison, MS) artist, massage therapist, permaculturist and yoga practitioner. Dedicated to spreading conscious awareness and mastering my crafts. My best friend, art partner and mom died May 24, 2011. I still live and work on Lake Castle. **p. 202**

Evelyn Terranova (Heber City, UT) Natural health practitioner, artist, astrologer. moonbeamgallery.com **p. 2**

Felicity Nightingale (Fort William, UK) is an artist and illustrator in the Highlands of Scotland. Her paintings and drawings explore the whispering of shadows and the sacred in everything. flickofpaint.co.uk Felicity@flickofpaint.co.uk **p. 106**

Francene Hart (Honaunau, HI) is an internationally recognized Visionary Artist whose work utilizes the wisdom and symbolic imagery of Sacred Geometry, reverence for the natural environment, and the interconnectedness among all things to create watercolor paintings of beauty and spirit. **p. 33**

Gaia Orion (Orillia, ON, Canada) explores healing and natural spiritual themes that manifest in symbolic and archetypal images in her artwork. These images arise from her quest to understand life and her interest in ancient and sacred forms of art. artbygaia.com **p. 124, 179**

Galloway Quena Crain (Alpine, CA) is a poet, contra dance caller, and youth leadership facilitator. She is also a lover of movement, and a budding fiddler. By the time she turns 30 she wants to be able to ride a unicycle, perform in community theatre and sing in harmony. **p. 34, 93**

Gennifer Weaver (Stoughton, WI) aspires to "live simply so that others may simply live." She is passionate about wildcrafting and urban homesteading, engaging in permaculture, primitive skills, soap-making, and fiber arts. She raises chickens and children in Southern Wisconsin. **p. 164**

Giita Priebe (Eugene, OR) co-facilitates Feminine Mysticism programs with her Acarya, Karerii Blochlinger, as part of Ananda Seva Mission. Programs include women's retreats, healing workshops, study groups, women's ceremonies and women's celebrations. giitapriebe@gmail.com **p. 49**

Ginger Salkowski (Manzanita, OR) A biodynamic farmer growing vegetables on the Oregon coast. revolutiongardens.com **p. 99**

Gretchen Butler (Cazadero, CA) Artist and gardener, lives in a remote area of N. California. Before escaping S. California's wildfires in '03, she participated in many peace and social justice actions. See her memoir, *Wild Plum Café*. canyonstudio@gretchenbutler.com, gretchenbutler.com **p. 89, 130, 143**

Gretchen Lawlor (Seattle, WA and Tepoztlan, Mexico) A passionate astrologer for 40 years, I love to assist We'Mooners around the world navigate opportunities and challenges with grace and right timing. Emotional, relational, health, creativity, professional issues. Consultations, apprenticeships, workshops—in person and by phone and internet. Phone: 206.391.8681 Email: light@whidbey.com Website: gretchenlawlor.com **p. 20, 27, 47, 61, 73, 83, 97, 109, 121, 133, 149, 159, 169, 181**

Grete Boann Perry (Newport, OR) Painter, potter, deep sea sailor, tree planter, wild crafter, food grower. Protecting 160 acres of beautiful forest habitat in perpetuity by creating and putting Conservation Easements on deeds. Living simply, deepening understanding by practicing loving kindness. HealingSpiritScapes.com **p. 174**

Hawk Madrone (Myrtle Creek, OR) has been living at Fly Away Home, women's land in Southern Oregon, for 38 years. The author of *Weeding at Dawn: A Lesbian Country Life*, she is a writer, photographer, gardener, woodworker, with her animal companions always close by. **p. 165**

Heather Roan Robbins (St. Paul, MN) Ceremonialist, spiritual counselor and astrologer for 30+ years, writes weekly Starcodes for We'Moon and practices in St. Paul, Santa Fe, and NYC. roanrobbins.com **p. 12, 15, 21**

Heather Taylor (Olympia, WA) is a visual artist and mother of 3. See more of her iconic mandala of the sacred feminine at fullcirclemandalas.com or preview her children's book at loveisacircle.com. Blessings. **p. 178**

Holly Wilkinson (Richmond, VT) is a writer and reflector who listens to people's stories as they seek to make a living and a vibrant life. From dusk to dawn, she listens to Earth's whispers and flocks of images that arrive. **p. 41**

Irene Ingalls (Seattle, WA) I create intuitive transformational art using Light language—the language of Source Energy—benevolent, full of love and support. It is my joy to bring these messages through, weaving them into healing, inspiring art. Lightlanguageart.com **p. 228**

J.ellen Cooper (Brampton, ON, Canada) A biologist by trade, she digests her insight into deep ecology and natural processes by spinning poetry, paintings, and sculpture, and by sharing the wonder with her children. j.ellencooper@gmail.com **p. 143, 155**

Jakki Moore (Oslo, Norway) is an artist and illustrator. She also makes animated films. Creator of "The Sheela" cards, she leads workshops in Ireland using Sheela-na-Gigs as metaphors. jakkimooreart@yahoo.com, jakkiart.com **p. 114**

Jane Gray (Portland, OR) I am a banjo playing, book binding, fementation enthusiast residing at The Planet Repair Institute, a radical homestead and permaculture demonstration site. planetrepair@riseup.net, planetrepair.wordpress.com **p. 59**

Janice Lore (Tofino, BC, Canada) is a writer and performer from British Columbia, Canada. Her work has appeared in anthologies and literary magazines, and on the radio. She is a founding member of Performance Anxiety, a performance poetry collective. janicelore.ca **p. 113, 173**

Janine Canan (Sonoma, CA) is the author of 20 books including *Ardor: Poems of Life*, and the award-winning anthologies, *Messages from Amma* and *She Rises like the Sun*. Janine is a Psychiatrist and consultant for Embracing the World. Please visit JanineCanan.com. **p. 37, 80, 177**

Janine Jackson (Miami, FL) has created in various aspects for many years, using acrylic paints, pen and pencil, illustration software applications and image-editing programs. Her tools assist her in constructing works that focus on the power and beauty found in life. **p. 56**

Jayme Dee (Myrtle Creek, OR) I am fully creative; my life is filled with many projects; drawing, painting, singing, dancing and being—just a few of many. **p. 85**

Jaymie Johnson (Nelson, BC, Canada) My images aim to invoke a sense of wonder and gratitude for the human experience. The relation between mind, body, spirit is my main source of inspiration. jaymiejohnson.ca, jaymsmj@hotmail.com **p. 74**

Jeanette M. French (Gresham, OR) Life purpose—inspiring relationship with spirit through portals of light, love, joy, beauty, harmony, compassion, hope & gratitude. jonfrench@frontier.com, jeanette-french.artistwebsites.com **p. 65**

Jennifer Rain Crosby (N. San Juan, CA) With our hearts we repattern the inner and outer worlds. May we all have the courage to follow our heart's wisdom! Still living and making art in the woods of the San Juan Ridge. jenniferrain.com **p. 36, 147**

Jo Jayson (Harrison, NY) Spiritual artist and teacher of Goddess and Divine Feminine themes. Her work embodies and carries the essence of the sacred feminine which she channels. She offers prints, cards, candles and more. jojayson.com **p. 168**

Joanne Rocky Delaplaine (Bethesda, MD) is the daughter of the night and the mother of astonishment. She watches birds, grows zinnias, quilts dreams and words, and teaches yoga. Peace is her prayer. **p. 94, 95**

Johari Harris (Stone Mountain, GA) ever thankful to the Eternal One for the gift of the Spirit that is art-making. johariharris7@yahoo.com, AfraSpiritArts.com **p. 161**

Julie Dillon (Cameron Park, CA) is a freelance fantasy and scifi artist living in Northern California. You can see more of her work at juliedillonart.com. **front cover**

Julie O. (Quebec, Canada) My creations are prayers of gratitude and offerings to the spirit world. May we celebrate and feel our connections to the Divine energy. Visit: solmundoart.com **p. 12**

June Boe (Salt Spring Island, BC, Canada) has been painting for 60 years, and is influenced by having lived in Greece, Egypt and Morocco. Past lives: Greek woman holding dominion over a sector of grape-growing land; Amazonian woman living in Croatia; wild, strong warrior woman living before recorded history. **p. 121, 172**

Kara Tosto (Clovis, CA) I am a spinner, weaver, creator of magic. I paint with intention, and thrive on creating joy and happiness with my art. Contact me at: daisymoonsong@aol.com **p. 151**

Karen Clarke (Squamish, BC, Canada) In the state of open consciousness between dreaming and waking early in the morning, this poem came to me. I lay waiting for my daughter to awaken. The sun was slowly brightening my room through the curtains. **p. 69**

Kat Beyer (WI & CA) is an artist and author of *The Demon Catchers of Milan* (Egmont USA, 2012). She plays music with her family, practices fire-staff, and lives part-time in a tiny house on wheels. katspaw.com **p. 17, 181**

Katharine Saunders (Palo Alto, CA) is a kinky, queer and irreverent teacher, parent, poet and photographer living in the San Francisco Bay area. She is very fond of chocolate and things that sparkle. **p. 144**

Katheryn M. Trenshaw (Totnes, Devon, UK) director of Passionate Presence Center for Creative Expression. She believes in making life an art and welcomes everyone who wants to reach deeper to find that part of themselves they long for. katheryntrenshaw.com, passionatepresence.org, post@ktrenshaw.com **p. 48**

Kathy Crabbe (Temecula, CA) is a Creative Soul Guide, artist and writer who empowers women to live the life of their dreams through intuitive readings, e-classes, inspirational art and online resources. She lives surrounded by ancient oaks and elfin forests. KathyCrabbe.com **p. 140**

Katja Maria Lewek (Goppeln, Germany) hopes to inspire you on your own creative journey. She facilitates workshops on intuitive painting and launching into the creative journey. More info at: katja-lewek.de **p. 166**

Katya Sabaroff Taylor (Tallahassee, FL) is enjoying her "golden years," still writing, teaching, gardening and beachcombing along the Gulf waters. As a haikuist, she knows that what passes as ordinary is also extraordinary. creativeartsandhealing.com **p. 129**

Kay Kemp (Houston, TX) creates mixed media collage and painting to touch the heart and stir the soul. She guides others in finding their true voices of self-expression at her Wild Heart Art studio (wildheartart.com). kaykemp.com **p. 51, 128**

Kersten Christianson (Sitka, AK) is a raven-watching, moon-gazing Alaskan who teaches high school English and French, and composes rough draft poetry. She lives with her partner Bruce, daughter Rie, and yellow lab, Odin. Kersten is also a co-editor of the journal, *Alaska Women Speak.* **p. 187**

Khara Scott-Bey (Berkeley, CA) is an artist and art therapist who believes whole heartedly that it is through creativity and creative expression that the world will be healed. Her work is her spirit manifested, her activism is her homage to her ancestry. livetobecome.etsy.com, livetobecome.com **p. 3**

Kit Skeoch (Berkeley, CA) lives in a magical garden with her beloved cat. Visitors welcome. rainhaiyade@gmail.com, sacredvisions.org **p. 61, 139**

Krista Lynn Brown (Santa Rosa, CA) My work is influenced by the shapes and metaphors of nature, mythic elements of story and dream, feminine perspective, spiritual folk art, emotional and sexual energies, dark underbellies and folk magic. devaluna.com **p. 69**

Laurie Bauers (Hakalau, HI) is currently loving life, in gratitude, with her family. Constantly awed by Mother Earth's beauty, she gleefully paints in a harmonious relationship with Her. etsy.com/shop/ArtbyLaurieCrain **p. 107**

Liliana Darwin López (Eugene, OR) I am an academic, activist and poet, who strives to nurture beauty and justice in all my manifestations. I am mother to a teenage son, Sereno, who is my greatest teacher. **p. 90**

Lilly Rose (Austin, TX) A lover living in the big city of Austin, TX. Chaser of beauty and happiness, writer, grower, swimmer, dancer, and supporter of people enduring unfair and hard lives. Participates in creative and intellectual enhancement, and as much music and culture as possible. **p. 126**

Linda Albert (Longboat Key, FL) holds a Master Certification in Neuro-Linguistics and is a trained Jungian Archetypal Pattern Analyst. Recipient of numerous prizes, including the *Atlanta Review*'s International Merit Award, her work has been published internationally in various journals, magazines and anthologies. lindaalbert.net **p. 40, 167**

Linda Brunner (Stockton, MO) can be reached through her website at ourgreenthumbfarm.com. **p. 71**

Lindy Kehoe (Gold Hill, OR) With heart wings unfurled, it is my great joy to offer these painting portals up to the awakening of Gaia Sophia in us all. lindykehoe.com **p. 116**

Lisa O'Connor (Tuckahoe, NY) shares with her clients an eclectic toolbox amassed over 20 years of spiritual practice and study. She is dedicated to providing a safe and supportive environment that allows for greater self awareness, personal growth and transformation. yoursoulsmiles.com **p. 37**

Lisa Noble (Burien, WA) is a writer and artist. She has recently completed her first Young Adult Novel: *The Charman Chronicles: The Book of Fire*, available from her on-line shop, as are images of her paintings which have appeared in We'Moon over the years. cafepress.com/lisanoble (thecharmangallery/goddesswithin) **p. 8, 135**

Lisette Costanzo (St. Catharines, ON, Canada) is an Intuitive Artist and Metaphysicist. She's just completed her Reiki Masters which will further aid her metaphysical research. metaphysics@hotmail.ca **p. 15, 136**

Liz Atticus Ferrie (Jackson, CA) Traveling artist and nature enthusiast. Enjoys exploring nature with others, swimming in rivers, planting gardens, sharing global community. Inspired by music to create art and dance, these are my meditations. Give thanks to mother earth and all her blessings! **p. 39**

Lupen Grainne (Graton, CA) I am a multi-media artist. My love of plants, the natural world, and celebrating expressions of the feminine spirit are reflected in my work. ArtGardenSpiral.com **p. 96**

Luz-Maria López (Covington, LA) paints images inspired by her Latin American/ Mayan ancestry, her childhood memories and stories from everywhere. She is a Magna Cum Laude graduate with a BA in Fine Art. Her work is exhibited nationally and has won a number of awards. **p. 29**

Lynn Dewart (San Diego, CA) Artist, Teacher, Expressive Art Therapist in training. Healing and wholeness of women and of the planet are my passion. lynndewart.com **p. 206**

Lynn Flory (Craftsbury Common, VT) is a potter and writer, who can be found at her studio and gallery, Mill Village Pottery, working from her heart and spirit. **p. 101**

Maj Ikle (Wales, UK) is a women's film writer living off grid on women's land in Wales. maj_ikle@yahoo.co.uk **p. 86**

Mama Donna Henes (Brooklyn, NY) is a renowned urban shaman, author, and spiritual teacher. A ritual expert, she has published four books and writes for the *Huffington Post, Beliefnet* and films. cityshaman@aol.com, donnahenes.net **p. 55**

Mara Berendt Friedman (Lorane, OR) Flowing in creation's river, dwelling in a forest cave, flying with inspiration—life is Beautiful!! For over two decades, Mara has celebrated the Divine Feminine through her paintings. For a free catalogue, email: stream@newmoonvisions.com Website: newmoonvisions.com **p. 54, 125**

Mara Berendt Friedman and Trinity Harris are co-creators of *Rainbow Warrior Awaken! Your Journey of Guidance and Healing*. This unique divination tool is an inspiring blend of beauty and wisdom and flows from the power of the Sacred Feminine. rainbowwarriorawaken.com **p. 54, 125**

Maria Silmon (Somerset, UK) I live between the ancient Isle of Avalon and the open road. I honor solar festivals and moon phases, using photography/video to express my wonder of our Divine Mother Planet—awesome plants, trees, creatures. Me+camera+undergrowth=Bliss!! mariasilmon.co.uk **p. 123**

Marla Faith (Nashville, TN) is a painter and poet, teaches Art History and directs the Marnie Sheridan Gallery at Harpeth Hall School. Creating art is an important part of her spiritual path, and a way to bring positive energy into the world. marlafaith.com **p. 123**

marna (Portland, OR) whirls dervishes and verves poems in the Pacific Cascadia bioregion while serving the womyn-arts nonprofit, Moonifest (moonifest.org), and founding The Institute of Earth Regenerative Studies: earthregenerative.org **p. 156, 180**

Mary Ruff—Gentle Doe (Longview, TX) As artist and therapeutic massage therapist, I practice the art of blended vision in my work and life. divaart.net **p. 134**

Marysia Miernowska (Santa Monica, CA) is an artist and herbalist trained in Plant Spirit Medicine. Her art and life are inspired by the vibrant beauty in nature, people and Spirit. m.mierno@gmail.com, miernowska.com, mmierno.wix.com/fineart Facebook:Marysia Miernowska ART. Goddess bless! **p. 132**

Max Dashú (Oakland, CA) is a history sibyl, founder of the Suppresed History Archives, artist, and teacher of global women's history and heritages. (online courses and webcasts— see suppressedhistories.net) Her new dvd is *Woman Shaman: The Ancients!* **p. 31**

Maya Fink (Trångsund, Sweden and California) holds a BA in English Creative Writing from San Francisco State University. She follows the cosmos as a writer and educator. Her poetry is inspired by mysticism, herstory, wisdom, and love. buskeratheart@gmail.com **p. 184**

Medea Benjamin (Washington, DC) cofounder of CODEPINK and Global Exchange. She is author/editor of eight books—her latest: *Drone Warfare: Killing by Remote Control*. She campaigns to get lethal drones out of the hands of the CIA. Her articles appear in outlets such as *The Huffington Post, CommonDreams, Alternet* and *OpEd News*. medea@codepink.org **p. 105**

Meganne Forbes (Carpinteria, CA) I am a visionary watercolor artist who paints what I love. Devotional images intertwining with nature delight me, spirit moves me, and the love of family and friends nourish me. Peace and love for all, please. meganneforbes.com **p. 63, 81**

Meghan Oona Clifford (Madison, WI) MFA, I studied at Evergreen and the San Francisco Art Institute. My current series, Illuminated Portraiture, explores new mythical archetypes, modes of revelry, and paths to bliss. Love and Blessings! realeyesgallery.blogspot.com **p. 104**

Melissa Harris (West Hurley, NY) Artist and intuitive, offers art-making and psychic development classes, spirit essence portraits and artwork, and products featuring her visionary art. melissaharris.com **p. 145**

Melissa Ireland (Cerrillos, NM) Living off the grid, learning, listening, loving, and grateful. melissaireland.com **p. 155**

Melissa Myers (Avila, Spain) Poet, Yoga Teacher, Reiki Master/Teacher/Practitioner and Transpersonal Therapist living in a little town in the mountains. Available for sessions by phone or Skype. Remember the love we are. azlightworker@yahoo.com **p. 76**

Modupe (Hamburg, Germany) is a double water spirit and mother. Dancing, dreaming, drawing and writing lead her into this great, wide and beautiful world. Enchanted by creation. miss_modupe@yahoo.com **p. 47, 50, 82, 149**

Monika Steinhoff (Santa Fe, NM) My work comes from my observations of life, from dreams, meditation and art history. It has been in many museum shows, one solo. I also show in Europe and have opened a gallery featuring magic realism and outsider art. **p. 19, 43**

MoonCat! (Atlantic Beach, Florida) Traveling Astrologer, Artist, Radio dj, Photographer, Jewelry Creator, PostCard Sender, GoddessCard Inventor, Seer of Patterns, Adventurer, Sagittarius, Moon in Capricorn, Rising Scorpio. See CatOvertheMoon.com or LifeMapAstrology.com or write me: mooncatastrology@yahoo.com or lifemapastrology@gmail.com **p. 203**

Musawa (Estacada, OR/Tesuque, NM) I have retired from the business of Mother Tongue Ink, and have more time to devote to writing and other creative work. I am especially interested in using video to document wemoon culture in the making, and in creating viable alternatives for wemoon to grow old on land in community with womyn of all ages. **p. 6, 9, 25, 188**

Myshkin (Wolf Creek, OR) Working, writing, singing, touring. Loving the land, the road, the art, and sweet beings everywhere. myshkinsrubywarblers.com **p. 189**

nancy holley (Ashland, OR) is living, laughing, crying and trying to practice happiness, right work, and realistic recycling and composting. Happily entranced by artistic process and the art and sacred nature of Hawaiian hula, she is constantly humbled by her own subjectivity. nancyholley@opendoor.com **p. 160**

Nancy Watterson (Oakland, OR) I am artist, mother, grandmother, teacher and gardener. In these ways I connect to the eternal and send my arrows into the future. Wherever I go I find powerful women who are quietly nurturing and creating the becoming world. nwattersonscharf.com **p. 111, 146, 159**

Patrice Haan (Oakland, CA) is a harper, singer, songwriter, composer and wordsmith, devoted to the healing presence of listening. For more information about her four albums of music, visit: patricehaan.com. **p. 79, 170, 178**

Petra LeFaye (Eppstein, Germany) is an artist intending to communicate, connect and contribute to soul-healing by art. She loves playing harp, collecting stones and feathers, being in touch with Mother Earth. petralefaye.de **p. 103**

Pi Luna (Santa Fe, NM) has her MFA from Goddard College in Interdisciplinary Art. pi-luna.blogspot.com **p. 55, 177, 185**

Purple Moose (Midvale, UT) Living and loving in Midvale, Utah. **p. 64**

Rachel Kaiser (Great Falls, MT) lives and works as an artist with her daughter, Zoe. She is known for her large public murals as well as her hand-made tiles, drawings, paintings, and hand-carved wooden sculptures. You are welcome to contact her via e-mail at starfly27@hotmail.com. **p. 137**

Rae Abileah (El Granada, CA) is an activist and writer. She served as co-director and national organizer with CodePink Women for Peace for eight and a half ruckus-raising years. rae@raeabileah.com, codepink.org **p. 105**

rain crowe (Portland, OR) A spell-telling priestess, artist, and community process facilitator who dances the magics and rituals of decolonizing—re-membering ourselves as the land alive. Her journey's prayer: collective liberation from the legacy of Empire culture, and the concurrent regeneration of nascent Earth cultures. callingourselveshome.weebly.com **p. 53, 153**

Renée Hummel (Boulder, CO) Perennials in this lifetime's garden include deep appreciation of nature, eclectic spirituality rooted in a moment of grace, and the joy of receiving words and inspirations that sometimes grow into poems. thismysticnature.com **p. 63, 119, 131**

Rhea Giffin (Coeur d'Alene, ID) Curiously weaving observations and quirky irony into story, Rhea Giffin's art is an unexpected frolicsome escape from the ordinary, imbued with layers of much more than what first meets the eye. rheagiffin.com **p. 40**

Robin Rose Bennett (Hewitt, NJ) Green witch and author of *Healing Magic: A Green Witch Guidebook to Conscious Living*, and the forthcoming book, *Green Treasures: Herbal Medicines from Mother Earth*. A gifted herbalist and loving teacher, Robin founded WiseWoman Healing Ways in 1986. RobinRoseBennett.com **p. 45, 151**

Robyn Waters (Hillsboro, OR) is exercising a new creative muscle by writing a collection of Young Adult S.F./Fantasy stories that she's also using all the old, standby muscles to illustrate. She's almost having too much fun! Check her website for hysterical outbursts: robynwaters.com. **p. 77**

Rose Flint (Somerset, UK) is a priestess of Avalon and Ceremonist, a poet and activist. She writes for the Goddess, for the concept of a Motherworld; details of her new fifth collection of Goddess and earth-centred poems, invocations and prayers are on poetrypf.co.uk. **p. 29, 53, 70, 89, 107, 125, 146, 161, 179**

Sandra Pastorius aka Laughing Giraffe (Ashland, OR) delights in the "Yoga of Kinship." I offer Astrological consultations in person or by phone (mention We'Moon for a special discount.) I'd love to speak about *Living the Wheel* Astrology to your group. Contact me for info on readings, lectures & workshops: laughinggiraffe@yahoo.com 541-482-0529. Peace Be! **p.18, 24**

Sandra Stanton (Farmington, ME) The most recent paintings, the "Shared Consciousness" series, explore the web of connections among people, other species and Mother Earth. sandrastanton.com and goddessmyths.com **p. 72**

Sandra Ure Griffin (Rock Hill, MO) is the author and illustrator of *Earth Circles* and other works. sandrauregriffin.com and artworkforpeace.com **p. 42, 95, 127**

Shae Savoy (Seattle, WA) has a deep and abiding love for We'Moon. She is rooted in the Pacific Northwest and teaches at Bent Writing Institute. A Tarot practitioner and poet-priestess, she believes there's nothing that can't be healed with deep listening and love medicine. shaesavoy.com **p. 50, 117**

Sophia Kelly Shultz (Pottsville, PA) Freelance artist, ritualist, realist, spiritualist. sophianan@aol.com, badgersoph.deviantart.com **p. 87**

Sophia Rosenberg (Lasqueti Island, BC, Canada) lives "off the grid." To see more of her work, go to sophiarosenberg.com. **p. 88**

Stephanie Wilson (Philadelphia, PA) She was visiting the Planet Repair Institute while she was studying wild bees in the Zumwalt Prairie of eastern Oregon. Sounds mystical? It certainly was. smwilson@email.wm.edu **p. 59**

Sue Burns (Portland, OR) is a feminist, pro-choice mother, herbalist, writer, swimmer, reader, witch, lover, activist. She is a veteran of high-school classrooms and independent bookstores. She believes in love, magick, grief, accountability, and family. She loves you. **p. 30**

Sulis Sarasvati (Santa Fe, NM) is a yogini, dreamer, healer, priestess, and minister. She cultivates a deepening openness and a fierce softness through many offerings at laughingtreespace.com. **p. 106**

Susa Silvermarie (Asheville, NC) My desire for adventure being stronger than my limitations, I sally forth in spite of them. Blessings and Balance to you. Visit me at ssilvermarie@gmail.com. **p. 39**

Susan Baylies (Durham, NC) puts her artwork on T-shirts and also makes a lunar phase card available from snakeandsnake.com. **p. 224**

Susan Levitt (San Francisco, CA) is an author and counselor who follows her We'Moon calendar every day! Susan reads tarot, is an astrologer, and does feng shui consultations. Visit susanlevitt.com for more mooney info. **p. 7, 19**

Tari Muñiz (Lansing, MI) I am a writer and a witch. Mostly, I am a gardener, a person trying to see love lurking everywhere. **p. 147**

Tatiana Leaf (Kamuela, HI) works with birthing mothers in Hawaii. Her paintings honor the sacredness of the human being, the human family, the mother earth, the deep feminine soul and glorifies the essential spirit of oneness shining through the veils of difference. **p. 108**

Teresa Gagné (Saskatoon, SK, Canada) Grounded by the earth, and often singing while she works, Teresa creates ceramic objects to be used for ritual, function and to enhance the environment. tgagneceramics.com **p. 118**

Teresa Honey Youngblood (Fayetteville, AR) lives and works in the southern Ozarks with children, stories, pictures, thread, and vegetables. She can be reached at teresa.youngblood@gmail.com. **p. 67**

Tessa Helweg-Larsen (Victoria, BC, Canada) I create art as an expression of my love and concern for my bioregion. I strive to be environmentally and socially sustainable by living in community, growing food, practicing herbalism and appreciating the wildness around me. pug@email.com, tessahl.blogspot.com **p. 131**

Toni Truesdale (Pecos, NM) Muralist / illustrator / painter / teacher / writer. tonitruesdale.com & trues@cybermesa.com **p. 97**

Venus Zephyr (Shutesbury, MA) is an Artist, Activist, Spoken Word Poet, Wise Womyn Herbalist, Birth Doula and Mother to Sela Jade. Venus uses art as a tool for alternative education, social change, collective transformation, and ecstatic experience in resurrecting the collective power of all people. Contact: soulflowerbirth@gmail.com or boneflowerbotanika.com **p. 110**

Wolfsong (Tillamook, OR) coyotemoon.net, rhonda@coyotemoon.net **p. 120**

ERRORS/CORRECTIONS FOR LAST YEAR'S WE'MOON

We have corrections to note about We'Moon 2013:

On page 19 in Susan Levitt's feature article "The Year Of the Serpent," 2012 is listed as a year of the Serpent. The year noted should be, of course, 2013.

On page 71, "Oregon Flower Harvest," the artist's name is missing. The credit should read, © Betty LaDuke 2010.

On page 111, in Catherine Henderson's poem "Los Parteras de la Puerta," we made typographical errors in the words, "Nourishing" and "Transition."

On Page 197, in Gretchen Lawlor's byline, we misprinted her email address. Contact her at light@whidbey.com for astrological consultations, apprenticeships, workshops. You can also reach Gretchen through her website at: www.gretchenlawlor.com

On page 204, the email address for Teresa Gagné is incorrect and should read: tgagne@sasktel.net

Send your feedback and insights to mothertongue@wemoon.ws

WE'MOON ANCESTORS

We honor wemoon who have gone between the worlds of life and death recently, beloved contributors to wemoon culture who continue to bless us from the other side. We appreciate receiving notice of their passing.

Deborah Wyatt (1947-2011) was a nationally recognized artist whose work graced the pages of We'Moon, usually with art co-created with her daughter, Emelie Hebert. Deborah's artistry will continue to be treasured, beyond her lifetime.

Fields Lost, Found Forever
◻ Emily Hebert and Deborah Wyatt 2005

Gerda Lerner (1920-2012) Women's Studies pioneer, scholar and teacher, Gerda taught the first-ever women's history course ('63), created the first graduate program in Women's History ('72), and co-founded NOW. Her many scholarly publications include *The Creation of Patriarchy* ('86). She was instrumental in changing the intellectual discourse of her times.

Julia Penelope (1941-2013) was an influential lesbian-feminist theorist, contributing especially to lesbian-separatist culture. Writer, linguist, teacher, publisher, she authored/co-authored many books (e.g., *Speaking Freely, The Original Coming Out Stories*) that made creative intellectual space for lesbian-feminist thinking.

Patricia Monaghan (1946-2012) was a Goddess scholar, accomplished poet, activist and leader in the women's spirituality movement. She published over 20 books, and is most well known for *The Goddess Path*, and *Encyclopedia of Goddesses and Heroines*. Patricia was a professor of Interdisciplinary Studies, a vintner, and co-founder of The Black Earth Institute, a think-tank connecting art & spirit, earth & society.

Rebecca Tarbotton (1973-2012) died in a swimming accident, a profound loss for environmental and social justice movements. Director of Rainforest Action Network, Becky was a brilliant activist, leading innovative work to combat climate change, protect forests and human rights.

Rosemary Keefe Curb (1940-2012) was co-editor of *Lesbian Nuns: Breaking Silence* (1985), a groundbreaking anthology of writings by current/former nuns. Translated around the world, the book caused a media storm and catapulted the word "lesbian" into public discourse. Rosemary was a revered women's studies professor and women's rights activist.

Shanti Soule (1951-2012) was a Buddhist teacher, a professional gourmet cook, and an activist beloved in feminist and spiritual communities. She worked for many years at Vipassana Meditation centers; she was especially committed to her service of cooking at retreats for cancer patients. Shanti nourished people physically and spiritually throughout her life.

Shulamith Firestone (1945-2012) was a radical feminist thinker who broke new intellectual ground in the burgeoning Women's Liberation Movement in 1970 with her book *The Dialectic of Sex: The Case for Feminist Revolution*. She argued that sexual inequity would not truly be available until advanced reproductive technologies freed women from childbearing. Her ideas remained out of vogue for decades, but some of them have begun to manifest in contemporary society. She was a founder of Redstockings, and other radical feminist groups.

Sunlight (1923-2012) aka Dorothy Lane, was a beloved land dyke in Mendocino County, CA. She was a prolific writer, published three books, and left much unpublished fiction, poetry and reflection. Sunlight was an activist and healer, committed to the earth, to women's community, and to her path of sobriety. She inspired and guided countless others along that pathway.

KNOW YOURSELF—MAP OF PLANETARY ASPECTS

Most people, when considering astrology's benefits, are familiar with their Sun Sign; however, each of the planets within our solar system has a specific part to play in the complete knowledge of "The Self." Here is a quick run-down of our planets' astrological effects:

☉ **The Sun** represents our soul purpose. It is what we are here on Earth to do or accomplish, and it informs how we go about that task. It answers the age-old question "Why am I here?"

☽ **The Moon** represents our capacity to feel or empathize with those around us and within our own soul as well. It awakens our intuitive and emotional body.

☿ **Mercury** is "The Thinker," and involves our communication skills: what we say, our words, our voice, and our thoughts, including the Teacher/Student, Master/Apprentice mode. Mercury affects how we connect with all the media tools of the day—our computers, phones and even the postal, publishing and recording systems!

♀ **Venus** is our recognition of love, art and beauty. Venus is harmony in its expressed form, as well as compassion, bliss and acceptance.

♂ **Mars** is our sense of "Get Up and GO!" It is the capacity to take action and do; it represents being in motion. It can also affect our temperament.

♃ **Jupiter** is our quest for truth, living the belief systems that we hold and walking the path of what those beliefs say about us. It involves an ever expanding desire to educate the Self through knowledge toward higher law, the adventure and opportunity of being on that road—sometimes literally entailing travel and foreign or international culture, language and/or customs.

♄ **Saturn** is the task master: active when we set a goal or plan then work strongly and steadily toward achieving what we have set out to do. Saturn takes life seriously along the way and can be rather stern, putting on an extra load of responsibility and effort.

⚷ **Chiron** is the "Wounded Healer." It relates to what we have brought into this lifetime in order to learn how to fix it, to perfect it, make it the best that it can possibly be! This is where we compete with ourselves to better our own previous score. In addition, it connects to our health-body—physiological and nutritional.

♅ **Uranus** is our capacity to experience "The Revolution," freedom to do things our own way, exhibiting our individual expression or even "Going Rogue" as we blast towards a future collective vision. Uranus inspires individual inclination to "Let me be ME" and connect to an ocean of humanity doing the same.

♆ **Neptune** is the spiritual veil, our connection to our inner psychology and consciousness, leading to the experience of our soul. Psychic presence and mediumship are influenced here too.

♇ Pluto is transformation, death/rebirth energy—to the extreme. In order for the butterfly to emerge, the caterpillar that it once was must completely give up its life! No going back; burn the bridge down; the volcano of one's own power explodes. Stand upon the mountain top and catch the lightning bolt in your hand!

In addition, we must consider our Rising Sign! This Sign is calculated using the time of day that we came into being, in relationship to the rotation of the earth. It describes how we relate to the external world and how it relates back to us—what we look like, how others see us and how we see ourselves.

Moon Moon Moon
© *Lynn Dewart 1997*

It is the combination of all of these planetary elements that makes us unique among all other persons alive! We are like snowflakes in that way! Sharing a Sun sign is not enough to put you in a singular category. Here's to our greater understanding! Know Yourself!

MoonCat! © Mother Tongue Ink 2011

GODDESS PLANETS: CERES, PALLAS, JUNO AND VESTA

"Asteroids" are small planets, located between the inner, personal planets (Sun to Mars) that move more swiftly through the zodiac, and the outer, social and collective planets (Jupiter to Pluto) whose slower movements mark generational shifts. Ceres, Pallas, Juno and Vesta are faces of the Great Goddess who is reawakening in our consciousness now, quickening abilities so urgently needed to solve our many personal, social, ecological and political problems.

Ceres (Goddess of corn and harvest) symbolizes our ability to nourish ourselves and others in a substantial and metaphoric way. As in the Greek myth of Demeter and Persephone, she helps us to let go and die, to understand mother-daughter dynamics, to re-parent ourselves and to educate by our senses.

Juno (partner of Jupiter) shows us what kind of committed partnership we long for, our own individual way to find fulfillment in personal and professional partnering. She wants partners to be team-workers, with equal rights and responsibilities.

Pallas (Athena) is a symbol for our creative intelligence and often hints at the sacrifice of women's own creativity or the lack of respect for it. She brings to the fore father-daughter issues, and points to difficulties in linking head, heart and womb.

Vesta (Vestal Virgin/Fire Priestess) reminds us first and foremost that we belong to ourselves and are allowed to do so! She shows us how to regenerate, to activate our passion, and how to carefully watch over our inner fire in the storms of everyday life.

excerpt Beate Metz © Mother Tongue Ink 2009

2014 ASTEROID EPHEMERIS

2014	Ceres *1	Pallas 2	Juno **3	Vesta *4
JAN 1	22≏00.5	13m35.9	29♊52.1	18≏12.6
11	24 53.4	13R38.5	4♋21.4	21 25.5
21	27 22.4	12 37.9	9 02.0	24 15.7
31	29 23.2	10 36.1	13 52.4	26 37.5
FEB 10	0m51.0	7 45.1	18 52.6	28 25.9
20	1 41.7	4 27.5	24 00.2	29 35.1
MAR 2	1R51.5	3 11.1	29 14.9	29R59.4
12	1 18.8	28≏22.9	4♋36.0	29R35.4
22	0 05.6	26 21.2	10 02.4	28 23.2
APR 1	28≏18.2	25 13.3	15 33.8	26 28.9
11	26 08.5	24D59.4	21 09.5	24 06.2
21	23 52.6	25 34.0	26 48.8	21 55.8
MAY 1	21 46.9	26 50.2	2♋31.3	19 19.1
11	20 06.3	28 41.4	8 16.3	17 35.5
21	19 00.2	1m01.1	14 03.1	16 36.7
31	18 32.9	3 44.0	19 51.1	16D27.1
JUN 10	18D45.1	6 46.2	25 40.0	17 06.2
20	19 34.1	10 03.8	1♌28.5	18 29.6
30	20 56.1	13 34.4	7 16.2	20 13.8
JUL 10	22 47.0	17 15.6	13 01.9	23 07.4
20	25 02.5	21 05.6	18 44.9	26 11.1
30	27 39.0	25 03.2	24 24.0	29 38.4
AUG 9	0m33.3	29 07.0	29 58.0	3m25.7
19	3 42.3	3♏16.0	5♍25.5	7 29.5
29	7 04.0	7 29.5	10 45.1	11 47.5
SEP 8	10 36.1	11 46.6	15 54.7	16 17.4
18	14 17.0	16 06.7	20 52.7	20 57.3
28	18 05.3	20 29.3	25 36.6	25 45.8
OCT 8	21 59.6	24 53.5	0≏03.1	0≏41.6
18	25 58.8	29 18.8	4 09.5	5 43.4
28	0♏01.9	3m44.2	7 51.7	10 50.4
NOV 7	4 07.9	8 10.2	11 04.8	16 01.5
17	8 15.9	12 34.6	13 43.9	21 16.0
27	12 25.2	16 57.3	15 42.8	26 33.1
DEC 7	16 34.8	21 17.1	16 55.4	1♏52.0
17	20 43.4	25 33.1	17R17.0	7 12.1
27	24 50.9	29 44.1	16 44.4	12 32.7
JAN 6	28♏55.8	3m48.6	15♊20.5	17♏53.1

(continued — 2015)

	Ceres 1	Pallas 2	Juno 3	Vesta 4
JAN 1	01♐07.1	22♏28.4	15♊18.3	00♑53.8
21	00 07.7	21 10.9	08 57.0	01 51.9
FEB 10	00♐02.3	16 33.1	04 04.1	02 07.0
MAR 2	00N37.5	08 43.2	02 49.5	01 16.3
22	01 53.2	00♐22.0	00N35.8	00N30.0
APR 11	03 44.4	06N58.3	04 00.1	02 32.8
MAY 1	03 44.4	13 47.0	07 11.0	03 47.4
21	03 08.1	13 47.7	09 56.4	03 47.4
JUN 10	01 26.7	14 30.0	12 04.8	01 44.2
30	01S00.1	14 04.1	13 26.6	01S02.2
JUL 20	03 53.6	12 52.3	13 55.5	04 23.5
AUG 9	07 00.0	11 17.2	13 21.1	08 00.5
29	10 08.8	09 16.5	12 13.4	11 37.8
SEP 18	13 11.8	07 18.3	10 14.7	15 02.6
OCT 8	16 01.9	05 28.2	07 46.9	18 03.2
28	18 32.9	03 56.1	05 00.4	20 39.7
NOV 17	20 39.6	02 51.6	02 39.7	22 10.3
DEC 7	22 18.1	02 23.4	00 56.2	23 00.1
27	23S26.3	02N38.7	00N22.8	23S00.1

2014	Psyche 16	Eros **433	Lilith 1181	Toro **1685
JAN 1	2♊13.8	14m32.1	20♈00.6	9♑25.7
11	6 08.8	22 14.4	18♈34.3	16 38.6
21	10 03.1	29 37.5	16 32.0	24 15.7
31	13 55.8	6♐40.4	14 08.6	2♒20.2
FEB 10	17 45.6	13 21.4	11 43.8	10 55.7
20	21 31.5	19 39.2	9 37.1	20 06.2
MAR 2	25 12.3	25 32.3	8 02.9	29 55.5
12	28 46.5	0♑57.8	7 09.7	10♓26.4
22	2♊12.6	5 53.3	6D59.8	21 39.8
APR 1	5 29.0	10 18.6	7 30.9	3♈34.1
11	8 33.5	13 56.3	8 39.1	16 03.3
21	11 24.0	16 52.3	10 19.3	28 57.0
MAY 1	13 57.8	18 54.0	12 26.2	12♉01.1
11	16 11.8	19 51.4	14 55.6	24 59.5
21	18 02.9	19R35.3	17 43.2	7♊33.7
31	19 27.1	17 59.9	20 45.8	19 44.1
JUN 10	20 27.7	15 06.2	24 00.7	1♋14.5
20	20 40.5	11 12.4	27 25.5	12 00.4
30	20R24.1	6 51.2	0♉58.3	22 07.7
JUL 10	19 31.4	2 45.5	4 37.6	1♌36.4
20	18 05.9	29♐30.6	8 22.0	10 29.6
30	16 14.7	26 34.4	11 06.0	18 51.1
AUG 9	14 10.7	26 34.4	16 01.9	26 44.4
19	12 07.8	26D51.3	19 55.4	4m12.9
29	10 20.7	28 06.6	23 50.4	11 19.8
SEP 8	9 01.6	0♑10.7	27 46.0	18 07.7
18	8 18.3	2 54.3	1♊41.5	24 39.1
28	8D14.0	6 10.6	5 36.3	0m56.1
OCT 8	8 49.1	9 54.2	9 29.5	7 00.2
18	10 00.0	14 00.2	13 20.8	12 54.4
28	11 45.8	18 25.7	17 08.0	18 35.2
NOV 7	14 00.4	23 08.2	20 51.4	24 07.9
17	16 40.3	28 05.4	24 29.5	29 31.7
27	19 42.3	3♒16.2	28 01.2	4m47.0
DEC 7	23 03.1	8 39.3	1♊24.9	9 53.7
17	26 39.8	14 13.9	4 39.2	14 51.9
27	0♊30.0	19 59.6	7 42.1	19 41.4
JAN 6	4♊31.5	25♒59.5	10m31.3	24♏21.3

(continued — 2015)

	Psyche 16	Eros 433	Lilith 1181	Toro 1685
JAN 1	21♒22.3	23♒36.0	09♏06.5	22♑41.3
21	21 03.7	29 11.5	09 08.8	19 52.9
FEB 2	20 18.3	32 59.6	09 58.7	15 07.9
MAR 11	19 10.2	35 10.2	11 00.1	08 15.3
APR 11	17 45.8	36 07.3	11 42.3	03♒00N32.2
MAY 1	16 13.8	36 23.5	11 51.0	10 10.8
11	13 32.9	36 51.0	10 19.5	17 22.5
JUN 12	12 51.9	36 52.3	08 44.0	22 37.3
JUL 20	12 56.0	35 08.8	06 40.9	19 05.5
AUG 9	13 49.9	31 28.4	04 15.2	13 54.6
SEP 18	15 18.3	27 42.2	01 32.2	08 10.5
OCT 28	17 57.6	20 59.6	07 26.0	08 11.8
NOV 16	16 7.7	16 33.9	13 14.0	11 51.8
DEC 27	14 27.7	09 45.6	18 55.4	15 48.7
	12S04.8	09S45.6	18S04.7	24S04.7

2014	Sappho 80	Amor **1221	Pandora 55	Icarus 1566
JAN 1	13♐56.3	28♑00.3	28♊32.1	3m37.6
11	18 56.3	28♑51.4	3m05.1	9 00.5
21	23 16.8	0♒20.3	7 41.5	14 53.0
31	27 55.9	2 24.7	12 20.8	21 23.4
FEB 10	2♑33.3	4 59.9	17 02.0	28 44.2
20	7 07.5	8 01.5	21 44.3	7♈15.2
MAR 2	11 38.3	11 26.2	26 27.0	17 30.5
12	16 03.9	15 11.3	1♋09.5	0♉34.7
22	20 23.0	19 14.4	5 50.4	16 12.3
APR 1	24 34.1	23 34.1	10 29.6	2♊10.4
11	28 34.9	28 09.3	15 06.1	15♊40.4
21	2♒23.1	2♓58.5	19 38.9	26 37.1
MAY 1	5 55.6	8 00.5	24 07.2	4♋56.7
11	9 08.3	13 21.2	28 29.8	0 32.0
21	11 57.2	18 53.6	2♌45.6	25♊27.1
31	14 16.4	24 40.7	6 53.1	18 27.9
JUN 10	15 59.8	0♈43.1	10 50.5	9 01.0
20	17 01.1	7 01.1	14 36.1	27♉33.4
30	17R14.1	13 37.1	18 07.5	15 40.8
JUL 10	16 35.8	20 30.8	21 25.2	8 29.5
20	15 09.0	27 43.6	24 15.2	28♉28.4
30	13 04.1	5♉16.0	26 44.3	23 18.8
AUG 9	10 42.8	13 06.9	28 44.6	20 42.5
19	8 26.9	21 21.7	0♎10.7	19 42.0
29	6 44.2	0♊06.0	0 58.7	19D51.8
SEP 8	5 51.4	9 06.1	1R02.9	20 53.7
18	5D55.8	18 26.5	0 23.6	22 34.5
28	6 57.6	28 05.1	29♍02.4	24 45.7
OCT 8	8 53.6	7♋58.4	27 08.2	27 20.9
18	11 33.5	18 02.1	24 55.7	0♎15.6
28	14 53.6	28 10.9	22 43.4	3 26.9
NOV 7	18 46.4	8m18.8	20 50.4	6 52.5
17	23 05.6	18 20.0	19 31.5	10 30.9
27	27 46.7	28 09.0	18 54.5	14 21.7
DEC 7	2♓45.5	7♍40.9	19D03.0	18 22.7
17	7 58.1	16 52.3	19 54.8	22 35.4
27	13 24.2	25 41.1	21 35.4	26 58.4
JAN 6	18♓54.5	4♍05.5	23♍31.4	1♏36.6

(continued — 2015)

	Sappho 80	Amor 1221	Pandora 55	Icarus 1566
JAN 1	19♒49.1	01♑11.4	25♍09.9	30♏31.7
21	19 57.6	00♑36.5	22 46.7	27 04.8
FEB 10	18 01.4	05 41.5	19 46.2	12 50.7
MAR 2	15 59.3	08 32.9	16 27.7	06N12.1
APR 11	13 21.2	13 38.6	09 08.5	04 46.2
MAY 1	10 06.7	15 12.7	05 47.9	06S09.7
21	06 56.3	16 12.3	03 15.2	06 22.7
JUN 10	03 41.9	16 12.3	01 53.0	04 36.2
30	00 11.3	16 04.4	01 07.1	01 31.3
JUL 20	00N16.7	15 04.4	00 51.8	04 30.0
AUG 9	00S15.7	12 34.9	01 55.0	04 30.4
SEP 18	06 44.0	02 29.7	07 41.5	34 07.1
OCT 7	07 38.6	02 48.5	12 10.3	34 36.1
NOV 17	07 14.5	12 30.7	11 22.1	33 27.4
DEC 7	05 42.3	16 31.4	11 55.5	30 40.3
27	03S14.2	16S35.5	12N59.3	30S56.0

2014	Diana 78	Hidalgo 944	Urania 30	Chiron 2060
JAN 1	25♒19.3	29♏28.4	17♉30.7	9♓58.4
11	28 39.0	0♐58.2	22 00.0	10 23.7
21	2♓06.9	2 25.2	26 15.3	10 53.1
31	5 41.6	3 47.8	0♊26.8	11 27.7
FEB 10	9 21.9	5 04.6	4 33.1	12 00.8
20	13 06.4	6 14.0	8 33.1	12 37.7
MAR 2	16 54.4	7 14.5	12 25.3	13 16.4
12	20 44.7	8 04.5	16 08.0	13 55.3
22	24 36.5	8 42.5	19 39.3	14 30.6
APR 1	28 29.1	9 07.3	22 57.0	15 06.4
11	2♈21.5	9 17.5	25 58.1	15 40.1
21	6 13.3	9R12.7	28 39.8	16 10.9
MAY 1	10 03.3	8 51.4	0♊58.8	16 37.3
11	13 50.4	8 14.7	2 49.0	17 01.2
21	17 33.9	7 23.3	4 07.6	17 20.2
31	21 12.9	6 18.9	4 49.2	17 34.2
JUN 10	24 47.8	5 04.2	4R49.5	17 42.5
20	28 14.9	3 42.7	4 06.5	17R45.3
30	1♉33.3	2 18.6	2 41.6	17R43.1
JUL 10	4 41.5	0 56.1	0 41.2	17 35.2
20	7 36.9	29♏39.5	28♉13.8	17 22.3
30	10 16.9	28 30.1	25 56.9	17 05.1
AUG 9	14 36.5	26 34.8	21 56.6	16 43.3
19	16 07.7	26 37.0	20 06.7	15 51.4
29	17 30.7	26D27.5	20♉44.7	15 23.8
SEP 8	17R09.7	27 00.6	22 34.7	14 29.1
18	16 48.3	27 39.3	24 30.0	15 43.0
28	16 11.7	28 33.7	26 51.2	13 26.2
OCT 8	9 46.6	0♐48.1	3 25.2	13 14.7
18	7 21.9	2 10.5	11 16.0	13 06.3
28	5 19.6	3 40.2	06N30.2	13D06.1
NOV 7	3 55.2	5 15.5	15 36.3	14 03.0
17	3 16.9	6 55.0	20 10.1	13 20.0
27	3D27.2	37.4	24 43.4	13 36.7
JAN 6	4♉24.7	10♐21.1	29♉23.9	13♓57.2

(continued — 2015)

	Diana 78	Hidalgo 944	Urania 30	Chiron 2060
JAN 1	12♒29.6	59♏46.3	24♉12.0	03♓15.4
21	09 46.4	60 10.4	24 19.9	01 50.4
FEB 10	06 48.0	60 58.1	23 42.0	00 42.8
MAR 2	00 12.6	61 58.1	14 43.4	01 03.5
APR 11	03♈N15.2	61 44.1	20 08.8	01 26.6
MAY 1	06 35.9	60 37.2	21 22.5	02 07.5
JUN 10	09 41.9	56 18.2	21 10.5	03 27.7
JUL 10	19 36.6	60 57.8	23 44.3	04 30.6
AUG 9	22 46.1	26 34.8	20 56.9	05 51.5
SEP 18	28 33.9	26 37.0	20 03.3	05 23.8
OCT 7	02 22.7	26 27.5	19 29.1	05 08.1
NOV 17	07 24.0	24 43.2	21 10.1	13 22.0
DEC 27	23N41.6	60S38.7	12S14.0	02S08.0

2014 Planetary Ephemeris (Noon GMT*)

LONGITUDE — JANUARY 2014

Day	Sid.Time	☉	0 hr ☽	Noon ☽	True ☊	☿	♀	♂	♃	♄	♅	♆	♇
1 W	6 42 17	10♑28 43	3♑47 6	11♑25 58	5♏33.1	12♑ 4.9	26♑53.9	11♎38.6	16♋ 7.0	20♏21.5	8♈40.6	3♓13.6	11♑15.4
2 Th	6 46 14	11 29 54	19 6 9	26 46 9	5R 23.2	13 41.9	26R 28.6	12 5.2	15R 59.0	20 26.9	8 41.4	3 15.2	11 17.5
3 F	6 50 10	12 31 5	4♒24 31	11♒59 50	5 12.6	15 19.2	26 1.2	12 31.5	15 50.9	20 32.2	8 42.2	3 16.7	11 19.6
4 Sa	6 54 7	13 32 16	19 30 52	26 56 33	5 2.8	16 56.9	25 32.0	12 57.5	15 42.8	20 37.5	8 43.1	3 18.3	11 21.7
5 Su	6 58 3	14 33 26	4♓16 3	11♓28 48	4 54.9	18 34.9	25 1.1	13 23.3	15 34.7	20 42.7	8 44.0	3 20.0	11 23.8
6 M	7 2 0	15 34 36	18 34 26	25 32 49	4 49.6	20 13.3	24 28.7	13 48.9	15 26.5	20 47.8	8 44.9	3 21.6	11 26.0
7 Tu	7 5 56	16 35 46	2♈24 0	9♈ 8 13	4 46.7	21 51.9	23 54.9	14 14.2	15 18.4	20 52.9	8 46.0	3 23.3	11 28.1
8 W	7 9 53	17 36 55	15 45 50	22 17 15	4D 45.9	23 31.0	23 20.0	14 39.3	15 10.3	20 57.9	8 47.0	3 25.0	11 30.2
9 Th	7 13 49	18 38 4	28 43 1	5♉ 3 40	4R 46.1	25 10.3	22 44.2	15 4.1	15 2.2	21 2.8	8 48.1	3 26.7	11 32.3
10 F	7 17 46	19 39 12	11♉19 46	17 31 54	4 46.0	26 50.0	22 7.9	15 28.7	14 54.2	21 7.7	8 49.3	3 28.5	11 34.4
11 Sa	7 21 43	20 40 20	23 40 35	29 46 23	4 44.5	28 29.9	21 31.1	15 53.0	14 46.1	21 12.4	8 50.5	3 30.3	11 36.5
12 Su	7 25 39	21 41 28	5♊49 45	11♊51 8	4 40.6	0♒10.0	20 54.2	16 17.0	14 38.1	21 17.2	8 51.8	3 32.1	11 38.5
13 M	7 29 36	22 42 35	17 50 56	23 49 30	4 33.8	1 50.4	20 17.5	16 40.7	14 30.1	21 21.8	8 53.1	3 33.9	11 40.6
14 Tu	7 33 32	23 43 41	29 47 8	5♋44 7	4 23.8	3 30.9	19 41.1	17 4.1	14 22.2	21 26.3	8 54.5	3 35.7	11 42.7
15 W	7 37 29	24 44 47	11♋40 39	17 36 57	4 11.3	5 11.4	19 5.4	17 27.3	14 14.4	21 30.8	8 55.9	3 37.6	11 44.8
16 Th	7 41 25	25 45 52	23 33 11	29 29 30	3 56.9	6 52.0	18 30.7	17 50.2	14 6.5	21 35.2	8 57.3	3 39.5	11 46.8
17 F	7 45 22	26 46 57	5♌26 3	11♌22 59	3 41.8	8 32.4	17 57.0	18 12.7	13 58.8	21 39.5	8 58.8	3 41.4	11 48.9
18 Sa	7 49 18	27 48 2	17 20 28	23 18 39	3 27.2	10 12.5	17 24.8	18 35.0	13 51.1	21 43.8	9 0.4	3 43.3	11 50.9
19 Su	7 53 15	28 49 5	29 17 47	5♍18 4	3 14.2	11 52.2	16 54.1	18 56.9	13 43.5	21 47.9	9 2.0	3 45.2	11 53.0
20 M	7 57 12	29 50 9	11♍19 49	17 23 20	3 3.9	13 31.3	16 25.1	19 18.5	13 36.0	21 52.0	9 3.6	3 47.2	11 55.0
21 Tu	8 1 8	0♒51 12	23 28 59	29 37 11	2 56.5	15 9.5	15 58.1	19 39.8	13 28.5	21 56.0	9 5.3	3 49.1	11 57.0
22 W	8 5 5	1 52 14	5♎48 24	12♎ 3 6	2 52.2	16 46.7	15 33.1	20 0.7	13 21.2	21 59.9	9 7.0	3 51.1	11 59.1
23 Th	8 9 1	2 53 17	18 21 49	24 45 5	2 50.4	18 22.4	15 10.3	20 21.3	13 13.9	22 3.7	9 8.8	3 53.1	12 1.1
24 F	8 12 58	3 54 18	1♏13 27	7♏47 25	2 50.0	19 56.4	14 49.7	20 41.5	13 6.7	22 7.5	9 10.6	3 55.2	12 3.1
25 Sa	8 16 54	4 55 20	14 27 30	21 14 6	2 49.9	21 28.2	14 31.6	21 1.3	12 59.7	22 11.1	9 12.5	3 57.2	12 5.0
26 Su	8 20 51	5 56 20	28 7 33	5♐ 8 2	2 48.7	22 57.3	14 15.8	21 20.8	12 52.7	22 14.7	9 14.4	3 59.2	12 7.0
27 M	8 24 47	6 57 21	12♐15 36	19 30 5	2 45.3	24 23.3	14 2.5	21 39.9	12 45.9	22 18.2	9 16.3	4 1.3	12 9.0
28 Tu	8 28 44	7 58 20	26 51 7	4♑18 4	2 39.2	25 45.6	13 51.7	21 58.6	12 39.2	22 21.6	9 18.3	4 3.4	12 10.9
29 W	8 32 41	8 59 20	11♑50 6	19 26 8	2 30.4	27 3.4	13 43.4	22 16.9	12 32.6	22 24.9	9 20.4	4 5.5	12 12.9
30 Th	8 36 37	10 0 18	27 4 54	4♒44 58	2 19.5	28 16.0	13 37.6	22 34.8	12 26.2	22 28.1	9 22.4	4 7.6	12 14.8
31 F	8 40 34	11 1 15	12♒24 53	20 3 6	2 7.8	29 22.8	13D 34.3	22 52.3	12 19.8	22 31.2	9 24.6	4 9.7	12 16.7

LONGITUDE — FEBRUARY 2014

Day	Sid.Time	☉	0 hr ☽	Noon ☽	True ☊	☿	♀	♂	♃	♄	♅	♆	♇
1 Sa	8 44 30	12♒ 2 12	27♒38 13	5♓ 8 57	1♏56.7	0♓22.9	13♑33.4	23♎ 9.3	12♋13.7	22♏34.2	9♈26.7	4♓11.9	12♑18.6
2 Su	8 48 27	13 3 7	12♓34 10	19 53 0	1R 47.4	1 15.5	13 34.9	23 25.9	12R 7.6	22 37.1	9 28.9	4 14.0	12 20.5
3 M	8 52 23	14 4 1	27 4 49	4♈ 9 12	1 40.8	1 59.9	13 38.8	23 42.0	12 1.7	22 40.0	9 31.2	4 16.2	12 22.3
4 Tu	8 56 20	15 4 53	11♈ 6 0	17 55 16	1 36.9	2 35.1	13 45.0	23 57.7	11 56.0	22 42.7	9 33.4	4 18.4	12 24.2
5 W	9 0 16	16 5 44	24 37 11	1♉12 7	1D 35.5	3 0.6	13 53.5	24 12.9	11 50.4	22 45.4	9 35.8	4 20.5	12 26.0
6 Th	9 4 13	17 6 34	7♉40 32	14 2 59	1R 35.4	3R 15.8	14 4.2	24 27.7	11 45.0	22 47.9	9 38.1	4 22.7	12 27.8
7 F	9 8 10	18 7 23	20 20 4	26 32 25	1 35.5	3 20.2	14 17.1	24 41.9	11 39.7	22 50.4	9 40.5	4 24.9	12 29.6
8 Sa	9 12 6	19 8 9	2♊40 39	8♊45 25	1 34.6	3 13.7	14 32.0	24 55.7	11 34.6	22 52.7	9 42.9	4 27.1	12 31.4
9 Su	9 16 3	20 8 55	14 47 19	20 46 56	1 31.8	2 56.2	14 49.0	25 8.9	11 29.7	22 55.0	9 45.4	4 29.4	12 33.2
10 M	9 19 59	21 9 39	26 44 49	2♋41 28	1 26.3	2 28.2	15 8.0	25 21.7	11 24.9	22 57.1	9 47.9	4 31.6	12 34.9
11 Tu	9 23 56	22 10 21	8♋37 20	14 32 51	1 18.1	1 50.3	15 28.9	25 33.9	11 20.4	22 59.2	9 50.4	4 33.8	12 36.7
12 W	9 27 52	23 11 2	20 28 20	26 24 8	1 7.4	1 3.3	15 51.7	25 45.6	11 16.0	23 1.2	9 53.0	4 36.1	12 38.4
13 Th	9 31 49	24 11 41	2♌20 29	8♌17 38	0 55.0	0 8.6	16 16.2	25 56.8	11 11.7	23 3.0	9 55.6	4 38.3	12 40.1
14 F	9 35 45	25 12 19	14 15 46	20 15 3	0 41.8	29♒ 7.6	16 42.5	26 7.4	11 7.7	23 4.8	9 58.2	4 40.6	12 41.7
15 Sa	9 39 42	26 12 55	26 15 37	2♍17 36	0 29.1	28 2.1	17 10.5	26 17.4	11 3.8	23 6.4	10 0.9	4 42.8	12 43.4
16 Su	9 43 39	27 13 30	8♍21 9	14 26 22	0 17.9	26 54.0	17 40.0	26 26.8	11 0.1	23 8.0	10 3.6	4 45.1	12 45.0
17 M	9 47 35	28 14 3	20 33 26	26 42 29	0 8.9	25 45.0	18 11.1	26 35.7	10 56.6	23 9.5	10 6.3	4 47.3	12 46.6
18 Tu	9 51 32	29 14 35	2♎53 44	9♎ 7 23	0 2.6	24 36.9	18 43.7	26 44.0	10 53.3	23 10.8	10 9.1	4 49.6	12 48.2
19 W	9 55 28	0♓15 6	15 23 43	21 43 2	29♎59.2	23 31.4	19 17.8	26 51.6	10 50.2	23 12.1	10 11.9	4 51.9	12 49.8
20 Th	9 59 25	1 15 35	28 5 38	4♏31 53	29D 58.0	22 29.9	19 53.2	26 58.6	10 47.2	23 13.2	10 14.7	4 54.2	12 51.3
21 F	10 3 21	2 16 3	11♏ 2 8	17 36 46	29 58.4	21 33.5	20 29.9	27 5.0	10 44.5	23 14.3	10 17.5	4 56.4	12 52.8
22 Sa	10 7 18	3 16 30	24 16 8	1♐ 0 36	29R 59.3	20 43.2	21 7.9	27 10.8	10 41.9	23 15.2	10 20.4	4 58.7	12 54.3
23 Su	10 11 14	4 16 55	7♐50 24	14 45 46	29 59.5	19 59.7	21 47.2	27 15.9	10 39.5	23 16.1	10 23.3	5 1.0	12 55.8
24 M	10 15 11	5 17 20	21 46 47	28 53 27	29 58.2	19 23.3	22 27.6	27 20.3	10 37.4	23 16.8	10 26.2	5 3.3	12 57.3
25 Tu	10 19 8	6 17 42	6♑ 5 33	13♑22 46	29 54.8	18 54.3	23 9.1	27 24.0	10 35.4	23 17.5	10 29.2	5 5.6	12 58.7
26 W	10 23 4	7 18 4	20 44 33	28 10 12	29 49.2	18 32.6	23 51.7	27 27.0	10 33.6	23 18.0	10 32.2	5 7.8	13 0.1
27 Th	10 27 1	8 18 24	5♒38 48	13♒ 9 20	29 41.9	18 18.2	24 35.3	27 29.3	10 32.0	23 18.5	10 35.2	5 10.1	13 1.5
28 F	10 30 57	9 18 42	20 40 37	28 11 29	29 33.8	18D 10.8	25 19.9	27 30.9	10 30.7	23 18.8	10 38.2	5 12.4	13 2.9

Astro Data Dy Hr Mn	Planet Ingress Dy Hr Mn	Last Aspect Dy Hr Mn	☽ Ingress Dy Hr Mn	Last Aspect Dy Hr Mn	☽ Ingress Dy Hr Mn	☽ Phases & Eclipses Dy Hr Mn	Astro Data
☽0N 6 5:56	☿ ♒ 11 21:36	2 11:13 ♀ ☌	♒ 2 17:04	31 16:46 ♂ △	♓ 1 3:46	1 11:15 ● 10♑57	1 JANUARY 2014
☽0S 20 21:57	☉ ♒ 20 3:52	4 1:48 ♄ □	♓ 4 16:59	2 16:36 ♄ △	♈ 3 4:56	8 3:40 ☽ 17♈46	Julian Day # 41639
♃☍♇ 31 9:17	☿ ♓ 31 14:30	6 9:45 ♀ ✶	♈ 6 19:46	4 23:15 ♂ ☍	♉ 5 9:48	16 4:53 ○ 25♋58	Galactic Ctr 27♐02.7
♀ D 31 20:50		8 16:23 ☿ □	♉ 9 2:25	7 4:51 ♄ ☍	♊ 7 18:45	24 5:20 ☾ 4♏08	SVP 05♓03'41"
	☿ ♒ 13 3:31	11 10:59 ☿ △	♊ 11 12:27	9 21:10 ♂ △	♋ 10 6:34	30 21:40 ● 10♒55	Obliquity 23°26'07"
☽0N 2 16:36	☉ ♓ 18 18:01	12 21:34 ♂ △	♋ 14 0:26	12 10:52 ♂ □	♌ 12 19:16		⚷ Chiron 9♓58.3
☿ R 6 21:44	☊ ♎ 18 16:18	16 4:53 ☉ ☍	♌ 16 13:02	15 3:14 ☿ ☍	♍ 15 7:27	6 19:23 ☽ 17♉56	☽ Mean ☊ 4♏16.0
☽0S 17 4:34		18 8:53 ♄ □	♍ 19 1:25	17 5:06 ♄ ✶	♎ 17 18:24	14 23:54 ○ 26♌13	
♃□♅ 26 7:30		20 20:56 ♄ ✶	♎ 21 12:44	19 21:53 ♂ ☌	♏ 20 3:34	22 17:16 ☾ 3♐60	1 FEBRUARY 2014
☿ D 28 14:01		23 3:52 ♂ ☌	♏ 23 21:45	21 22:11 ♄ ☌	♐ 22 10:13		Julian Day # 41670
		25 13:56 ☿ □	♐ 26 3:14	24 9:26 ♂ ✶	♑ 24 13:51		Galactic Ctr 27♐02.8
		27 22:03 ☿ ✶	♑ 28 5:05	26 10:52 ♂ □	♒ 26 14:57		SVP 05♓03'36"
		29 16:48 ♂ □	♒ 30 4:34	28 10:56 ♂ △	♓ 28 14:54		Obliquity 23°26'07"
							⚷ Chiron 11♓29.1
							☽ Mean ☊ 2♏37.5

*Giving the positions of planets daily at noon, in LONGITUDE Greenwich Mean Time (UT)

Each planet's retrograde period is shaded gray.

2014 Planetary Ephemeris (Noon GMT*)

MARCH 2014

LONGITUDE

Day	Sid.Time	☉	0 hr ☽	Noon ☽	True ☊	☿	♀	♂	♃	♄	♅	♆	♇
1 Sa	10 34 54	10♓18 59	5♓40 40	13♓ 7 0	29♎25.9	18♒10.3	26♑ 5.5	27♎31.8	10♋29.5	23♏19.0	10♈41.3	5♓14.7	13♑ 4.2
2 Su	10 38 50	11 19 13	20 29 24	27 46 55	29R19.4	18 16.2	26 51.9	27R31.9	10R28.5	23R19.1	10 44.3	5 16.9	13 5.5
3 M	10 42 47	12 19 26	4♈58 46	12♈ 4 22	29 14.8	18 28.1	27 39.3	27 31.3	10 27.7	23 19.2	10 47.4	5 19.2	13 6.8
4 Tu	10 46 43	13 19 37	19 3 18	25 55 24	29D12.4	18 45.9	28 27.4	27 30.0	10 27.1	23 19.1	10 50.5	5 21.5	13 8.0
5 W	10 50 40	14 19 47	2♉40 36	9♉19 3	29 12.0	19 9.0	29 16.4	27 27.9	10 26.7	23 18.9	10 53.7	5 23.7	13 9.3
6 Th	10 54 36	15 19 54	15 51 0	22 16 51	29 12.9	19 37.1	0♒ 6.1	27 25.0	10D26.5	23 18.6	10 56.8	5 26.0	13 10.5
7 F	10 58 33	16 19 59	28 37 2	4♊52 6	29 14.4	20 10.0	0 56.6	27 21.4	10 26.5	23 18.2	11 0.0	5 28.2	13 11.6
8 Sa	11 2 30	17 20 2	11♊ 2 37	17 9 12	29R15.5	20 47.2	1 47.7	27 17.0	10 26.8	23 17.7	11 3.2	5 30.5	13 12.8
9 Su	11 6 26	18 20 2	23 12 28	29 13 2	29 15.6	21 28.5	2 39.6	27 11.8	10 27.2	23 17.1	11 6.4	5 32.7	13 13.9
10 M	11 10 23	19 20 1	5♋11 30	11♋ 8 29	29 14.0	22 13.6	3 32.1	27 5.9	10 27.8	23 16.4	11 9.7	5 35.0	13 15.0
11 Tu	11 14 19	20 19 58	17 4 31	23 0 9	29 10.8	23 2.2	4 25.2	26 59.2	10 28.6	23 15.6	11 12.9	5 37.2	13 16.1
12 W	11 18 16	21 19 52	28 55 53	4♌52 9	29 5.8	23 54.1	5 19.0	26 51.8	10 29.6	23 14.7	11 16.2	5 39.4	13 17.1
13 Th	11 22 12	22 19 44	10♌49 21	16 47 53	28 59.7	24 49.2	6 13.3	26 43.5	10 30.7	23 13.7	11 19.4	5 41.6	13 18.1
14 F	11 26 9	23 19 34	22 48 2	28 50 6	28 53.0	25 47.1	7 8.2	26 34.5	10 32.1	23 12.6	11 22.7	5 43.8	13 19.1
15 Sa	11 30 5	24 19 22	4♍54 16	11♍ 0 46	28 46.5	26 47.7	8 3.7	26 24.8	10 33.7	23 11.5	11 26.0	5 46.0	13 20.1
16 Su	11 34 2	25 19 8	17 9 45	23 21 18	28 40.7	27 51.0	8 59.7	26 14.3	10 35.4	23 10.2	11 29.4	5 48.2	13 21.0
17 M	11 37 59	26 18 51	29 35 34	5♎52 35	28 36.3	28 56.6	9 56.2	26 3.0	10 37.4	23 8.8	11 32.7	5 50.3	13 21.9
18 Tu	11 41 55	27 18 33	12♎12 27	18 35 13	28 33.5	0♓ 4.6	10 53.2	25 50.9	10 39.5	23 7.3	11 36.0	5 52.5	13 22.8
19 W	11 45 52	28 18 13	25 0 56	1♏29 41	28D32.3	1 14.7	11 50.6	25 38.2	10 41.9	23 5.7	11 39.4	5 54.6	13 23.6
20 Th	11 49 48	29 17 51	8♏ 1 33	14 36 35	28 32.6	2 26.9	12 48.6	25 24.7	10 44.4	23 4.0	11 42.7	5 56.8	13 24.4
21 F	11 53 45	0♈17 27	21 14 54	27 56 34	28 33.8	3 41.0	13 46.9	25 10.5	10 47.1	23 2.3	11 46.1	5 58.9	13 25.2
22 Sa	11 57 41	1 17 2	4♐41 41	11♐30 20	28 35.4	4 57.1	14 45.7	24 55.5	10 49.9	23 0.4	11 49.5	6 1.0	13 25.9
23 Su	12 1 38	2 16 35	18 22 33	25 18 23	28 36.8	6 15.0	15 44.9	24 39.9	10 53.0	22 58.5	11 52.9	6 3.1	13 26.7
24 M	12 5 34	3 16 6	2♑17 47	9♑20 40	28R37.4	7 34.6	16 44.5	24 23.6	10 56.3	22 56.4	11 56.3	6 5.2	13 27.4
25 Tu	12 9 31	4 15 35	16 26 52	23 36 8	28 36.9	8 56.0	17 44.5	24 6.7	10 59.7	22 54.3	11 59.7	6 7.3	13 28.0
26 W	12 13 28	5 15 3	0♒48 7	8♒ 2 23	28 35.4	10 19.0	18 44.9	23 49.1	11 3.3	22 52.1	12 3.1	6 9.3	13 28.6
27 Th	12 17 24	6 14 29	15 18 24	22 35 30	28 32.9	11 43.6	19 45.6	23 30.9	11 7.1	22 49.7	12 6.5	6 11.4	13 29.3
28 F	12 21 21	7 13 53	29 53 1	7♓10 10	28 30.0	13 9.8	20 46.6	23 12.1	11 11.0	22 47.3	12 9.9	6 13.4	13 29.8
29 Sa	12 25 17	8 13 15	14♓26 10	21 40 14	28 27.1	14 37.5	21 48.0	22 52.8	11 15.2	22 44.9	12 13.3	6 15.4	13 30.4
30 Su	12 29 14	9 12 35	28 51 35	5♈59 31	28 24.8	16 6.8	22 49.7	22 32.9	11 19.5	22 42.3	12 16.8	6 17.4	13 30.9
31 M	12 33 10	10 11 54	13♈ 3 24	20 2 40	28 23.2	17 37.5	23 51.6	22 12.6	11 23.9	22 39.6	12 20.2	6 19.4	13 31.3

APRIL 2014

LONGITUDE

Day	Sid.Time	☉	0 hr ☽	Noon ☽	True ☊	☿	♀	♂	♃	♄	♅	♆	♇
1 Tu	12 37 7	11♈11 10	26♈56 53	3♉45 47	28♎22.7	19♓ 9.7	24♒53.9	21♎51.8	11♋28.6	22♏36.9	12♈23.6	6♓21.4	13♑31.8
2 W	12 41 3	12 10 24	10♉29 8	17 6 53	28D23.0	20 43.4	25 56.4	21R30.6	11 33.4	22R34.1	12 27.0	6 23.3	13 32.2
3 Th	12 45 0	13 9 36	23 39 5	0♊ 5 53	28 24.0	22 18.5	26 59.2	21 9.0	11 38.4	22 31.2	12 30.5	6 25.2	13 32.6
4 F	12 48 56	14 8 46	6♊27 33	12 44 23	28 25.2	23 55.1	28 2.3	20 47.1	11 43.5	22 28.2	12 33.9	6 27.1	13 33.0
5 Sa	12 52 53	15 7 53	18 56 49	25 5 19	28 26.4	25 33.2	29 5.6	20 24.9	11 48.9	22 25.1	12 37.3	6 29.0	13 33.3
6 Su	12 56 50	16 6 59	1♋10 22	7♋12 31	28 27.4	27 12.7	0♓ 9.2	20 2.4	11 54.3	22 22.0	12 40.8	6 30.9	13 33.6
7 M	13 0 46	17 6 2	13 12 21	19 10 26	28R27.8	28 53.6	1 13.0	19 39.8	11 60.0	22 18.8	12 44.2	6 32.7	13 33.8
8 Tu	13 4 43	18 5 2	25 7 21	1♌ 3 42	28 27.7	0♈36.0	2 17.0	19 17.0	12 5.8	22 15.5	12 47.6	6 34.6	13 34.1
9 W	13 8 39	19 4 1	7♌ 0 2	12 56 55	28 27.2	2 19.9	3 21.3	18 54.0	12 11.7	22 12.2	12 51.0	6 36.4	13 34.3
10 Th	13 12 36	20 2 57	18 54 54	24 54 27	28 26.3	4 5.3	4 25.8	18 31.0	12 17.8	22 8.8	12 54.4	6 38.2	13 34.4
11 F	13 16 32	21 1 51	0♍56 4	7♍ 0 9	28 25.3	5 52.1	5 30.4	18 8.0	12 24.0	22 5.3	12 57.8	6 39.9	13 34.6
12 Sa	13 20 29	22 0 42	13 7 6	19 17 15	28 24.4	7 40.5	6 35.3	17 45.0	12 30.4	22 1.8	13 1.2	6 41.7	13 34.7
13 Su	13 24 25	22 59 32	25 30 51	1♎48 9	28 23.6	9 30.4	7 40.4	17 22.0	12 37.0	21 58.2	13 4.6	6 43.4	13 34.8
14 M	13 28 22	23 58 19	8♎ 9 17	14 34 22	28 23.2	11 21.8	8 45.7	16 59.2	12 43.7	21 54.5	13 8.0	6 45.1	13R34.8
15 Tu	13 32 19	24 57 4	21 3 26	27 36 29	28D22.9	13 14.7	9 51.1	16 36.5	12 50.5	21 50.8	13 11.4	6 46.7	13 34.8
16 W	13 36 15	25 55 47	4♏13 27	10♏54 12	28 22.9	15 9.2	10 56.8	16 13.9	12 57.5	21 47.0	13 14.8	6 48.4	13 34.8
17 Th	13 40 12	26 54 29	17 38 35	24 26 23	28 23.0	17 5.1	12 2.6	15 51.6	13 4.6	21 43.2	13 18.1	6 50.0	13 34.8
18 F	13 44 8	27 53 8	1♐17 23	8♐11 19	28R23.1	19 2.6	13 8.6	15 29.6	13 11.9	21 39.3	13 21.5	6 51.6	13 34.7
19 Sa	13 48 5	28 51 46	15 7 54	22 6 51	28 23.1	21 1.6	14 14.8	15 7.9	13 19.3	21 35.3	13 24.8	6 53.2	13 34.6
20 Su	13 52 1	29 50 22	29 7 51	6♑10 38	28 23.0	23 2.0	15 21.1	14 46.5	13 26.8	21 31.3	13 28.1	6 54.8	13 34.4
21 M	13 55 58	0♉48 57	13♑14 52	20 20 15	28 22.9	25 3.9	16 27.6	14 25.6	13 34.5	21 27.3	13 31.5	6 56.3	13 34.3
22 Tu	13 59 54	1 47 30	27 26 29	4♒33 16	28D22.8	27 7.1	17 34.2	14 5.0	13 42.3	21 23.2	13 34.8	6 57.8	13 34.1
23 W	14 3 51	2 46 1	11♒40 17	18 47 13	28 22.8	29 11.5	18 41.0	13 44.9	13 50.2	21 19.1	13 38.1	6 59.3	13 33.9
24 Th	14 7 48	3 44 30	25 53 46	2♓59 34	28 23.1	1♉17.1	19 48.0	13 25.3	13 58.2	21 14.9	13 41.3	7 0.8	13 33.6
25 F	14 11 44	4 42 58	10♓ 4 19	17 7 40	28 23.5	3 23.8	20 55.1	13 6.3	14 6.4	21 10.7	13 44.6	7 2.2	13 33.3
26 Sa	14 15 41	5 41 25	24 9 15	1♈ 8 43	28 24.2	5 31.3	22 2.3	12 47.7	14 14.7	21 6.5	13 47.8	7 3.6	13 33.0
27 Su	14 19 37	6 39 50	8♈ 5 43	14 59 55	28 24.8	7 39.6	23 9.6	12 29.8	14 23.1	21 2.2	13 51.1	7 5.0	13 32.7
28 M	14 23 34	7 38 13	21 51 0	28 38 39	28R25.2	9 48.3	24 17.1	12 12.5	14 31.7	20 57.9	13 54.3	7 6.3	13 32.3
29 Tu	14 27 30	8 36 34	5♉22 38	12♉ 2 44	28 25.2	11 57.4	25 24.7	11 55.9	14 40.4	20 53.6	13 57.5	7 7.6	13 31.9
30 W	14 31 27	9 34 54	18 38 46	25 10 38	28 24.6	14 6.4	26 32.4	11 39.9	14 49.1	20 49.2	14 0.7	7 8.9	13 31.4

Astro Data

Dy Hr Mn

♂ R 1 16:25
☽0N 2 4:03
♄ R 2 16:20
♃ D 6 10:43
☽0S 16 11:17
☽0N 29 14:06

☿0N 10 14:19
☽0S 12 18:57
♇ R 14 23:48
♃□♅ 20 7:30
♃☍♇ 20 23:27
♅□♇ 21 19:22
☽0N 25 21:49

Planet Ingress

Dy Hr Mn

♀ ♒ 5 21:04
☿ ♓ 17 22:25
☉ ♈ 20 16:58

♀ ♓ 5 20:32
☿ ♈ 7 15:36
☉ ♉ 20 3:57
☿ ♉ 23 9:17

Last Aspect Dy Hr Mn	☽ Ingress Dy Hr Mn
2 11:05 ♀ ⚹	♈ 2 15:41
4 17:32 ♀ □	♉ 4 19:13
6 13:56 ♄ ☍	♊ 7 2:38
9 7:54 ♂ △	♋ 9 13:34
11 19:52 ♂ □	♌ 12 2:10
14 7:25 ♂ ⚹	♍ 14 14:19
16 17:09 ☉ ☍	♎ 17 0:47
19 1:08 ♂ ☌	♏ 19 9:14
21 3:13 ♄ ☌	♐ 21 15:40
23 10:41 ♂ ⚹	♑ 23 20:04
25 12:36 ♂ □	♒ 25 22:40
27 13:14 ♂ △	♓ 28 0:12
29 13:45 ♄ △	♈ 30 1:55

Last Aspect Dy Hr Mn	☽ Ingress Dy Hr Mn
31 20:08 ♀ ⚹	♉ 1 5:21
3 6:44 ♀ □	♊ 3 11:49
5 14:56 ☿ □	♋ 5 21:41
7 18:15 ♄ △	♌ 8 9:51
10 6:27 ♄ □	♍ 10 22:09
12 17:13 ♄ ⚹	♎ 13 8:34
15 7:43 ☉ ☍	♏ 15 16:21
17 7:10 ♄ ☌	♐ 17 21:45
20 1:18 ☉ △	♑ 20 1:29
21 23:22 ☿ □	♒ 22 4:19
23 16:12 ♄ □	♓ 24 6:56
25 20:04 ♀ ☌	♈ 26 10:02
27 11:03 ♃ □	♉ 28 14:24
30 15:54 ♀ ⚹	♊ 30 20:57

☽ Phases & Eclipses

Dy Hr Mn

1 8:01 ● 10♓39
8 13:28 ☽ 17♊54
16 17:09 ○ 26♍02
24 1:47 ☾ 3♑21
30 18:46 ● 9♈59

7 8:32 ☽ 17♋27
15 7:43 ○ 25♎16
15 7:47 •T 1.290
22 7:53 ☾ 2♒07
29 6:15 ● 8♉52
29 6:04:33 •A non-C

Astro Data

1 MARCH 2014
Julian Day # 41698
Galactic Ctr 27♐02.8
SVP 05♓03'33"
Obliquity 23°26'07"
⚷ Chiron 13♓11.6
☽ Mean ☊ 1♏08.6

1 APRIL 2014
Julian Day # 41729
Galactic Ctr 27♐02.9
SVP 05♓03'31"
Obliquity 23°26'07"
⚷ Chiron 15♓06.4
☽ Mean ☊ 29♎30.0

*Giving the positions of planets daily at noon, in LONGITUDE Greenwich Mean Time (UT)

Each planet's retrograde period is shaded gray.

2014 Planetary Ephemeris (Noon GMT*)

LONGITUDE — MAY 2014

Day	Sid.Time	☉	0 hr ☽	Noon ☽	True ☊	☿	♀	♂	♃	♄	♅	♆	♇
1 Th	14 35 23	10♉33 11	1♊38 17	8♊ 1 46	28♎23.5	16♉15.2	27♓40.2	11♎24.6	14♋58.1	20♏44.8	14♈ 3.8	7♓10.2	13♑31.0
2 F	14 39 20	11 31 27	14 21 8	20 36 34	28R 21.8	18 23.4	28 48.1	11R 10.1	15 7.1	20R 40.4	14 7.0	7 11.4	13R 30.5
3 Sa	14 43 17	12 29 41	26 48 17	2♋56 33	28 19.8	20 30.7	29 56.1	10 56.3	15 16.2	20 36.0	14 10.1	7 12.7	13 30.0
4 Su	14 47 13	13 27 53	9♋ 1 45	15 4 14	28 17.7	22 36.9	1♈ 4.2	10 43.2	15 25.4	20 31.5	14 13.2	7 13.8	13 29.4
5 M	14 51 10	14 26 4	21 4 28	27 2 57	28 16.0	24 41.7	2 12.5	10 30.9	15 34.8	20 27.0	14 16.3	7 15.0	13 28.9
6 Tu	14 55 6	15 24 12	3♌ 0 11	8♌56 43	28 14.7	26 44.7	3 20.8	10 19.4	15 44.3	20 22.6	14 19.3	7 16.1	13 28.3
7 W	14 59 3	16 22 18	14 53 8	20 50 0	28D 14.2	28 45.7	4 29.2	10 8.6	15 53.8	20 18.1	14 22.4	7 17.2	13 27.7
8 Th	15 2 59	17 20 22	26 47 56	2♍47 29	28 14.5	0♊44.4	5 37.7	9 58.7	16 3.5	20 13.6	14 25.4	7 18.3	13 27.0
9 F	15 6 56	18 18 25	8♍49 16	14 53 50	28 15.5	2 40.7	6 46.3	9 49.5	16 13.3	20 9.1	14 28.4	7 19.3	13 26.3
10 Sa	15 10 52	19 16 25	21 1 43	27 13 24	28 17.0	4 34.2	7 55.0	9 41.2	16 23.1	20 4.6	14 31.3	7 20.3	13 25.6
11 Su	15 14 49	20 14 24	3♎29 21	9♎49 56	28 18.5	6 24.9	9 3.7	9 33.6	16 33.1	20 0.0	14 34.3	7 21.3	13 24.9
12 M	15 18 46	21 12 21	16 15 29	22 46 14	28R 19.7	8 12.6	10 12.6	9 26.9	16 43.1	19 55.5	14 37.2	7 22.2	13 24.1
13 Tu	15 22 42	22 10 16	29 22 18	6♏ 3 44	28 20.1	9 57.1	11 21.5	9 20.9	16 53.3	19 51.0	14 40.1	7 23.1	13 23.3
14 W	15 26 39	23 8 10	12♏50 28	19 42 19	28 19.5	11 38.4	12 30.5	9 15.8	17 3.6	19 46.5	14 43.0	7 24.0	13 22.5
15 Th	15 30 35	24 6 2	26 38 57	3♐39 59	28 17.6	13 16.3	13 39.6	9 11.5	17 13.9	19 42.0	14 45.8	7 24.9	13 21.7
16 F	15 34 32	25 3 52	10♐44 54	17 53 6	28 14.6	14 50.9	14 48.8	9 7.9	17 24.3	19 37.5	14 48.6	7 25.7	13 20.9
17 Sa	15 38 28	26 1 42	25 3 56	2♑16 41	28 10.8	16 21.9	15 58.1	9 5.1	17 34.8	19 33.1	14 51.4	7 26.5	13 20.0
18 Su	15 42 25	26 59 30	9♑30 38	16 45 5	28 6.8	17 49.5	17 7.4	9 3.2	17 45.4	19 28.6	14 54.1	7 27.2	13 19.1
19 M	15 46 21	27 57 17	23 59 20	1♒12 47	28 3.1	19 13.4	18 16.9	9 2.0	17 56.1	19 24.2	14 56.9	7 28.0	13 18.2
20 Tu	15 50 18	28 55 2	8♒24 52	15 35 6	28 0.5	20 33.7	19 26.4	9D 1.5	18 6.9	19 19.8	14 59.6	7 28.7	13 17.2
21 W	15 54 15	29 52 47	22 43 6	29 48 33	27D 59.1	21 50.3	20 35.9	9 1.9	18 17.8	19 15.3	15 2.2	7 29.3	13 16.2
22 Th	15 58 11	0♊50 30	6♓51 14	13♓51 0	27 59.0	23 3.2	21 45.6	9 2.9	18 28.7	19 11.0	15 4.9	7 29.9	13 15.2
23 F	16 2 8	1 48 12	20 47 45	27 41 24	27 60.0	24 12.3	22 55.3	9 4.8	18 39.7	19 6.6	15 7.5	7 30.5	13 14.2
24 Sa	16 6 4	2 45 54	4♈31 59	11♈19 27	28 1.4	25 17.5	24 5.0	9 7.4	18 50.8	19 2.3	15 10.1	7 31.1	13 13.2
25 Su	16 10 1	3 43 34	18 3 51	24 45 11	28R 2.7	26 18.9	25 14.9	9 10.7	19 2.0	18 58.0	15 12.6	7 31.6	13 12.1
26 M	16 13 57	4 41 13	1♉23 28	7♉58 43	28 3.0	27 16.3	26 24.8	9 14.8	19 13.2	18 53.7	15 15.1	7 32.1	13 11.1
27 Tu	16 17 54	5 38 52	14 30 54	21 0 3	28 1.8	28 9.6	27 34.7	9 19.6	19 24.6	18 49.5	15 17.6	7 32.6	13 10.0
28 W	16 21 50	6 36 29	27 26 8	3♊49 10	27 58.7	28 58.8	28 44.7	9 25.1	19 35.9	18 45.3	15 20.0	7 33.1	13 8.8
29 Th	16 25 47	7 34 5	10♊ 9 8	16 26 4	27 53.8	29 43.8	29 54.8	9 31.3	19 47.4	18 41.1	15 22.4	7 33.5	13 7.7
30 F	16 29 44	8 31 40	22 40 0	28 51 2	27 47.4	0♋24.6	1♉ 4.9	9 38.2	19 59.0	18 37.0	15 24.8	7 33.8	13 6.5
31 Sa	16 33 40	9 29 14	4♋59 16	11♋ 4 52	27 40.0	1 1.0	2 15.1	9 45.8	20 10.6	18 32.9	15 27.1	7 34.2	13 5.4

LONGITUDE — JUNE 2014

Day	Sid.Time	☉	0 hr ☽	Noon ☽	True ☊	☿	♀	♂	♃	♄	♅	♆	♇
1 Su	16 37 37	10♊26 47	17♋ 8 3	23♋ 9 4	27♎32.4	1♋33.0	3♉25.4	9♎54.1	20♋22.2	18♏28.9	15♈29.4	7♓34.5	13♑ 4.2
2 M	16 41 33	11 24 18	29 8 12	5♌ 5 51	27R 25.3	2 0.6	4 35.6	10 3.0	20 34.0	18R 24.9	15 31.7	7 34.7	13R 3.0
3 Tu	16 45 30	12 21 48	11♌ 2 23	16 58 17	27 19.5	2 23.6	5 46.0	10 12.6	20 45.8	18 21.0	15 33.9	7 35.0	13 1.7
4 W	16 49 26	13 19 17	22 54 2	28 50 10	27 15.3	2 42.0	6 56.4	10 22.8	20 57.6	18 17.1	15 36.1	7 35.2	13 0.5
5 Th	16 53 23	14 16 45	4♍47 16	10♍45 55	27D 13.1	2 55.8	8 6.8	10 33.7	21 9.5	18 13.3	15 38.3	7 35.4	12 59.2
6 F	16 57 19	15 14 12	16 46 45	22 50 22	27 12.5	3 4.9	9 17.3	10 45.2	21 21.5	18 9.5	15 40.4	7 35.5	12 58.0
7 Sa	17 1 16	16 11 37	28 57 25	5♎ 8 30	27 13.2	3R 9.5	10 27.8	10 57.3	21 33.5	18 5.8	15 42.5	7 35.6	12 56.7
8 Su	17 5 13	17 9 1	11♎24 14	17 45 8	27 14.4	3 9.5	11 38.4	11 9.9	21 45.6	18 2.1	15 44.5	7 35.7	12 55.4
9 M	17 9 9	18 6 24	24 11 43	0♏44 22	27R 15.2	3 5.0	12 49.0	11 23.2	21 57.8	17 58.5	15 46.5	7R 35.7	12 54.0
10 Tu	17 13 6	19 3 46	7♏23 25	14 9 3	27 14.8	2 56.2	13 59.6	11 37.0	22 10.0	17 55.0	15 48.4	7 35.7	12 52.7
11 W	17 17 2	20 1 7	21 1 18	28 0 5	27 12.5	2 43.2	15 10.4	11 51.4	22 22.2	17 51.5	15 50.4	7 35.7	12 51.4
12 Th	17 20 59	20 58 27	5♐ 5 7	12♐15 54	27 8.0	2 26.2	16 21.1	12 6.3	22 34.5	17 48.1	15 52.2	7 35.7	12 50.0
13 F	17 24 55	21 55 47	19 31 49	26 52 4	27 1.5	2 5.6	17 31.9	12 21.8	22 46.9	17 44.8	15 54.1	7 35.6	12 48.6
14 Sa	17 28 52	22 53 5	4♑15 42	11♑41 41	26 53.5	1 41.6	18 42.8	12 37.8	22 59.3	17 41.5	15 55.9	7 35.5	12 47.3
15 Su	17 32 48	23 50 23	19 8 53	26 36 13	26 45.1	1 14.7	19 53.7	12 54.3	23 11.7	17 38.3	15 57.6	7 35.3	12 45.9
16 M	17 36 45	24 47 41	4♒ 2 34	11♒26 58	26 37.1	0 45.2	21 4.6	13 11.3	23 24.2	17 35.2	15 59.3	7 35.1	12 44.5
17 Tu	17 40 42	25 44 58	18 48 31	26 6 28	26 30.7	0 13.7	22 15.6	13 28.8	23 36.7	17 32.1	16 1.0	7 34.9	12 43.0
18 W	17 44 38	26 42 15	3♓20 16	10♓29 29	26 26.4	29♊40.7	23 26.7	13 46.8	23 49.3	17 29.1	16 2.6	7 34.7	12 41.6
19 Th	17 48 35	27 39 31	17 33 51	24 33 16	26D 24.3	29 6.8	24 37.8	14 5.3	24 1.9	17 26.2	16 4.2	7 34.4	12 40.2
20 F	17 52 31	28 36 47	1♈27 45	8♈17 22	26 23.9	28 32.4	25 48.9	14 24.2	24 14.6	17 23.4	16 5.8	7 34.1	12 38.7
21 Sa	17 56 28	29 34 3	15 2 20	21 42 52	26R 24.4	27 58.3	27 0.1	14 43.6	24 27.3	17 20.6	16 7.2	7 33.7	12 37.3
22 Su	18 0 24	0♋31 19	28 19 14	4♉51 42	26 24.7	27 25.0	28 11.4	15 3.5	24 40.0	17 17.9	16 8.7	7 33.4	12 35.8
23 M	18 4 21	1 28 35	11♉20 34	17 46 6	26 23.7	26 53.0	29 22.6	15 23.8	24 52.8	17 15.3	16 10.1	7 33.0	12 34.4
24 Tu	18 8 17	2 25 51	24 8 31	0♊28 3	26 20.6	26 22.9	0♊34.0	15 44.5	25 5.6	17 12.8	16 11.5	7 32.5	12 32.9
25 W	18 12 14	3 23 6	6♊44 54	12 59 14	26 14.8	25 55.3	1 45.3	16 5.7	25 18.5	17 10.4	16 12.8	7 32.1	12 31.4
26 Th	18 16 11	4 20 21	19 11 10	25 20 50	26 6.3	25 30.6	2 56.7	16 27.3	25 31.4	17 8.0	16 14.1	7 31.6	12 29.9
27 F	18 20 7	5 17 36	1♋28 21	7♋33 48	25 55.6	25 9.2	4 8.2	16 49.3	25 44.3	17 5.7	16 15.3	7 31.0	12 28.5
28 Sa	18 24 4	6 14 51	13 37 20	19 39 2	25 43.4	24 51.5	5 19.7	17 11.7	25 57.2	17 3.5	16 16.5	7 30.5	12 27.0
29 Su	18 28 0	7 12 6	25 39 4	1♌37 36	25 30.7	24 37.8	6 31.2	17 34.5	26 10.2	17 1.4	16 17.6	7 29.9	12 25.5
30 M	18 31 57	8 9 20	7♌34 51	13 31 3	25 18.6	24 28.4	7 42.7	17 57.8	26 23.2	16 59.4	16 18.7	7 29.3	12 24.0

Astro Data (Dy Hr Mn)	Planet Ingress (Dy Hr Mn)	Last Aspect (Dy Hr Mn)	☽ Ingress (Dy Hr Mn)	Last Aspect (Dy Hr Mn)	☽ Ingress (Dy Hr Mn)	☽ Phases & Eclipses (Dy Hr Mn)	Astro Data
♀0N 6 2:54	♀ ♈ 3 1:22	1 23:33 ♅ ⚹	♋ 3 6:14	1 6:33 ♃ ☌	♌ 2 1:44	7 3:16 ☽ 16♌30	1 MAY 2014
☽0S 10 3:44	☿ ♊ 7 14:58	5 8:47 ☿ ⚹	♌ 5 17:57	3 14:43 ♄ □	♍ 4 14:21	14 19:17 ○ 23♏55	Julian Day # 41759
♂ D 20 1:32	☉ ♊ 21 3:00	7 10:52 ♄ □	♍ 8 6:25	6 9:14 ♃ ⚹	♎ 7 2:02	21 13:00 ☾ 0♓24	Galactic Ctr 27♐03.0
☽0N 23 3:59	☿ ♋ 29 9:13	9 22:09 ♄ ⚹	♎ 10 17:20	8 19:48 ♃ □	♏ 9 10:39	28 18:41 ● 7♊21	SVP 05♓03'28"
♃△♄ 24 17:48	♀ ♉ 29 1:47	12 0:52 ♃ □	♏ 13 1:08	11 2:22 ♃ △	♐ 11 15:24		Obliquity 23°26'07"
		14 19:17 ☉ ☍	♐ 15 5:45	13 4:13 ☉ ☍	♑ 13 17:06		⚷ Chiron 16♓38.2
☽0S 6 13:01	☿ ♊ 17 10:06	16 7:44 ☿ ☍	♑ 17 8:13	15 6:36 ♃ ☍	♒ 15 17:28	5 20:40 ☽ 15♍06	☽ Mean ☊ 27♎54.7
☿ R 7 11:58	☉ ♋ 21 10:52	19 7:03 ☉ △	♒ 19 9:59	17 18:08 ☿ △	♓ 17 18:27	13 4:13 ○ 22♐06	
♆ R 9 19:51	♀ ♊ 23 12:35	20 22:22 ☿ △	♓ 21 12:19	19 19:07 ☿ □	♈ 19 21:27	19 18:40 ☾ 28♓24	1 JUNE 2014
♃□♆ 12 2:13		23 6:27 ☿ □	♈ 23 16:02	21 22:25 ☿ ⚹	♉ 22 3:04	27 8:10 ● 5♋37	Julian Day # 41790
☽0N 19 10:22		25 15:59 ☿ ⚹	♉ 25 21:29	24 1:50 ♃ ⚹	♊ 24 11:07		Galactic Ctr 27♐03.1
		27 9:11 ♃ ⚹	♊ 28 4:49	26 11:57 ☿ ☌	♋ 26 21:07		SVP 05♓03'23"
		29 10:00 ♅ ⚹	♋ 30 14:14	29 1:04 ♃ ☌	♌ 29 8:44		Obliquity 23°26'06"
							⚷ Chiron 17♓35.1
							☽ Mean ☊ 26♎16.2

*Giving the positions of planets daily at noon, in LONGITUDE Greenwich Mean Time (UT)

Each planet's retrograde period is shaded gray.

2014 Planetary Ephemeris (Noon GMT*)

JULY 2014 — LONGITUDE

Day	Sid.Time	☉	0 hr ☽	Noon ☽	True ☊	☿	♀	♂	♃	♄	♅	♆	♇
1 Tu	18 35 53	9♋ 6 34	19♌26 31	25♌21 35	25♎ 8.1	24♊23.6	8♊54.3	18♎21.4	26♋36.2	16♏57.5	16♈19.7	7♓28.6	12♑22.5
2 W	18 39 50	10 3 47	1♍16 38	7♍12 7	24R 59.9	24D 23.4	10 6.0	18 45.3	26 49.3	16R 55.7	16 20.7	7R 28.0	12R 21.0
3 Th	18 43 46	11 1 0	13 8 30	19 6 21	24 54.4	24 28.1	11 17.7	19 9.7	27 2.4	16 53.9	16 21.7	7 27.3	12 19.5
4 F	18 47 43	11 58 13	25 6 13	1♎ 8 42	24 51.4	24 37.7	12 29.4	19 34.4	27 15.5	16 52.3	16 22.6	7 26.5	12 18.0
5 Sa	18 51 40	12 55 26	7♎14 26	13 24 4	24D 50.3	24 52.2	13 41.1	19 59.5	27 28.6	16 50.7	16 23.4	7 25.8	12 16.5
6 Su	18 55 36	13 52 38	19 38 14	25 57 34	24R 50.2	25 11.8	14 52.9	20 24.9	27 41.8	16 49.3	16 24.2	7 25.0	12 15.0
7 M	18 59 33	14 49 50	2♏22 41	8♏54 7	24 50.1	25 36.4	16 4.7	20 50.6	27 54.9	16 47.9	16 25.0	7 24.2	12 13.5
8 Tu	19 3 29	15 47 2	15 32 20	22 17 42	24 48.9	26 6.1	17 16.6	21 16.7	28 8.1	16 46.6	16 25.7	7 23.3	12 12.0
9 W	19 7 26	16 44 14	29 10 26	6♐10 35	24 45.6	26 40.8	18 28.5	21 43.2	28 21.3	16 45.4	16 26.3	7 22.4	12 10.5
10 Th	19 11 22	17 41 25	13♐18 1	20 32 23	24 39.8	27 20.4	19 40.4	22 9.9	28 34.5	16 44.3	16 26.9	7 21.5	12 9.0
11 F	19 15 19	18 38 37	27 53 8	5♑19 26	24 31.6	28 4.9	20 52.4	22 36.9	28 47.8	16 43.3	16 27.5	7 20.6	12 7.5
12 Sa	19 19 15	19 35 49	12♑50 18	20 24 33	24 21.5	28 54.4	22 4.4	23 4.3	29 1.0	16 42.4	16 28.0	7 19.7	12 6.0
13 Su	19 23 12	20 33 1	28 0 52	5♒37 51	24 10.7	29 48.7	23 16.5	23 32.0	29 14.3	16 41.6	16 28.5	7 18.7	12 4.5
14 M	19 27 9	21 30 13	13♒14 9	20 48 25	24 0.4	0♋47.7	24 28.6	23 59.9	29 27.6	16 40.9	16 28.9	7 17.7	12 3.0
15 Tu	19 31 5	22 27 25	28 19 27	5♓46 13	23 51.9	1 51.5	25 40.8	24 28.1	29 40.9	16 40.3	16 29.3	7 16.7	12 1.6
16 W	19 35 2	23 24 38	13♓ 7 52	20 23 48	23 45.8	2 59.9	26 52.9	24 56.7	29 54.2	16 39.8	16 29.6	7 15.6	12 0.1
17 Th	19 38 58	24 21 52	27 33 34	4♈36 59	23 42.3	4 12.9	28 5.2	25 25.5	0♌ 7.5	16 39.4	16 29.9	7 14.5	11 58.6
18 F	19 42 55	25 19 6	11♈33 59	18 24 42	23 40.9	5 30.3	29 17.5	25 54.6	0 20.8	16 39.0	16 30.1	7 13.4	11 57.2
19 Sa	19 46 51	26 16 21	25 9 21	1♉48 16	23 40.7	6 52.2	0♋29.8	26 23.9	0 34.1	16 38.8	16 30.3	7 12.3	11 55.7
20 Su	19 50 48	27 13 37	8♉21 50	14 50 28	23 40.5	8 18.5	1 42.1	26 53.5	0 47.4	16D 38.7	16 30.4	7 11.2	11 54.3
21 M	19 54 44	28 10 53	21 14 37	27 34 44	23 39.1	9 48.9	2 54.5	27 23.4	1 0.8	16 38.6	16 30.5	7 10.0	11 52.8
22 Tu	19 58 41	29 8 10	3♊51 14	10♊ 4 31	23 35.5	11 23.4	4 7.0	27 53.6	1 14.1	16 38.7	16R 30.5	7 8.8	11 51.4
23 W	20 2 38	0♌ 5 28	16 14 58	22 22 55	23 29.2	13 1.8	5 19.5	28 24.0	1 27.5	16 38.9	16 30.5	7 7.6	11 50.0
24 Th	20 6 34	1 2 47	28 28 40	4♋32 30	23 20.1	14 44.0	6 32.0	28 54.7	1 40.8	16 39.1	16 30.4	7 6.4	11 48.6
25 F	20 10 31	2 0 7	10♋34 37	16 35 14	23 8.5	16 29.7	7 44.6	29 25.6	1 54.1	16 39.5	16 30.3	7 5.1	11 47.2
26 Sa	20 14 27	2 57 27	22 34 33	28 32 44	22 55.4	18 18.7	8 57.2	29 56.8	2 7.5	16 39.9	16 30.1	7 3.8	11 45.8
27 Su	20 18 24	3 54 48	4♌29 56	10♌26 20	22 41.8	20 10.8	10 9.8	0♏28.3	2 20.8	16 40.5	16 29.9	7 2.5	11 44.5
28 M	20 22 20	4 52 9	16 22 5	22 17 25	22 28.7	22 5.6	11 22.5	0 59.9	2 34.2	16 41.1	16 29.7	7 1.2	11 43.1
29 Tu	20 26 17	5 49 31	28 12 31	4♍ 7 39	22 17.3	24 2.9	12 35.3	1 31.8	2 47.5	16 41.9	16 29.4	6 59.9	11 41.8
30 W	20 30 13	6 46 54	10♍ 3 6	15 59 13	22 8.3	26 2.3	13 48.0	2 4.0	3 0.8	16 42.7	16 29.0	6 58.5	11 40.4
31 Th	20 34 10	7 44 18	21 56 21	27 54 55	22 2.0	28 3.6	15 0.8	2 36.3	3 14.1	16 43.7	16 28.6	6 57.2	11 39.1

AUGUST 2014 — LONGITUDE

Day	Sid.Time	☉	0 hr ☽	Noon ☽	True ☊	☿	♀	♂	♃	♄	♅	♆	♇
1 F	20 38 7	8♌41 42	3♎55 24	9♎58 18	21♎58.4	0♌ 6.3	16♋13.7	3♏ 8.9	3♌27.5	16♏44.7	16♈28.1	6♓55.8	11♑37.8
2 Sa	20 42 3	9 39 6	16 4 9	22 13 31	21D 57.1	2 10.1	17 26.5	3 41.7	3 40.8	16 45.8	16R 27.6	6R 54.4	11R 36.5
3 Su	20 46 0	10 36 32	28 27 0	4♏45 12	21 57.0	4 14.6	18 39.5	4 14.8	3 54.0	16 47.1	16 27.1	6 53.0	11 35.2
4 M	20 49 56	11 33 58	11♏ 8 43	17 38 6	21R 57.3	6 19.7	19 52.4	4 48.0	4 7.3	16 48.4	16 26.5	6 51.5	11 34.0
5 Tu	20 53 53	12 31 24	24 13 52	0♐56 28	21 56.7	8 24.8	21 5.4	5 21.5	4 20.6	16 49.8	16 25.8	6 50.1	11 32.7
6 W	20 57 49	13 28 52	7♐46 15	14 43 23	21 54.5	10 29.9	22 18.4	5 55.2	4 33.8	16 51.4	16 25.1	6 48.6	11 31.5
7 Th	21 1 46	14 26 20	21 47 56	28 59 44	21 50.0	12 34.6	23 31.5	6 29.0	4 47.1	16 53.0	16 24.4	6 47.1	11 30.3
8 F	21 5 42	15 23 49	6♑18 24	13♑43 18	21 43.2	14 38.8	24 44.6	7 3.1	5 0.3	16 54.7	16 23.6	6 45.6	11 29.1
9 Sa	21 9 39	16 21 18	21 13 38	28 48 19	21 34.7	16 42.2	25 57.7	7 37.4	5 13.5	16 56.5	16 22.8	6 44.1	11 28.0
10 Su	21 13 36	17 18 49	6♒26 7	14♒ 5 41	21 25.4	18 44.6	27 10.9	8 11.8	5 26.7	16 58.4	16 21.9	6 42.6	11 26.8
11 M	21 17 32	18 16 20	21 45 33	29 24 18	21 16.5	20 46.1	28 24.1	8 46.5	5 39.8	17 0.4	16 21.0	6 41.1	11 25.7
12 Tu	21 21 29	19 13 53	7♓ 0 33	14♓33 3	21 9.0	22 46.3	29 37.4	9 21.3	5 53.0	17 2.5	16 20.1	6 39.5	11 24.6
13 W	21 25 25	20 11 27	22 0 44	29 22 43	21 3.7	24 45.4	0♌50.7	9 56.3	6 6.1	17 4.7	16 19.1	6 38.0	11 23.5
14 Th	21 29 22	21 9 2	6♈38 21	13♈47 13	21 0.8	26 43.2	2 4.0	10 31.5	6 19.2	17 6.9	16 18.0	6 36.4	11 22.4
15 F	21 33 18	22 6 38	20 49 5	27 43 56	21D 0.0	28 39.6	3 17.4	11 6.9	6 32.3	17 9.3	16 16.9	6 34.8	11 21.3
16 Sa	21 37 15	23 4 17	4♉31 53	11♉13 12	21 0.5	0♍34.6	4 30.8	11 42.4	6 45.3	17 11.7	16 15.8	6 33.2	11 20.3
17 Su	21 41 11	24 1 56	17 48 14	24 17 25	21R 1.2	2 28.2	5 44.3	12 18.1	6 58.3	17 14.3	16 14.6	6 31.7	11 19.3
18 M	21 45 8	24 59 38	0♊41 15	7♊ 0 14	21 1.2	4 20.5	6 57.8	12 54.1	7 11.3	17 16.9	16 13.4	6 30.1	11 18.3
19 Tu	21 49 5	25 57 21	13 14 54	19 25 45	20 59.6	6 11.3	8 11.3	13 30.1	7 24.3	17 19.6	16 12.1	6 28.5	11 17.3
20 W	21 53 1	26 55 5	25 33 19	1♋38 3	20 55.9	8 0.7	9 24.9	14 6.4	7 37.2	17 22.4	16 10.8	6 26.8	11 16.4
21 Th	21 56 58	27 52 51	7♋40 25	13 40 49	20 50.0	9 48.7	10 38.5	14 42.8	7 50.1	17 25.3	16 9.5	6 25.2	11 15.5
22 F	22 0 54	28 50 39	19 39 39	25 37 14	20 42.1	11 35.2	11 52.2	15 19.4	8 3.0	17 28.3	16 8.1	6 23.6	11 14.6
23 Sa	22 4 51	29 48 28	1♌33 54	7♌29 56	20 32.9	13 20.4	13 5.9	15 56.2	8 15.9	17 31.4	16 6.7	6 22.0	11 13.7
24 Su	22 8 47	0♍46 19	13 25 33	19 21 1	20 23.3	15 4.2	14 19.6	16 33.1	8 28.7	17 34.6	16 5.2	6 20.3	11 12.8
25 M	22 12 44	1 44 11	25 16 32	1♍12 19	20 14.0	16 46.7	15 33.4	17 10.2	8 41.4	17 37.8	16 3.7	6 18.7	11 12.0
26 Tu	22 16 40	2 42 5	7♍ 8 33	13 5 27	20 6.0	18 27.8	16 47.2	17 47.5	8 54.2	17 41.1	16 2.2	6 17.0	11 11.2
27 W	22 20 37	3 40 0	19 3 16	25 2 12	19 59.9	20 7.5	18 1.0	18 24.9	9 6.8	17 44.6	16 0.6	6 15.4	11 10.4
28 Th	22 24 34	4 37 57	1♎ 2 33	7♎ 4 35	19 55.9	21 46.0	19 14.9	19 2.5	9 19.5	17 48.1	15 59.0	6 13.7	11 9.7
29 F	22 28 30	5 35 55	13 8 38	19 15 2	19D 54.0	23 23.1	20 28.8	19 40.2	9 32.1	17 51.6	15 57.3	6 12.1	11 8.9
30 Sa	22 32 27	6 33 54	25 24 12	1♏36 32	19 53.9	24 58.9	21 42.8	20 18.1	9 44.7	17 55.3	15 55.6	6 10.5	11 8.2
31 Su	22 36 23	7 31 55	7♏52 27	14 12 26	19 54.9	26 33.4	22 56.7	20 56.2	9 57.2	17 59.0	15 53.9	6 8.8	11 7.5

Astro Data Dy Hr Mn	Planet Ingress Dy Hr Mn	Last Aspect Dy Hr Mn	☽ Ingress Dy Hr Mn	Last Aspect Dy Hr Mn	☽ Ingress Dy Hr Mn	☽ Phases & Eclipses Dy Hr Mn
☿ D 1 12:51	☿ ♋ 13 4:46	1 10:01 ☿ ⚹	♍ 1 21:25	2 2:59 ♀ □	♏ 3 2:58	5 12:00 ☽ 13♎24
☽0S 3 21:48	♃ ♌ 16 10:32	4 4:22 ♃ ⚹	♎ 4 9:44	4 17:44 ♀ △	♐ 5 10:20	12 11:26 ○ 20♑03
☽0N 16 18:28	♀ ♋ 18 14:07	6 15:32 ♃ □	♏ 6 19:35	6 14:53 ♅ △	♑ 7 13:40	19 2:09 ☾ 26♈21
♄ D 20 20:36	☉ ♌ 22 21:42	8 22:34 ♃ △	♐ 9 1:26	9 8:10 ♀ ☍	♒ 9 13:53	26 22:43 ● 3♌52
♅ R 22 2:54	♂ ♏ 26 2:26	11 0:20 ☿ ☍	♑ 11 3:26	10 22:13 ☿ ☍	♓ 11 12:56	
☽0S 31 5:24	☿ ♌ 31 22:47	13 1:57 ♃ ☍	♒ 13 3:08	12 16:02 ♄ △	♈ 13 13:01	4 0:51 ☽ 11♏36
		14 19:24 ♀ △	♓ 15 2:41	15 15:51 ☿ △	♉ 15 15:59	10 18:10 ○ 18♒02
☽0N 13 4:31	♀ ♌ 12 7:25	17 0:58 ♀ □	♈ 17 4:08	17 12:27 ☉ □	♊ 17 22:42	17 12:27 ☾ 24♉32
♃⚻♆ 15 4:13	☿ ♍ 15 16:45	19 2:19 ♂ ☍	♉ 19 8:44	20 2:55 ☉ ⚹	♋ 20 8:46	25 14:14 ● 2♍19
☽0S 27 11:52	☉ ♍ 23 4:47	21 14:14 ☉ ⚹	♊ 21 16:37	21 19:35 ♄ △	♌ 22 20:50	
		24 0:54 ♂ △	♋ 24 3:00	24 8:27 ♄ □	♍ 25 9:34	
		25 13:54 ☿ ☌	♌ 26 14:56	27 2:30 ☿ ☌	♎ 27 21:55	
		28 0:39 ♄ □	♍ 29 3:38	29 16:01 ♀ ⚹	♏ 30 8:54	
		31 14:49 ☿ ⚹	♎ 31 16:10			

Astro Data

1 JULY 2014
Julian Day # 41820
Galactic Ctr 27♐03.1
SVP 05♓03'18"
Obliquity 23°26'06"
⚷ Chiron 17♓42.5R
☽ Mean ☊ 24♎40.9

1 AUGUST 2014
Julian Day # 41851
Galactic Ctr 27♐03.2
SVP 05♓03'14"
Obliquity 23°26'06"
⚷ Chiron 17♓00.8R
☽ Mean ☊ 23♎02.4

*Giving the positions of planets daily at noon, in LONGITUDE Greenwich Mean Time (UT)

Each planet's retrograde period is shaded gray.

2014 Planetary Ephemeris (Noon GMT*)

LONGITUDE — SEPTEMBER 2014

Day	Sid.Time	☉	0 hr ☽	Noon ☽	True ☊	☿	♀	♂	♃	♄	♅	♆	♇
1 M	22 40 20	8♍29 57	20♏36 56	27♏ 6 23	19♎56.4	28♍ 6.6	24♌10.7	21♏34.4	10♌ 9.6	18♏ 2.9	15♈52.1	6♓ 7.2	11♑ 6.9
2 Tu	22 44 16	9 28 1	3♐41 14	10♐21 52	19R57.4	29 38.6	25 24.8	22 12.7	10 22.1	18 6.8	15R50.3	6R 5.5	11R 6.3
3 W	22 48 13	10 26 6	17 8 35	24 1 37	19 57.3	1♎ 9.2	26 38.8	22 51.2	10 34.4	18 10.8	15 48.5	6 3.9	11 5.7
4 Th	22 52 9	11 24 13	1♑ 1 5	8♑ 6 57	19 55.8	2 38.5	27 52.9	23 29.8	10 46.8	18 14.8	15 46.7	6 2.2	11 5.1
5 F	22 56 6	12 22 20	15 19 1	22 36 56	19 52.6	4 6.6	29 7.1	24 8.6	10 59.0	18 19.0	15 44.8	6 0.6	11 4.6
6 Sa	23 0 2	13 20 30	0♒ 0 5	7♒27 45	19 48.2	5 33.3	0♍21.2	24 47.5	11 11.3	18 23.2	15 42.9	5 59.0	11 4.1
7 Su	23 3 59	14 18 40	14 59 0	22 32 44	19 43.1	6 58.7	1 35.4	25 26.5	11 23.4	18 27.5	15 40.9	5 57.3	11 3.6
8 M	23 7 56	15 16 53	0♓ 7 46	7♓42 50	19 38.1	8 22.8	2 49.6	26 5.7	11 35.5	18 31.8	15 39.0	5 55.7	11 3.1
9 Tu	23 11 52	16 15 6	15 16 42	22 48 6	19 34.0	9 45.5	4 3.9	26 45.0	11 47.6	18 36.3	15 37.0	5 54.1	11 2.7
10 W	23 15 49	17 13 22	0♈15 57	7♈39 15	19 31.3	11 6.7	5 18.1	27 24.4	11 59.6	18 40.8	15 34.9	5 52.5	11 2.3
11 Th	23 19 45	18 11 39	14 57 9	22 9 2	19D30.1	12 26.6	6 32.4	28 3.9	12 11.5	18 45.4	15 32.9	5 50.9	11 1.9
12 F	23 23 42	19 9 59	29 14 26	6♉13 6	19 30.3	13 44.9	7 46.8	28 43.6	12 23.4	18 50.0	15 30.8	5 49.3	11 1.6
13 Sa	23 27 38	20 8 20	13♉ 4 55	19 49 56	19 31.5	15 1.8	9 1.2	29 23.4	12 35.2	18 54.7	15 28.7	5 47.7	11 1.3
14 Su	23 31 35	21 6 44	26 28 22	3♊ 0 31	19 33.1	16 17.0	10 15.6	0♐ 3.4	12 47.0	18 59.5	15 26.5	5 46.1	11 1.0
15 M	23 35 31	22 5 10	9♊26 46	15 47 34	19 34.4	17 30.6	11 30.0	0 43.5	12 58.7	19 4.4	15 24.4	5 44.6	11 0.7
16 Tu	23 39 28	23 3 38	22 3 26	28 14 53	19R35.0	18 42.4	12 44.5	1 23.6	13 10.3	19 9.3	15 22.2	5 43.0	11 0.5
17 W	23 43 25	24 2 8	4♋22 29	10♋26 48	19 34.6	19 52.5	13 59.0	2 4.0	13 21.8	19 14.3	15 20.0	5 41.4	11 0.3
18 Th	23 47 21	25 0 40	16 28 21	22 27 41	19 33.0	21 0.6	15 13.5	2 44.4	13 33.3	19 19.4	15 17.8	5 39.9	11 0.1
19 F	23 51 18	25 59 14	28 25 19	4♌21 44	19 30.3	22 6.6	16 28.0	3 25.0	13 44.7	19 24.5	15 15.6	5 38.4	11 0.0
20 Sa	23 55 14	26 57 51	10♌17 22	16 12 40	19 27.0	23 10.5	17 42.6	4 5.7	13 56.1	19 29.7	15 13.3	5 36.9	10 59.9
21 Su	23 59 11	27 56 29	22 8 0	28 3 44	19 23.3	24 12.1	18 57.2	4 46.5	14 7.3	19 35.0	15 11.0	5 35.4	10 59.8
22 M	0 3 7	28 55 10	4♍ 0 11	9♍57 39	19 19.8	25 11.2	20 11.8	5 27.4	14 18.5	19 40.3	15 8.7	5 33.9	10 59.8
23 Tu	0 7 4	29 53 52	15 56 24	21 56 40	19 16.9	26 7.7	21 26.5	6 8.4	14 29.7	19 45.7	15 6.4	5 32.4	10D59.8
24 W	0 11 0	0♎52 37	27 58 40	4♎ 2 37	19 14.7	27 1.2	22 41.2	6 49.6	14 40.7	19 51.1	15 4.1	5 31.0	10 59.8
25 Th	0 14 57	1 51 24	10♎ 8 42	16 17 7	19D13.6	27 51.7	23 55.9	7 30.9	14 51.6	19 56.6	15 1.7	5 29.5	10 59.8
26 F	0 18 54	2 50 12	22 28 3	28 41 41	19 13.4	28 38.9	25 10.6	8 12.3	15 2.5	20 2.2	14 59.4	5 28.1	10 59.9
27 Sa	0 22 50	3 49 3	4♏58 13	11♏17 50	19 13.9	29 22.5	26 25.3	8 53.8	15 13.3	20 7.8	14 57.0	5 26.7	11 0.0
28 Su	0 26 47	4 47 55	17 40 46	24 7 12	19 15.0	0♏ 2.1	27 40.1	9 35.4	15 24.0	20 13.4	14 54.7	5 25.3	11 0.1
29 M	0 30 43	5 46 49	0♐37 23	7♐11 30	19 16.2	0 37.5	28 54.9	10 17.2	15 34.6	20 19.2	14 52.3	5 23.9	11 0.3
30 Tu	0 34 40	6 45 46	13 49 46	20 32 21	19 17.3	1 8.2	0♎ 9.7	10 59.0	15 45.1	20 24.9	14 49.9	5 22.6	11 0.5

LONGITUDE — OCTOBER 2014

Day	Sid.Time	☉	0 hr ☽	Noon ☽	True ☊	☿	♀	♂	♃	♄	♅	♆	♇
1 W	0 38 36	7♎44 43	27♐19 24	4♑11 3	19♎17.9	1♏34.0	1♎24.5	11♐40.9	15♌55.6	20♏30.8	14♈47.5	5♓21.2	11♑ 0.7
2 Th	0 42 33	8 43 43	11♑ 7 18	18 8 9	19R18.1	1 54.3	2 39.4	12 23.0	16 5.9	20 36.7	14R45.1	5R19.9	11 1.0
3 F	0 46 29	9 42 44	25 13 27	2♒23 0	19 17.8	2 8.8	3 54.2	13 5.1	16 16.2	20 42.6	14 42.6	5 18.6	11 1.3
4 Sa	0 50 26	10 41 47	9♒36 28	16 53 23	19 17.1	2R17.0	5 9.1	13 47.4	16 26.3	20 48.6	14 40.2	5 17.4	11 1.6
5 Su	0 54 23	11 40 52	24 13 10	1♓35 11	19 16.2	2 18.5	6 24.0	14 29.7	16 36.4	20 54.6	14 37.8	5 16.1	11 2.0
6 M	0 58 19	12 39 58	8♓58 37	16 22 37	19 15.4	2 12.8	7 38.9	15 12.2	16 46.3	21 0.7	14 35.4	5 14.9	11 2.4
7 Tu	1 2 16	13 39 6	23 46 19	1♈ 8 46	19 14.8	1 59.5	8 53.8	15 54.7	16 56.2	21 6.8	14 32.9	5 13.7	11 2.8
8 W	1 6 12	14 38 16	8♈29 5	15 46 23	19D14.5	1 38.4	10 8.7	16 37.4	17 5.9	21 13.0	14 30.5	5 12.5	11 3.2
9 Th	1 10 9	15 37 28	22 59 52	0♉ 8 52	19 14.4	1 9.3	11 23.7	17 20.1	17 15.6	21 19.2	14 28.1	5 11.3	11 3.7
10 F	1 14 5	16 36 43	7♉12 47	14 11 10	19 14.5	0 32.1	12 38.6	18 2.9	17 25.1	21 25.5	14 25.7	5 10.2	11 4.2
11 Sa	1 18 2	17 35 59	21 3 43	27 50 14	19 14.7	29♎46.9	13 53.6	18 45.8	17 34.5	21 31.8	14 23.2	5 9.0	11 4.7
12 Su	1 21 58	18 35 18	4♊30 42	11♊ 5 11	19R14.8	28 54.3	15 8.6	19 28.8	17 43.9	21 38.2	14 20.8	5 8.0	11 5.3
13 M	1 25 55	19 34 39	17 33 51	23 57 1	19 14.9	27 54.8	16 23.6	20 11.9	17 53.1	21 44.6	14 18.4	5 6.9	11 5.9
14 Tu	1 29 51	20 34 2	0♋15 2	6♋28 20	19 14.8	26 49.5	17 38.6	20 55.1	18 2.2	21 51.0	14 16.0	5 5.8	11 6.5
15 W	1 33 48	21 33 27	12 37 24	18 42 48	19D14.7	25 39.8	18 53.7	21 38.4	18 11.2	21 57.5	14 13.6	5 4.8	11 7.2
16 Th	1 37 45	22 32 55	24 45 3	0♌44 45	19 14.7	24 27.4	20 8.8	22 21.8	18 20.1	22 4.0	14 11.2	5 3.8	11 7.9
17 F	1 41 41	23 32 25	6♌42 29	12 38 50	19 14.8	23 14.1	21 23.8	23 5.2	18 28.9	22 10.5	14 8.8	5 2.9	11 8.6
18 Sa	1 45 38	24 31 58	18 34 22	24 29 39	19 15.2	22 2.0	22 38.9	23 48.8	18 37.5	22 17.1	14 6.4	5 1.9	11 9.4
19 Su	1 49 34	25 31 32	0♍25 13	6♍21 35	19 15.8	20 53.4	23 54.0	24 32.4	18 46.0	22 23.7	14 4.0	5 1.0	11 10.1
20 M	1 53 31	26 31 9	12 19 13	18 18 34	19 16.5	19 50.1	25 9.2	25 16.1	18 54.4	22 30.4	14 1.7	5 0.1	11 10.9
21 Tu	1 57 27	27 30 48	24 20 1	0♎23 57	19 17.3	18 54.2	26 24.3	25 59.9	19 2.7	22 37.0	13 59.3	4 59.3	11 11.8
22 W	2 1 24	28 30 29	6♎30 38	12 40 22	19 17.9	18 7.2	27 39.4	26 43.8	19 10.8	22 43.8	13 57.0	4 58.5	11 12.6
23 Th	2 5 20	29 30 12	18 53 20	25 9 43	19R18.2	17 30.2	28 54.6	27 27.8	19 18.8	22 50.5	13 54.6	4 57.7	11 13.5
24 F	2 9 17	0♏29 57	1♏29 37	7♏53 7	19 17.9	17 4.1	0♏ 9.7	28 11.8	19 26.7	22 57.3	13 52.3	4 56.9	11 14.4
25 Sa	2 13 14	1 29 45	14 20 13	20 50 55	19 17.0	16D49.3	1 24.9	28 56.0	19 34.5	23 4.1	13 50.0	4 56.1	11 15.4
26 Su	2 17 10	2 29 34	27 25 9	4♐ 2 52	19 15.6	16 45.8	2 40.1	29 40.2	19 42.1	23 10.9	13 47.8	4 55.4	11 16.4
27 M	2 21 7	3 29 25	10♐43 56	17 28 15	19 13.7	16 53.5	3 55.3	0♑24.5	19 49.6	23 17.8	13 45.5	4 54.8	11 17.4
28 Tu	2 25 3	4 29 18	24 15 40	1♑ 6 2	19 11.6	17 11.9	5 10.5	1 8.9	19 56.9	23 24.7	13 43.3	4 54.1	11 18.4
29 W	2 29 0	5 29 12	7♑59 11	14 54 59	19 9.7	17 40.2	6 25.7	1 53.3	20 4.1	23 31.6	13 41.1	4 53.5	11 19.5
30 Th	2 32 56	6 29 9	21 53 14	28 53 47	19 8.4	18 17.8	7 40.9	2 37.9	20 11.2	23 38.5	13 38.9	4 52.9	11 20.6
31 F	2 36 53	7 29 6	5♒56 25	13♒ 0 57	19D 7.9	19 3.7	8 56.1	3 22.5	20 18.1	23 45.5	13 36.7	4 52.4	11 21.7

Astro Data Dy Hr Mn	Planet Ingress Dy Hr Mn	Last Aspect Dy Hr Mn	☽ Ingress Dy Hr Mn	Last Aspect Dy Hr Mn	☽ Ingress Dy Hr Mn	☽ Phases & Eclipses Dy Hr Mn	Astro Data
☿0S 2 2:54	☿ ♎ 2 5:39	1 15:41 ☿ ⚹	♐ 1 17:18	30 3:30 ♃ △	♑ 1 4:42	2 11:12 ☽ 9♐55	1 SEPTEMBER 2014
♃⚻♇ 5 10:24	♀ ♍ 5 17:08	3 18:07 ♀ △	♑ 3 22:16	2 16:19 ♄ ⚹	♒ 3 8:01	9 1:39 ○ 16♓19	Julian Day # 41882
☽0N 9 15:31	♂ ♐ 13 21:58	5 15:09 ♂ ⚹	♒ 5 24:00	4 18:33 ♄ □	♓ 5 9:25	16 2:06 ☾ 23♊09	Galactic Ctr 27♐03.3
☽0S 23 18:05	☉ ♎ 23 2:30	7 17:20 ♂ □	♓ 7 23:48	6 19:39 ♄ △	♈ 7 10:08	24 6:15 ● 1♎08	SVP 05♓03'11"
♇ D 23 0:37	☿ ♏ 27 22:40	9 19:11 ♂ △	♈ 9 23:34	8 14:21 ♃ △	♉ 9 11:45		Obliquity 23°26'06"
♃△♅ 25 18:20	♀ ♎ 29 20:53	11 0:59 ♅ ☌	♉ 12 1:18	11 0:50 ♄ ☍	♊ 11 15:52	1 19:34 ☽ 8♑33	⚷ Chiron 15♓43.5R
		13 13:32 ☉ △	♊ 14 6:27	13 17:59 ☿ △	♋ 13 23:31	8 10:52 ○ 15♈05	☽ Mean ☊ 21♎23.9
♀0S 2 11:49	☿ ♎ 10 17:28	16 2:06 ☉ □	♋ 16 15:25	15 23:28 ☿ □	♌ 16 10:30	8 10:56 ● T 1.166	
☿ R 4 17:03	☉ ♏ 23 11:58	18 18:39 ☉ ⚹	♌ 19 3:11	18 13:11 ☉ ⚹	♍ 18 23:09	15 19:13 ☾ 22♋21	1 OCTOBER 2014
☽0N 7 1:56	♀ ♏ 23 20:53	21 4:34 ☿ ⚹	♍ 21 15:55	21 3:31 ♂ □	♎ 21 11:13	23 21:58 ● 0♏25	Julian Day # 41912
☽0S 21 1:14	♂ ♑ 26 10:44	23 12:16 ♀ ☌	♎ 24 4:00	23 17:23 ♂ ⚹	♏ 23 21:11	23 21:45:39 ● P 0.811	Galactic Ctr 27♐03.3
☿ D 25 19:18		26 12:40 ☿ ☌	♏ 26 14:30	25 16:12 ♄ ☌	♐ 26 4:41	31 2:49 ☽ 7♒36	SVP 05♓03'08"
		28 20:32 ♀ ⚹	♐ 28 22:51	27 16:19 ♃ △	♑ 28 10:04		Obliquity 23°26'06"
				30 3:02 ♄ ⚹	♒ 30 13:53		⚷ Chiron 14♓21.4R
							☽ Mean ☊ 19♎48.6

*Giving the positions of planets daily at noon, in LONGITUDE Greenwich Mean Time (UT)

Each planet's retrograde period is shaded gray.

2014 Planetary Ephemeris (Noon GMT*)

NOVEMBER 2014 LONGITUDE

Day	Sid.Time	☉	0 hr ☽	Noon ☽	True ☊	☿	♀	♂	♃	♄	♅	♆	♇
1 Sa	2 40 49	8♏29 6	20♒ 7 9	27♒14 45	19♎ 8.2	19♎57.2	10♏11.3	4♑ 7.1	20♌24.8	23♏52.4	13♈34.6	4♓51.8	11♑22.8
2 Su	2 44 46	9 29 7	4♓23 27	11♓32 57	19 9.3	20 57.3	11 26.6	4 51.8	20 31.4	23 59.4	13R 32.5	4R 51.3	11 24.0
3 M	2 48 43	10 29 9	18 42 52	25 52 46	19 10.7	22 3.2	12 41.8	5 36.6	20 37.9	24 6.4	13 30.4	4 50.9	11 25.2
4 Tu	2 52 39	11 29 13	3♈ 2 14	10♈10 44	19 11.9	23 14.3	13 57.0	6 21.5	20 44.2	24 13.5	13 28.3	4 50.5	11 26.4
5 W	2 56 36	12 29 19	17 17 47	24 22 51	19R 12.6	24 29.6	15 12.2	7 6.4	20 50.4	24 20.5	13 26.3	4 50.1	11 27.7
6 Th	3 0 32	13 29 26	1♉25 23	8♉24 53	19 12.1	25 48.7	16 27.5	7 51.4	20 56.4	24 27.6	13 24.2	4 49.7	11 28.9
7 F	3 4 29	14 29 35	15 20 51	22 12 51	19 10.3	27 11.0	17 42.7	8 36.5	21 2.3	24 34.6	13 22.3	4 49.4	11 30.2
8 Sa	3 8 25	15 29 46	29 0 31	5♊43 32	19 7.3	28 35.9	18 58.0	9 21.6	21 8.0	24 41.7	13 20.3	4 49.1	11 31.6
9 Su	3 12 22	16 29 59	12♊21 43	18 54 56	19 3.1	0♏ 3.1	20 13.2	10 6.8	21 13.5	24 48.8	13 18.4	4 48.8	11 32.9
10 M	3 16 18	17 30 14	25 23 10	1♋46 29	18 58.4	1 32.0	21 28.5	10 52.0	21 18.9	24 55.9	13 16.5	4 48.6	11 34.3
11 Tu	3 20 15	18 30 30	8♋ 5 4	14 19 10	18 53.7	3 2.5	22 43.7	11 37.3	21 24.1	25 3.0	13 14.6	4 48.4	11 35.7
12 W	3 24 12	19 30 49	20 29 6	26 35 19	18 49.6	4 34.2	23 59.0	12 22.7	21 29.1	25 10.2	13 12.8	4 48.2	11 37.1
13 Th	3 28 8	20 31 10	2♌38 15	8♌38 26	18 46.6	6 6.8	25 14.3	13 8.1	21 34.0	25 17.3	13 11.0	4 48.1	11 38.6
14 F	3 32 5	21 31 32	14 36 25	20 32 50	18D 45.0	7 40.3	26 29.6	13 53.5	21 38.7	25 24.4	13 9.3	4 48.0	11 40.0
15 Sa	3 36 1	22 31 56	26 28 17	2♍23 23	18 44.8	9 14.3	27 44.9	14 39.1	21 43.3	25 31.6	13 7.5	4 48.0	11 41.5
16 Su	3 39 58	23 32 22	8♍18 47	14 15 8	18 45.8	10 48.8	29 0.2	15 24.7	21 47.7	25 38.7	13 5.8	4D 47.9	11 43.0
17 M	3 43 54	24 32 50	20 13 3	26 13 6	18 47.4	12 23.6	0♐15.4	16 10.3	21 51.9	25 45.9	13 4.2	4 47.9	11 44.6
18 Tu	3 47 51	25 33 20	2♎15 54	8♎21 56	18 49.2	13 58.7	1 30.7	16 56.0	21 55.9	25 53.0	13 2.6	4 48.0	11 46.1
19 W	3 51 47	26 33 52	14 31 42	20 45 35	18R 50.2	15 33.9	2 46.1	17 41.7	21 59.7	26 0.2	13 1.0	4 48.0	11 47.7
20 Th	3 55 44	27 34 25	27 3 58	3♏27 4	18 50.0	17 9.2	4 1.4	18 27.5	22 3.4	26 7.3	12 59.5	4 48.2	11 49.3
21 F	3 59 41	28 35 0	9♏55 3	16 28 0	18 47.9	18 44.5	5 16.7	19 13.4	22 6.9	26 14.5	12 58.0	4 48.3	11 50.9
22 Sa	4 3 37	29 35 37	23 5 53	29 48 33	18 43.9	20 19.8	6 32.0	19 59.3	22 10.2	26 21.6	12 56.5	4 48.5	11 52.6
23 Su	4 7 34	0♐36 15	6♐35 45	13♐27 10	18 38.0	21 55.1	7 47.3	20 45.3	22 13.3	26 28.8	12 55.1	4 48.7	11 54.2
24 M	4 11 30	1 36 54	20 22 21	27 20 51	18 30.9	23 30.4	9 2.6	21 31.3	22 16.3	26 35.9	12 53.7	4 49.0	11 55.9
25 Tu	4 15 27	2 37 35	4♑22 6	11♑25 34	18 23.4	25 5.5	10 18.0	22 17.3	22 19.0	26 43.1	12 52.4	4 49.2	11 57.6
26 W	4 19 23	3 38 17	18 30 41	25 36 53	18 16.3	26 40.6	11 33.3	23 3.4	22 21.6	26 50.2	12 51.1	4 49.6	11 59.3
27 Th	4 23 20	4 39 1	2♒43 40	9♒50 34	18 10.7	28 15.5	12 48.6	23 49.6	22 24.0	26 57.3	12 49.9	4 49.9	12 1.1
28 F	4 27 16	5 39 45	16 57 12	24 3 12	18 7.0	29 50.3	14 3.9	24 35.8	22 26.2	27 4.4	12 48.7	4 50.3	12 2.8
29 Sa	4 31 13	6 40 30	1♓ 8 20	8♓12 21	18D 5.3	1♐25.1	15 19.2	25 22.0	22 28.2	27 11.5	12 47.5	4 50.7	12 4.6
30 Su	4 35 10	7 41 16	15 15 7	22 16 29	18 5.4	2 59.7	16 34.6	26 8.2	22 30.0	27 18.6	12 46.4	4 51.2	12 6.4

DECEMBER 2014 LONGITUDE

Day	Sid.Time	☉	0 hr ☽	Noon ☽	True ☊	☿	♀	♂	♃	♄	♅	♆	♇
1 M	4 39 6	8♐42 3	29♓16 23	6♈14 43	18♎ 6.4	4♐34.2	17♐49.9	26♑54.5	22♌31.6	27♏25.7	12♈45.3	4♓51.7	12♑ 8.2
2 Tu	4 43 3	9 42 51	13♈11 24	20 6 19	18R 7.3	6 8.7	19 5.2	27 40.9	22 33.0	27 32.7	12R 44.3	4 52.2	12 10.0
3 W	4 46 59	10 43 40	26 59 22	3♉50 23	18 7.1	7 43.1	20 20.5	28 27.2	22 34.3	27 39.8	12 43.3	4 52.8	12 11.8
4 Th	4 50 56	11 44 30	10♉39 12	17 25 37	18 4.8	9 17.4	21 35.8	29 13.6	22 35.3	27 46.8	12 42.4	4 53.4	12 13.7
5 F	4 54 52	12 45 21	24 9 24	0♊50 19	17 59.9	10 51.6	22 51.1	0♒ 0.1	22 36.2	27 53.8	12 41.5	4 54.0	12 15.6
6 Sa	4 58 49	13 46 13	7♊28 8	14 2 38	17 52.5	12 25.9	24 6.4	0 46.5	22 36.8	28 0.8	12 40.7	4 54.6	12 17.4
7 Su	5 2 45	14 47 6	20 33 36	27 0 54	17 42.9	14 0.1	25 21.7	1 33.0	22 37.3	28 7.7	12 39.9	4 55.3	12 19.3
8 M	5 6 42	15 48 0	3♋24 24	9♋44 4	17 32.0	15 34.3	26 37.0	2 19.6	22R 37.5	28 14.7	12 39.2	4 56.1	12 21.2
9 Tu	5 10 39	16 48 55	15 59 56	22 12 4	17 20.8	17 8.5	27 52.3	3 6.1	22 37.6	28 21.6	12 38.5	4 56.8	12 23.2
10 W	5 14 35	17 49 51	28 20 39	4♌25 56	17 10.3	18 42.8	29 7.6	3 52.7	22 37.5	28 28.5	12 37.9	4 57.6	12 25.1
11 Th	5 18 32	18 50 48	10♌28 14	16 27 56	17 1.6	20 17.1	0♑22.8	4 39.3	22 37.2	28 35.4	12 37.3	4 58.5	12 27.0
12 F	5 22 28	19 51 46	22 25 30	28 21 26	16 55.2	21 51.4	1 38.1	5 25.9	22 36.7	28 42.2	12 36.8	4 59.3	12 29.0
13 Sa	5 26 25	20 52 45	4♍16 18	10♍10 42	16 51.3	23 25.9	2 53.4	6 12.6	22 35.9	28 49.1	12 36.3	5 0.2	12 31.0
14 Su	5 30 21	21 53 46	16 5 17	22 0 43	16D 49.7	25 0.4	4 8.7	6 59.3	22 35.0	28 55.8	12 35.8	5 1.1	12 32.9
15 M	5 34 18	22 54 47	27 57 41	3♎56 53	16 49.6	26 35.0	5 24.0	7 46.0	22 33.9	29 2.6	12 35.4	5 2.1	12 34.9
16 Tu	5 38 14	23 55 49	9♎58 59	16 4 40	16R 50.1	28 9.7	6 39.3	8 32.7	22 32.6	29 9.3	12 35.1	5 3.1	12 36.9
17 W	5 42 11	24 56 53	22 14 35	28 29 17	16 50.1	29 44.6	7 54.6	9 19.5	22 31.1	29 16.0	12 34.8	5 4.1	12 38.9
18 Th	5 46 8	25 57 57	4♏49 20	11♏15 10	16 48.6	1♑19.6	9 9.8	10 6.3	22 29.4	29 22.7	12 34.6	5 5.2	12 41.0
19 F	5 50 4	26 59 2	17 47 6	24 25 22	16 44.7	2 54.7	10 25.1	10 53.1	22 27.5	29 29.4	12 34.4	5 6.2	12 43.0
20 Sa	5 54 1	28 0 8	1♐10 2	8♐ 1 1	16 38.0	4 29.9	11 40.4	11 39.9	22 25.4	29 36.0	12 34.3	5 7.4	12 45.0
21 Su	5 57 57	29 1 15	14 58 4	22 0 46	16 28.8	6 5.4	12 55.7	12 26.8	22 23.1	29 42.5	12D 34.2	5 8.5	12 47.1
22 M	6 1 54	0♑ 2 22	29 8 31	6♑20 38	16 17.6	7 40.9	14 11.0	13 13.6	22 20.6	29 49.0	12 34.2	5 9.7	12 49.1
23 Tu	6 5 50	1 3 30	13♑36 13	20 54 23	16 5.6	9 16.6	15 26.2	14 0.5	22 18.0	29 55.5	12 34.2	5 10.9	12 51.2
24 W	6 9 47	2 4 38	28 14 7	5♒34 27	15 54.2	10 52.4	16 41.5	14 47.4	22 15.1	0♐ 2.0	12 34.3	5 12.1	12 53.2
25 Th	6 13 43	3 5 47	12♒54 28	20 13 16	15 44.6	12 28.3	17 56.8	15 34.3	22 12.0	0 8.4	12 34.4	5 13.4	12 55.3
26 F	6 17 40	4 6 56	27 30 9	4♓44 29	15 37.6	14 4.3	19 12.0	16 21.3	22 8.8	0 14.8	12 34.6	5 14.7	12 57.4
27 Sa	6 21 37	5 8 4	11♓55 46	19 3 41	15 33.5	15 40.3	20 27.2	17 8.2	22 5.4	0 21.1	12 34.8	5 16.0	12 59.5
28 Su	6 25 33	6 9 13	26 8 1	3♈ 8 41	15D 31.8	17 16.3	21 42.5	17 55.2	22 1.8	0 27.4	12 35.1	5 17.4	13 1.5
29 M	6 29 30	7 10 21	10♈ 5 39	16 59 0	15R 31.6	18 52.3	22 57.7	18 42.1	21 58.0	0 33.6	12 35.5	5 18.8	13 3.6
30 Tu	6 33 26	8 11 30	23 48 52	0♉35 23	15 31.5	20 28.2	24 12.9	19 29.1	21 54.0	0 39.8	12 35.9	5 20.2	13 5.7
31 W	6 37 23	9 12 38	7♉18 43	13 59 1	15 30.1	22 3.9	25 28.1	20 16.0	21 49.9	0 45.9	12 36.3	5 21.6	13 7.8

Astro Data Dy Hr Mn	Planet Ingress Dy Hr Mn	Last Aspect Dy Hr Mn	☽ Ingress Dy Hr Mn	Last Aspect Dy Hr Mn	☽ Ingress Dy Hr Mn	☽ Phases & Eclipses Dy Hr Mn	Astro Data
☽0N 3 10:33	☿ ♏ 8 23:10	1 6:23 ♄ □	♓ 1 16:38	30 20:48 ♄ △	♈ 1 1:15	6 22:24 ○ 14♉26	1 NOVEMBER 2014
♆ D 16 7:07	♀ ♐ 16 19:05	3 9:06 ♄ △	♈ 3 18:54	3 2:43 ♂ □	♉ 3 5:16	14 15:17 ☾ 22♌10	Julian Day # 41943
☽0S 17 9:54	☉ ♐ 22 9:39	5 13:26 ☿ ☍	♉ 5 21:34	5 6:46 ♄ ☍	♊ 5 10:29	22 12:33 ● 0♐07	Galactic Ctr 27♐03.4
♄∠♇ 27 16:48	☿ ♐ 28 2:27	7 16:18 ♄ ☍	♊ 8 1:46	7 9:53 ♀ ☍	♋ 7 17:35	29 10:07 ☽ 7♓06	SVP 05♓03'05"
☽0N 30 17:22		9 16:23 ♃ ⚹	♋ 10 8:39	10 0:16 ♄ △	♌ 10 3:15		Obliquity 23°26'06"
	♂ ♒ 4 23:58	12 9:17 ♄ △	♌ 12 18:45	12 12:50 ♄ □	♍ 12 15:20	6 12:28 ○ 14♊18	⚷ Chiron 13♓20.8R
♄⚻♅ 3 10:47	♀ ♑ 10 16:43	15 2:54 ♀ □	♍ 15 7:09	15 2:12 ♄ ⚹	♎ 15 4:06	14 12:52 ☾ 22♍26	☽ Mean ☊ 18♎10.0
♃ R 8 20:42	☿ ♑ 17 3:54	17 11:12 ♄ ⚹	♎ 17 19:31	17 5:41 ☉ ⚹	♏ 17 14:53	22 1:37 ● 0♑06	
☽0S 14 19:35	☉ ♑ 21 23:04	19 14:26 ♃ ⚹	♏ 20 5:32	19 21:12 ♄ ☌	♐ 19 21:56	28 18:33 ☽ 6♈56	1 DECEMBER 2014
♅□♇ 15 5:15	♄ ♐ 23 16:35	22 5:54 ♄ ☌	♐ 22 12:20	21 12:36 ♃ △	♑ 22 1:26		Julian Day # 41973
♅ D 21 22:46		24 3:17 ♃ △	♑ 24 16:33	23 3:18 ♀ ☌	♒ 24 2:53		Galactic Ctr 27♐03.5
☽0N 27 23:59		26 15:31 ☿ ⚹	♒ 26 19:24	25 15:12 ♃ ☍	♓ 26 4:08		SVP 05♓03'01"
		28 17:15 ♄ □	♓ 28 22:04	27 15:45 ♀ ⚹	♈ 28 6:36		Obliquity 23°26'05"
				30 0:47 ♀ □	♉ 30 10:57		⚷ Chiron 13♓07.2
							☽ Mean ☊ 16♎34.7

*Giving the positions of planets daily at noon, in LONGITUDE Greenwich Mean Time (UT)

Each planet's retrograde period is shaded gray.

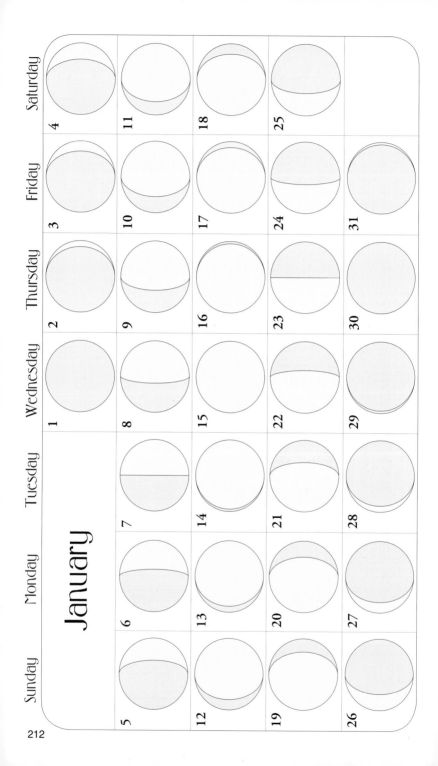

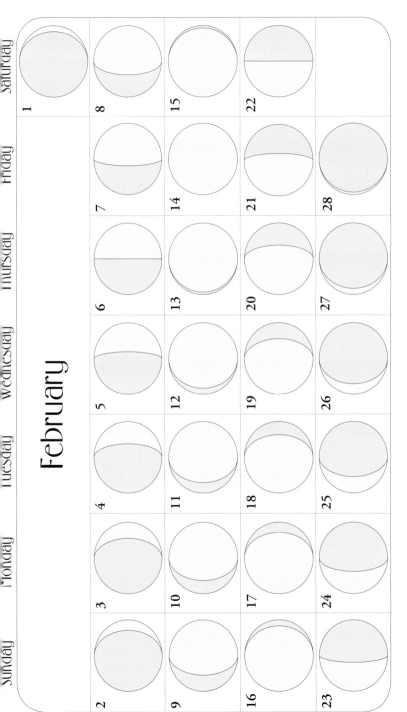

February

Sunday	Monday	Tuesday	Wednesday	Thursday	Friday	Saturday
						1
2	3	4	5	6	7	8
9	10	11	12	13	14	15
16	17	18	19	20	21	22
23	24	25	26	27	28	

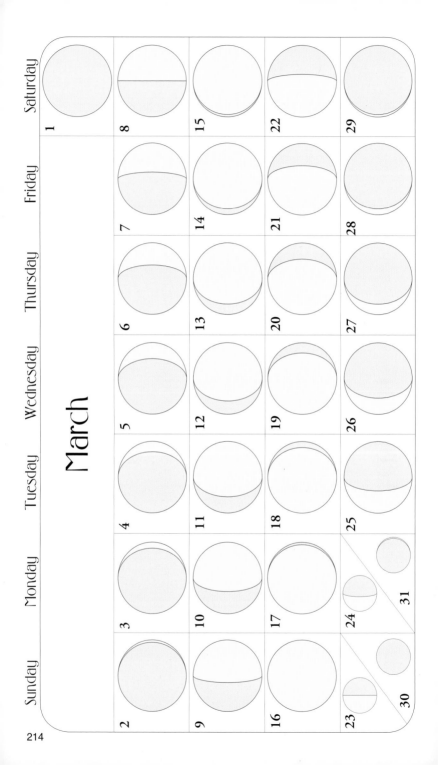

March

Sunday	Monday	Tuesday	Wednesday	Thursday	Friday	Saturday
						1
2	3	4	5	6	7	8
9	10	11	12	13	14	15
16	17	18	19	20	21	22
23	24	25	26	27	28	29
30	31					

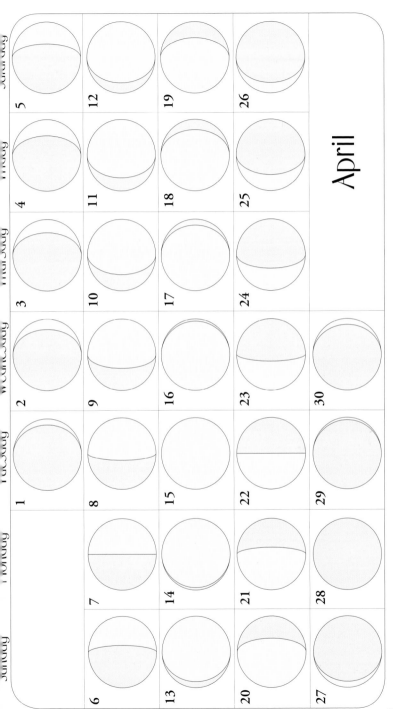

April

215

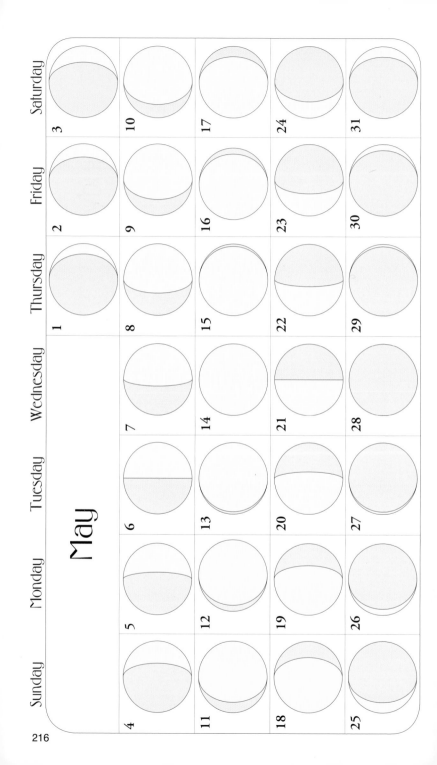

May

Sunday	Monday	Tuesday	Wednesday	Thursday	Friday	Saturday
				1	2	3
4	5	6	7	8	9	10
11	12	13	14	15	16	17
18	19	20	21	22	23	24
25	26	27	28	29	30	31

June

217

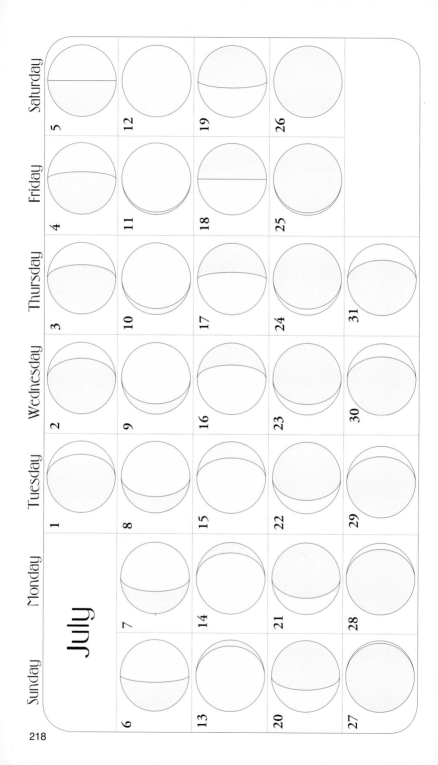

218

August

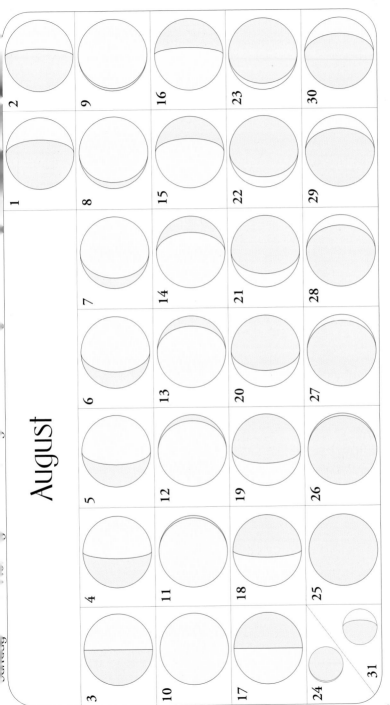

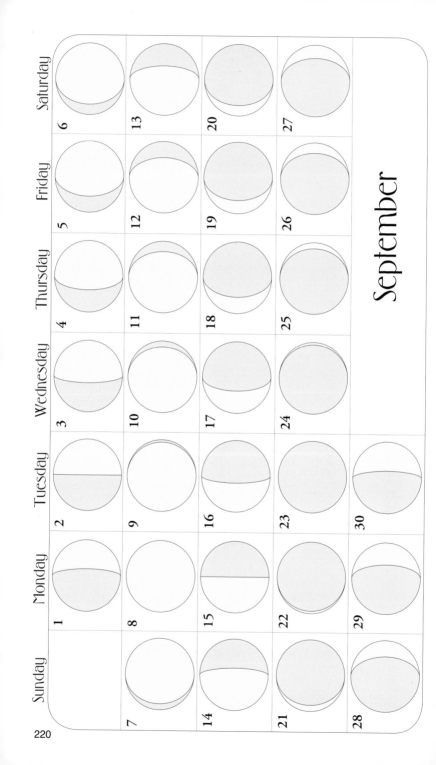

September

Sunday	Monday	Tuesday	Wednesday	Thursday	Friday	Saturday
	1	2	3	4	5	6
7	8	9	10	11	12	13
14	15	16	17	18	19	20
21	22	23	24	25	26	27
28	29	30				

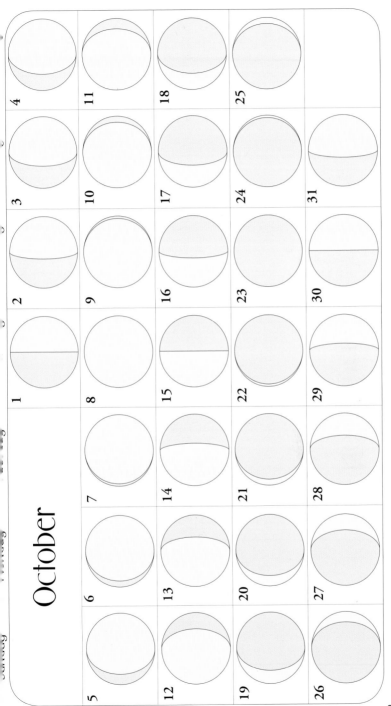

October

November

Sunday	Monday	Tuesday	Wednesday	Thursday	Friday	Saturday
2	3	4	5	6	7	1
9	10	11	12	13	14	8
16	17	18	19	20	21	15
23	24	25	26	27	28	22
30						29

222

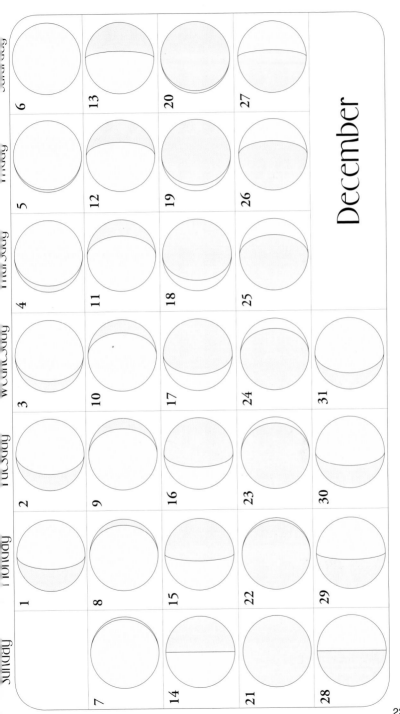

December

Eclipse Key: ☾=Solar ☽=Lunar **A**=Annular **T**=Total **P** = Partial
Lunar Eclipses are visible wherever it is night and cloud free around time of full moon.

Attn: All times on this page in EST

Eastern Standard Time (-5 from GMT)

Add one hour during Daylight Savings.

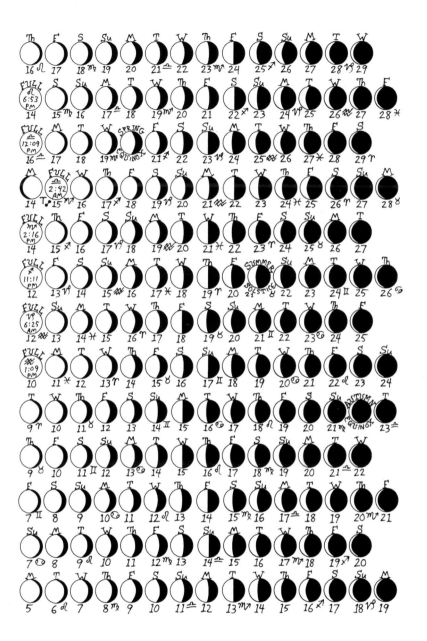

2014 LUNAR PHASES

© Susan Baylies, reproduced with permission

This format available on cards from: **http://snakeandsnake.com**

Snake and Snake Productions 3037 Dixon Rd Durham, NC 27707

WORLD TIME ZONES

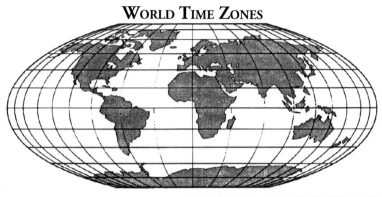

ID LW	NT BT	CA HT	YST	PST	MST	CST	EST	AST	BST	AT	WAT	GMT	CET	EET	BT	USSR Z3	USSR Z4	USSR Z5	SST	CCT	JST	GST	USSR Z10	ID LE
-12	-11	-10	-9	-8	-7	-6	-5	-4	-3	-2	-1	**0**	+1	+2	+3	+4	+5	+6	+7	+8	+9	+10	+11	+12
-4	-3	-2	-1	**0**	+1	+2	+3	+4	+5	+6	+7	+8	+9	+10	+11	+12	+13	+14	+15	+16	+17	+18	+19	+20

STANDARD TIME ZONES FROM WEST TO EAST CALCULATED FROM PST AS ZERO POINT:

IDLW:	International Date Line West	-4
NT/BT:	Nome Time/Bering Time	-3
CA/HT:	Central Alaska & Hawaiian Time	-2
YST:	Yukon Standard Time	-1
PST:	Pacific Standard Time	0
MST:	Mountain Standard Time	+1
CST:	Central Standard Time	+2
EST:	Eastern Standard Time	+3
AST:	Atlantic Standard Time	+4
NFT:	Newfoundland Time	+4 1/2
BST:	Brazil Standard Time	+5
AT:	Azores Time	+6
WAT:	West African Time	+7
GMT:	Greenwich Mean Time	+8
WET:	Western European Time (England)	+8
CET:	Central European Time	+9
EET:	Eastern European Time	+10

BT:	Bagdhad Time	+11
IT:	Iran Time	+11 1/2
USSR	Zone 3	+12
USSR	Zone 4	+13
IST:	Indian Standard Time	+13 1/2
USSR	Zone 5	+14
NST:	North Sumatra Time	+14 1/2
SST:	South Sumatra Time & USSR Zone 6	+15
JT:	Java Time	+15 1/2
CCT:	China Coast Time	+16
MT:	Moluccas Time	+16 1/2
JST:	Japanese Standard Time	+17
SAST:	South Australian Standard Time	+17 1/2
GST:	Guam Standard Time	+18
USSR	Zone 10	+19
IDLE:	International Date Line East	+20

HOW TO CALCULATE TIME ZONE CORRECTIONS IN YOUR AREA:

ADD if you are **east** of PST (Pacific Standard Time); **SUBTRACT** if you are **west** of PST on this map (see right-hand column of chart above).

All times in this calendar are calculated from the West Coast of North America where We'Moon is made. Pacific Standard Time (PST Zone 8) is zero point for this calendar, except during Daylight Saving Time (March 9–November 2, 2014, during which times are given for PDT Zone 7). If your time zone does not use Daylight Saving Time, add one hour to the standard correction during this time. At the bottom of each page, EST/EDT (Eastern Standard or Daylight Time) and GMT (Greenwich Mean Time) times are also given. For all other time zones, calculate your time zone correction(s) from this map and write it on the inside cover for easy reference.

SIGNS AND SYMBOLS AT A GLANCE

PLANETS

Personal Planets are closest to Earth.

⊙ **Sun**: self radiating outward, character, ego

☽ **Moon**: inward sense of self, emotions, psyche

☿ **Mercury**: communication, travel, thought

♀ **Venus**: relationship, love, sense of beauty, empathy

♂ **Mars**: will to act, initiative, ambition

Asteroids are between Mars and Jupiter and reflect the awakening of feminine-defined energy centers in human consciousness. See "Goddess Planets" (p.27).

Social Planets are between personal and outer planets.

♃ **Jupiter**: expansion, opportunities, leadership

♄ **Saturn**: limits, structure, discipline

Note: The days of the week are named in various languages after the above seven heavenly bodies.

⚷ **Chiron**: is a small planetary body between Saturn and Uranus representing the wounded healer.

Transpersonal Planets are the outer planets.

♅ **Uranus**: cosmic consciousness, revolutionary change

♆ **Neptune**: spiritual awakening, cosmic love, all one

♇ **Pluto**: death and rebirth, deep, total change

ZODIAC SIGNS

♈ Aries

♉ Taurus

♊ Gemini

♋ Cancer

♌ Leo

♍ Virgo

♎ Libra

♏ Scorpio

♐ Sagittarius

♑ Capricorn

♒ Aquarius

♓ Pisces

ASPECTS

Aspects show the angle between planets; this informs how the planets influence each other and us. **We'Moon** lists only significant aspects:

☌ CONJUNCTION (planets are 0–5° apart)
   linked together, energy of aspected planets is mutually enhancing

☍ OPPOSITION (planets are 180° apart)
   polarizing or complementing, energies are diametrically opposite

△ TRINE (planets are 120° apart)
   harmonizing, energies of this aspect are in the same element

□ SQUARE (planets are 90° apart)
   challenging, energies of this aspect are different from each other

✶ SEXTILE (planets are 60° apart)
   cooperative, energies of this aspect blend well

⚻ QUINCUNX (planets are 150° apart)
   variable, energies of this aspect combine contrary elements

OTHER SYMBOLS

☽ v/c–Moon is "void of course" from last lunar aspect until it enters new sign.

ApG–Apogee: Point in the orbit of a planet that's farthest from Earth.

PrG–Perigee: Point in the orbit of a planet that's nearest to Earth.

D or R–Direct or Retrograde: Describes when a planet moves forward (D) through the zodiac or appears to move backward (R).

2015

JANUARY
S	M	T	W	T	F	S
				1	2	3
4	5	6	7	8	9	10
11	12	13	14	15	16	17
18	19	20	21	22	23	24
25	26	27	28	29	30	31

FEBRUARY
S	M	T	W	T	F	S
1	2	3	4	5	6	7
8	9	10	11	12	13	14
15	16	17	18	19	20	21
22	23	24	25	26	27	28

MARCH
S	M	T	W	T	F	S
1	2	3	4	5	6	7
8	9	10	11	12	13	14
15	16	17	18	19	20	21
22	23	24	25	26	27	28
29	30	31				

APRIL
S	M	T	W	T	F	S
			1	2	3	4
5	6	7	8	9	10	11
12	13	14	15	16	17	18
19	20	21	22	23	24	25
26	27	28	29	30		

MAY
S	M	T	W	T	F	S
					1	2
3	4	5	6	7	8	9
10	11	12	13	14	15	16
17	18	19	20	21	22	23
24	25	26	27	28	29	30
31						

JUNE
S	M	T	W	T	F	S
	1	2	3	4	5	6
7	8	9	10	11	12	13
14	15	16	17	18	19	20
21	22	23	24	25	26	27
28	29	30				

JULY
S	M	T	W	T	F	S
			1	2	3	4
5	6	7	8	9	10	11
12	13	14	15	16	17	18
19	20	21	22	23	24	25
26	27	28	29	30	31	

AUGUST
S	M	T	W	T	F	S
						1
2	3	4	5	6	7	8
9	10	11	12	13	14	15
16	17	18	19	20	21	22
23	24	25	26	27	28	29
30	31					

SEPTEMBER
S	M	T	W	T	F	S
		1	2	3	4	5
6	7	8	9	10	11	12
13	14	15	16	17	18	19
20	21	22	23	24	25	26
27	28	29	30			

OCTOBER
S	M	T	W	T	F	S
				1	2	3
4	5	6	7	8	9	10
11	12	13	14	15	16	17
18	19	20	21	22	23	24
25	26	27	28	29	30	31

NOVEMBER
S	M	T	W	T	F	S
1	2	3	4	5	6	7
8	9	10	11	12	13	14
15	16	17	18	19	20	21
22	23	24	25	26	27	28
29	30					

DECEMBER
S	M	T	W	T	F	S
		1	2	3	4	5
6	7	8	9	10	11	12
13	14	15	16	17	18	19
20	21	22	23	24	25	26
27	28	29	30	31		

= NEW MOON, PST/PDT

Heart Flame
□ *Irene Ingalls 2007*

= FULL MOON, PST/PDT

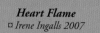

In the Spirit of We'Moon
Celebrating 30 Years
An Anthology of We'Moon Art and Writing

In the Spirit of We'Moon is a unique Anthology showcasing three decades of treasured art and writing from the We'Moon datebook. Curious about earlier We'Moons? Don't miss this cutting edge collection that celebrates the outpouring of We'Moon creativity from around the world, during an extraordinary period of women's history.

Hear the spirited voices of women making waves that have changed our world! The Anthology features vibrant offerings of art and writing from hundreds of beloved We'Moon contributors, and historical perspectives from founding editor Musawa, and others, sharing stories of We'Moon's colorful evolution. Open this book to any page for inspiration in your daily life. You won't want to put it down!

Softbound, 256 pages 8x10 $25.95

The beauty of We'Moon is the beauty of "oneness, putting all these nations under the same umbrella. I have absolute blessings for this Anthology. We can walk with this wisdom."

—Excerpt from a We'Moon review by Flordemayo, Mayan Grandmother from The International Council of Thirteen Indigenous Grandmothers

---

The Last Wild Witch
by Starhawk — illustrations by Lindy Kehoe
An Eco-Fable for Kids and Other Free Spirits

In the very heart of the last magic forest lived the last wild Witch. . .

This is the story of how the children of the perfect town let a little wildness get inside of them, found their joy and courage, and saved the last wild Witch and the last magic forest from disappearing. The first children's book by visionary author and earth activist **Starhawk**, magically illustrated by painter **Lindy Kehoe**, *The Last Wild Witch* is a fable for our time.

Hardcover, 34 pages 8x10 $18.95

For more information on how to order see page 231, or visit www.wemoon.ws

We'Moon 2014: Radical Balance

• **Datebook** The iconic feminist datebook, best-selling astrological moon calendar, earth-spirited handbook in natural rhythms, and visionary collection of women's creative work. Week-at-a-glance format. Choice of 3 bindings: Spiral, Sturdy Paperback Binding or Unbound. 8x5 1/4, 240 pages $18.95

• **Cover Poster** featuring "Planetary Alignment," a fantastical image of a confident *balancera*, tools for repair at the ready, by Julie Dillon. 11x17 $10

• **We'Moon on the Wall 2014** A gorgeous full color wall calendar featuring inspired art and writing from *We'Moon 2014*. With key astrological information, interpretive articles, lunar phases and signs. 12x12 $14.95

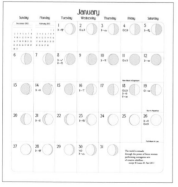

• **We'Moon 2014 Tote Bag** 100% Organic Cotton tote, proudly displaying the cover of *We'Moon 2014*. Perfect for stowing all of your goodies in style. 13x14 $12

• **Greeting Cards** An assortment of six gorgeous note cards featuring art from *We'Moon 2014*, with writings from each artist on the back. Wonderful to send for any occasion: Holy Day, Birthday, Anniversary, Sympathy, or just to say hello. Each pack is wrapped in biodegradable cellophane. Blank inside, 5x7, $9.95

• **In the Spirit of We'Moon ~ Celebrating 30 Years: An Anthology of We'Moon Art and Writing** $25.95 (See p. 229)

• **The Last Wild Witch** by **Starhawk**, illustrated by **Lindy Kehoe** An Eco-Fable for Kids and Other Free Spirits $18.95 (See p. 229)

• **Matriotism Poster** A large Cosmic-Mother image of peace by Kjersten Hallin deGaia, with a Virginia Woolf quote: "*...As a woman my country is the whole world.*" 19x27 $20

• **We'Moon Datebooks—Back Issues** Collector's editions of select past We'Moon datebooks and cards. Shop for them on our website. $10

All products printed in full color on recycled paper with low VOC soy-based ink.

Become a We'Moon Contributor!

Accepting contributions June through August 2014 for

We'Moon 2016: The 35ᵗʰ Edition!

Tentative Theme: Shake It Up!

Call for Contributions: Available in the spring of 2014

Due Date for all art and writing: September 1, 2014

Note: It is too late to contribute to

We'Moon 2015: Wild Card

We'Moon is an exploration of a world created in Her image. We welcome work by women. Our focus on womyn is an affirmation of the range and richness of a world where womyn are whole unto themselves. Many earth-based cultures traditionally have womyn-only spaces and times, which, through deepening the female experience, are seen to enhance womyn's contributions to the whole of society. We'Moon invites all womyn who love and honor womyn to join us in this spirit, and we offer what we create from such a space for the benefit of all beings.

We invite you to send in your art and writing for the 35ᵗʰ edition of We'Moon! Here's how:

Step 1: Visit www.wemoon.ws to download a Call for Contributions or send your request for a Call for Contributions, along with a self-addressed, stamped, business-size (9 ½" x 4") envelope to **We'Moon Submissions, 181 Brimstone Rd., Wolf Creek, OR 97497**. (If you are not within the U.S. you do not need to include postage.) The Call contains current information about the theme (it may change), how to submit your art and writing (with exact specifications), and terms of compensation. There are no jury fees. The Call comes out in the early Spring every year, as the Crocus begin to bloom.

Step 2: Fill in the accompanying Contributor's License, giving all the requested information, and return it with your art/writing and a self addressed envelope, by the due date. *No work will be accepted without a signed license!*

Step 3: Think ahead! To assure your work is considered for *We'Moon 2016*, get your submissions in by September 1, 2014.

Give We'Moon for the holidays!
and for special occasions all year 'round!

NOTES

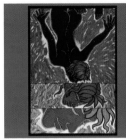

Point of Balance
© *Robyn Waters 2003*

The Bird Girls
© *Denise Kester 2012*

Notes

Illumination
© *Nancy Watterson 2010*

Blue Blue Hearts
© *Cori Caputo 2002*

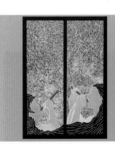

Mother Child Song
© Amy L. Alley 2009

Second Chakra
© *Beth Lenco 2000*